Physical Education and Movement in Waldorf Schools

I0808380

Disclaimer

A number of the activities in this book should only be carried out under the guidance of professionally trained and accredited instructors with the appropriate equipment. The Publisher accepts no liability for damages or injury of any kind.

Translated by Geoff Hunter

First published in German as *Der Sportunterricht an der Waldorfschule*
by Verlag Freies Geistesleben, Stuttgart in 2018
First published in English by Floris Books, Edinburgh in 2021

British Library CIP data available

ISBN 978-178250-714-7
Printed in Poland through Hussar

Floris Books supports sustainable forest management by
printing this book on materials made from wood that
comes from responsible sources and reclaimed material

FSC www.fsc.org MIX Paper from responsible sources FSC® C167221

Physical Education and Movement in Waldorf Schools

Edited by Gerlinde Idler and Lutz Gerding

Floris Books

Contents

Preface

Many children today live in a fast-moving, virtual world dominated by digital media and other forms of passive entertainment. This makes it all the more important that they receive a good schooling in physical education (P.E.) and movement. A young person caught up in the dynamics of sporting activity drinks from the spring which gives health and zest for life. When physically active, children have a direct and profound experience of who they are – spiritually, emotionally and physically. Games and physical movement activate each child's will, which places them anew in space and time. Waldorf education sets out to encourage this phenomenon of experiencing identity through physical activity by using a method of teaching P.E. that accords with children's stages of development. Wherever possible, Waldorf schools work according to the principle that teachers should seek to discover, support and encourage the 'person within the person'.

When teachers combine their study of anthroposophy (in particular Rudolf Steiner's *Study of Man*) with their first-hand experience of young people, they find ample scope for researching and developing P.E. lessons. This then has a knock-on effect on the rest of the children's learning experience. When the choice of a certain game in Class 3 or a particular exercise in the Upper School fits with the children's developmental stage, this creates enjoyment and encourages initiative within P.E. lessons. But it also helps bring children alive in their other lessons. Developmental resonances like these affect not only the quality of the will, but also the depth of children's awareness. When the children of Class 5 from different Waldorf schools meet to compete in the classical Greek pentathlon and live the Olympic ideal, three elements merge into one: the current developmental stage of the children, cultural history in the form of physical education, and community building.

Regional factors and the need to focus on particular physical activities in particular places combines with the aforementioned developmental approach to create a wide variety in P.E. lessons within different Waldorf schools. Where some Waldorf schools have built up a flourishing circus with a well-established tradition of regular, intensive training, others can boast of strong volleyball, basketball, running or dragon boat teams. This book illustrates this necessarily varied approach, while at the same time elaborating on the characteristic features of P.E. in Waldorf schools: from the inclusion of Bothmer exercises, which were devised in the early days of Waldorf education, to the holistic approach to child development, and interdisciplinary teaching. Between the diversity and the standard features, there are exciting opportunities for cultivating new pedagogical ideas.

Claus-Peter Röh, Florian Osswald

Foreword

At the beginning of the twentieth century, the first Waldorf school was founded in Stuttgart. From this one small seed, a worldwide network of over a thousand schools has grown, which are all working, across all cultures and five continents, towards one common aim: the healthy development of children.

The fundamental thing is not the shared curriculum, but rather a keen eye for children's needs. By observing individual children, we endeavour to find the appropriate educational method to fit the circumstances. Teaching does not take place on a school bench, but in a temporal and physical space in which children can develop. Movement education, and in particular physical education, can make an important contribution to understanding children and adolescents.

This book sets out to help teachers find the content and form that their pupils need. It offers an outline of many possible activities for each age group, while also surveying a wide variety of physical activities and games which can be taught at Waldorf schools, as well as providing examples of how to plan and carry out single lessons. These examples are not meant to be recipes. Their aim is to underline how what we do in P.E. lessons can boost the development of children and adolescents.

Gerlinde Idler, Lutz Gerding

Part One
Introduction

Fundamental Aspects of Physical Education in Waldorf Schools

Gerlinde Idler

The beginnings

Soon after the founding of the first Waldorf School in Stuttgart in 1919, the question of physical education arose. In German schools at that time, such lessons revolved around the so-called 'German gymnastics movement', or *turnverein*: a form of physical training developed by renowned teacher Friedrich Ludwig Jahn (1778–1852) that had unavoidably militaristic overtones. For Rudolf Steiner (1861–1925), this kind of exercise did not suit the holistic style of education he envisioned for the new school, and so he asked Fritz Graf von Bothmer (1883–1941) to devise a new way of teaching gymnastics. In 1922, von Bothmer took on the role of teaching P.E. Having studied Steiner's ideas on teaching based on his picture of the human being and how children develop, he invented something quite new: the Bothmer exercises. Over the next sixteen years he created a series of thirty different exercises, each of which took into consideration a particular stage in the development of children and young students. These form the basis for all lessons in physical education in Waldorf Schools.

For Bothmer, the following questions were of great importance:

- What is the value of practising certain sequences of movement?
- How should they be practised?
- Which qualities in movement do they improve?
- What effect do they have on the healthy development of children and adolescents?

These remain crucial questions concerning P.E. in Waldorf schools today. What's more, they are crucial questions for every subject and for every teacher who strives to work according to Steiner's picture of the human being.

General aspects

In Waldorf schools, the content of lessons is determined by the pupils' age and their level of development. The task of the teacher is to recognise which stage their pupils are at and to prepare lessons that will stimulate and encourage them accordingly. To do this, it is necessary to work thoroughly on Steiner's *Study of Man,* a series of lectures he gave for the future teachers of the first Waldorf school in 1919. A basic principle is that the children of one age group form a class and, as far as possible, remain together from Class 1 right through to Class 12. Due to the closeness of the age group, it is possible to address the class members as a fairly homogeneous group. In P.E., a holistic approach is used to help young people in all areas, and this is much easier in a homogeneous group than a heterogeneous one.

In his standard work on the Waldorf curriculum, Tobias Richter emphasises the fact that Waldorf schools look to encourage creativity and social competence as well as personal development:

> The free will to learn, to engage in research, to be creative, to be part of shaping society, all these things are to be fostered and sustained. In this way, education is acknowledged as an instrument for development and change.[1]

In selecting material for the various subjects, the Waldorf school teacher is guided by the 'exemplary principle'. The content of their lessons should stimulate a child's healthy development and as such the teacher takes on a great responsibility in preparing them. They have few guidelines to stick to and must decide for themselves, according to their own understanding of Waldorf teaching, what to do for each pupil, when to do it and how. On this point, Tobias Richter writes:

> Academic freedom is the human precondition for achieving an authentic 'education towards freedom' ... But the choice of what to do in lessons must undergo careful examination as follows: which topics have a global dimension ... which ones are concerned with different cultures ... where do topical questions of the day find expression? An educational framework arises out of this which is truly alive, which can be expanded and updated, but which, on a human level, may be neither reduced nor restricted.[2]

Learning in school is just one stage in a process of lifelong learning, and all the subjects in Waldorf schools are there to provide life skills.[3] In practical terms this means responding to children and young

people according to their stage of development, while at the same time offering lesson content that is appropriate for the various age groups according to the anthroposophical description of the human being. If we can meet this challenge, then 'educating towards freedom' is not just a slogan. Each pupil will be able to develop their own capabilities individually.

P.E. and the Waldorf curriculum

For insight into the significance of P.E., a clearer picture emerges if we look at the status of individual subjects within the Waldorf School curriculum as a whole. All subjects can be divided into three categories: cognitive, practical craft and artistic. All subjects are of equal importance and work together to form a healthy, harmonious foundation for the pupils' development.

Cognitive subjects	Practical craft subjects	Artistic subjects
English	Needlework	Eurythmy
History	Woodwork	Music
Social studies	Art	P.E.
Geography	Gardening	
Sciences		
Maths		
Foreign languages		

One essential component in achieving this harmony is an effective, well-organised timetable. With this in mind, the school day always begins with a double lesson, the so-called 'main lesson' in Class 1 through to Class 12, in which pupils work intensively on one topic for several weeks: for example, in history they study Ancient Greece in Class 5, and the age of discovery and the voyages of Columbus in Class 7. After the morning break, further cognitive subjects are studied followed by a practical craft subject. The school day then ends with one of the artistic subjects. This ideal day, which in reality often varies, is repeated throughout the week.

In order for the P.E. teacher to prepare lessons that fit within this harmonious interplay of subjects, they should know which particular topic the pupils are busy with in the main lesson. Which project are they working on? Where are they in their development?

To achieve this continuity, all teachers working with any particular class have to be in constant contact with each other. Sitting in on other lessons can also help P.E. teachers in preparing their own lessons, as it lets them observe the pupils in a different learning environment.

It is essential that the class teacher and the subject teachers keep in mind how all the subjects complement each other – in particular when they are working with younger pupils. The older pupils have a greater self-awareness, and have experienced much more in all the various subjects. It is not as important for them that the school day form one homogeneous unit.

Rudolf Steiner's picture of the human being as the basis for P.E.

Waldorf education aims to stimulate and nourish the whole human being: everything the pupil experiences affects their entire being, so they need to be addressed in body, soul and intellect.

In the course of lectures he gave to teachers, collected under the title of *Study of Man*, Rudolf Steiner sets out how the college of teachers can strive to achieve this high ideal. [v] In many schools, grappling with the content of these lectures takes place in the so-called pedagogical conference and in reading groups with teachers and interested parents. Exchanging thoughts about these demanding texts is a valuable study aid in understanding how children develop, while also discovering their relevance to topical educational issues. Studying the texts alone can be an equally satisfying challenge, and teachers often find that they learn as much about themselves as about the various stages of childhood development. Working with this picture of the human being, the teacher becomes sensitive to the needs of their pupils, able to assess their potential and to understand what they need.

At the same time, the ability to work intensively on lesson preparation is enhanced if the teacher pursues some practical activity of their own. By following this path of self-education, the teacher is better able to respond to specific class situations.

Some terminology

The aim of the articles that appear later in this book is to stimulate interest in P.E. based on the principles of Waldorf education.

Although there isn't the room here to provide a full introduction to Waldorf education, there are some terms and concepts that Steiner used that need explaining:

- the seven-year cycles;
- thinking, feeling and willing;
- the four bodies;
- the twelve senses;
- the temperaments; and
- terms relating to P.E. in Steiner's picture of the human being.

The seven-year cycles

Steiner put forward the idea that a person's biography develops in seven-year periods. This is the ideal form of development, although individual biographical and cultural conditions may cause variations. Knowing about these seven-year cycles helps teachers find the right approach in teaching children and adolescents.

Thinking, feeling and willing

Steiner divided the human bodily organism into three interconnected parts: the sense-nervous system, the rhythmic system and the metabolic-limb system. This division corresponds to the three soul forces of thinking, feeling and willing. Thinking is related to the nerves and the senses and corresponds to imagining and discerning. The bodily seat of feeling lies in the rhythmic system of the heart and lungs and is reflected in the rhythms of life. The will is located in the metabolic-limb system and is the instigator of action. These soul forces must be seen as a whole, each one interwoven with the other two.

The four bodies

In his book *The Education of the Child*, which contains the fundamental essay 'The Education of the Child in the Light of Anthroposophy', Steiner sets out the principles of Waldorf education.[5] He describes how the human being that we see consists of four bodies drawn from four planes of being. Besides the physical body, with which we are all familiar, the human being also possesses an etheric body, an astral body and an 'I' or ego. These bodies must be seen as belonging together and not existing separately in the human being.

The writer and psychiatrist Rudolf Treichler writes:

> This picture shows us that we are not dealing with separate entities here … Just as with the threefold division of body, soul and spirit, so in further subdivisions the forces of the individual planes of being permeate each other … And just as with the limbs of our body, in some special way each entity explores and shapes the outside world.[6]

Roughly every seven years, from when we are born until around the age of twenty-one, the 'birth' of one of these bodies takes place, freeing up forces for further learning, growth and development. During the first seven years, physical bodily development is foremost. In the second seven-year period, following the birth of the etheric body and marked by the loss of the milk teeth, qualities of the soul are developed:

habits are formed, skills are honed. Finally, in the third seven-year period, with the onset of puberty and the birth of the astral body, the ability to form judgements is developed and spiritual development reaches a certain conclusion. The birth of the 'I' brings the process to fruition: it is time for the young adult, of their own free will, to shape their own future.

The twelve senses

Besides the five senses we are familiar with, Rudolf Steiner described a further seven, making twelve in total. They are divided into the 'lower senses' of touch, life, movement and balance, the 'middle senses' of smell, taste, sight and warmth, and the 'higher senses' of hearing, speech, thought and ego. They develop and are experienced differently in the various phases of life.

The lower senses play a special part in the first seven years of children's development. They are also known as the physical or bodily senses as they are used for perceiving one's own body. The middle senses are those of feeling and have to do with how a person relates to the world around them. They become significant in the second seven-year cycle. The higher senses, also called the spiritual or social senses by Steiner, address the inner life and reveal what is hidden.[7]

The temperaments

Steiner recommended that teachers use the classical doctrine of the four temperaments as a further aid to understanding children and their healthy development. This does not mean dividing children into rigid categories of sanguine, melancholic, phlegmatic and choleric. Instead it means that each child is supported in such a way that they are able to deal with their own particular disposition. It also helps the teacher choose more suitable lesson material and find the most appropriate teaching method.[8]

Terms relating to P.E. in Steiner's picture of the human being

The table below illustrates the terms developed by Steiner for the different age groups.[9] They can serve as a background for planning lessons appropriate to the particular stage of the child's development. These rather dry-looking terms can be studied by teachers and other interested parties in small working groups, so that they can be infused with life for daily use.

Willing													
1–6 years	Age	7	8	9	10	11	12	13	14	15	16	17	18
	Class	1	2	3	4	5	6	7	8	9	10	11	12
	Area of focus	Security	Security	Warmth	Breathing	Blood	Muscle	Sinew	Bone	Will	Feeling	Thinking	Consciousness
	Corresponding movement			Playing	Romping	Walking	Running	Jumping	Wrestling	Shot put	Discus	Javelin	Pentathlon
	Quality developed			Imitation	Rhythmical activity	Imaginative activity	Skill, dexterity	Acrobatics	Bearing	Strength	Prudence	Awareness	Overview

Some technical considerations

As is the case with other subjects, the P.E. teacher has to adapt to the given conditions. The planning of lessons must take account of the space: not every school has a separate sports hall, and when lessons take place in the school hall there may be conflicts of interest. It is the same with gymnastic equipment. While it is great to have everything at one's fingertips so that an idea can be implemented straight away, a lot of exercises are possible using the simplest of means. This calls for imagination, ingenuity and, above all, *patience*. But it does work, as everyday practice shows, and lessons given under the most difficult of conditions can be stimulating and exciting.

Structure and continuity in lessons are a challenge, because pupils normally only have P.E. once a week and pursuing a central theme is not easy. What makes matters worse is when lessons are cancelled. This is unavoidable but must be taken into account. School festivals and class trips all interrupt the course of lessons. It's all the more important that the structure of the lessons and the long-term planning for them go hand in hand. As with the main lesson, it is essential that P.E. lessons be planned and carried out as projects over several weeks, for example, learning to play handball in Class 7. Pupils remember more easily what they did in the previous lesson and immerse themselves more quickly in the various tasks. They can see the progress they're making, and they grow in confidence as their movements become more skilful and practised.

In Waldorf schools, younger pupils are taught all lessons using stories and imaginative pictures to help develop a healthy inner strength. This approach can be adapted for P.E. lessons by embedding games and exercises in pictures or stories, with the children playing various parts. The image or story becomes the basis for action, which the children carry out without thinking. This can even be effective for the warm-up session.

With the older pupils, the emphasis is on experience. It is not about communicating some insight which must then be put

into practice, but rather through the experience of movement the pupils are brought to an increased awareness of themselves. For the individual pupil, becoming aware of their own abilities and how they are developing is more important than acquiring new skills. Just as with other school subjects, P.E. lessons can and should encourage individualisation. Similarly, learning is reflected in what the individual pupil has accomplished. Variety, so often moaned about, is now a vital component of the lesson – it is the precondition for creating the ability to cooperate within a group.

We also have to consider how each lesson is structured. As in the other school subjects, there should be an element of giving and receiving, of tensing and letting go. One important rhythm that must not be overlooked is that of 'inhaling and exhaling'. This does not refer to actual breathing (although this would certainly reflect whether a P.E. lesson has a healthy balance or not), rather it means that having been emotionally involved in some particular unit of the lesson, the children must be helped to free themselves from it.

After a wild game of tag, do the teachers give the children an exercise that is quieter and slower, one that helps them calm down by decreasing their pulse rate and slowing their breathing? When the lesson comes to an end, do they have an exercise or a game at hand where you might hear a pin drop? Are there any exercises with calm, controlled movements, in which the pupils can immerse themselves?

In order for children to fully experience the quality of particular movements, it is necessary that there are exercises that lead to calm and concentrated learning, as well as those that are hectic and strenuous. In this respect, P.E. lessons rank alongside the cognitive subjects. Steiner divided the learning process into three stages and highlighted the important role that sleep plays. Because it isn't possible for the pupil to assimilate new material on the same day that they encounter it, it should be presented in as vivid and graphic a way as possible so that in the following stage, the pupil absorbs the material thoroughly. In the final stage, on the following day with a sleep in between, it has evolved into something which has been understood and properly grasped.[10]

P.E. teachers also take this three-step learning into account. Since the lessons generally have a weekly rhythm, the situation differs from that of the main lessons which take place every day. For P.E. lessons, it means getting to know a new exercise (immersion), then in the following week's lesson deepening the experience (practise) until finally the movement is performed and consolidated (for the older pupils, understood). This is one of the main reasons for P.E. lessons to be taught in project form.

When Steiner laid down the principles of co-educative teaching, he was more interested in the children's development than in the issue of gender equality. Although today nobody questions boys and girls learning to knit and sew together, often with physical education boys and girls are split up once puberty begins. Many Waldorf P.E. teachers adopt a firm standpoint on this. There are strong educational arguments for the sexes remaining together as much as possible, and for them to be taught by both male and female teachers. Certainly, there are single lessons, or times during the difficult phase of early puberty, when separating the sexes for a whilc may makc scnsc. But wc recommend keeping this as an exception to the rule.

When teaching children with additional support needs, it is important to consider what sort of conditions they require in order to feel comfortable and to fulfil their potential. A sports hall can be an enormous, intimidating place. Young children in the Lower School can find it hard to get their bearings at first, and any children with orientation problems are likely to find the space extremely daunting. The games and activities themselves must also be carefully considered. For example, many children find catching a ball challenging, but if a child has limited spatial perception it becomes almost impossible. P.E. lessons can be loud, boisterous and seemingly chaotic, which for some children can be an overwhelming experience.

Many other examples could be given, but the serious challenges they present are no reason to feel discouraged. Instead, everything must be done to ensure that teachers have the training and sometimes specialist support to deal responsibly with the situations they encounter, so that they can meet the individual needs of their students and enable them to fully integrate into the class community.

P.E. lessons in Waldorf Education, as with all the other subjects, are part of a larger educational picture. They are not primarily about communicating facts, but rather about creating the sort of learning atmosphere in which the young person can become a more mature, responsible individual, ready and willing to contribute to society. On their way to becoming adults, children should learn to face situations in which direct contact may initially be difficult, but which allow them to explore boundaries and set limits. The field of physical education should not shrink from this challenge.

Movement in Childhood

Dr Elisabeth Frank

What is movement?

We never associate life with movement more than when we see children in action. To observe children in the playground is to see a picture of pure motion: they run, climb, jump and whirl about, barge and jostle each other as they seek contact, fall over, get back up and continue running around. From an early age, children not only want to experience the world through movement, they want to shape it too, as can clearly be seen when they play with sand and water.

When children are in motion, they are simultaneously self-contained and part of the outside world. This apparent contradiction is best understood in the following way. Being self-contained, children can express their individuality through movement, and through that same movement also relate themselves to the world. This is particularly the case with small children, especially during the first year, when progress is rapid. Not only do infant bodies develop but also children's own personal ways of moving, which shows us how the spiritual individuality is gradually taking hold of and shaping the body it has inherited.

At the same time the outer world is experienced through movement. In his doctrine of the twelve senses (see p. 15 above), Rudolf Steiner points out how the sense of movement plays a large role in helping us learn about everything around us.

The physical body is what connects the inner self to the outer world. But it is not just a boundary or a place of encounter, it is also part of the outer world, which comprises all things material and living, including all people. With each movement, a person acts in this world, which in turn reappears in their inner self. Even the movements of other people are reflected in our own bodies, something that has been confirmed with the discovery of mirror neurons. These are nerve cells in the brain that imitate another person's actions as if the observer were doing them and not just watching.

Rudolf Steiner often mentions that we are part of the world around us, which is then in turn reflected inside us:

> Human beings are really always outside their bodies and their bodily functions with that part of them that is engaged in the cognitive process; they live inside the things under study ... And the fact that a person comes to know something is due to the reflection in their body of the experience they have inside things.[1]

With each movement, children place their own being in the outer world of movement and make it their home. They experience themselves among objects and people, and learn to understand those objects and others and their own selves through their movements. At the same time, the movements and actions of other people are reflected in the children's own bodies. A bond with and love for the world and the people in it begins to evolve. Proper, meaningful movement therefore helps children develop not only physical but also social skills.

The sense of movement

The sense of movement refers to one's own movement and not that of others, and always works in concert with other senses: for example, the senses of sight, of touch, and of balance. The sense of movement has the task of determining whereabouts in any given space my body is and what the relative positions of my limbs are. Where is above and below? What is the effect of gravity on my body? What is the position of my head, my torso, my arms and legs? Am I standing? Sitting? Lying down? Where is there contact with another object? How tense or relaxed are my muscles? In which direction must I move my body to catch a ball flying towards me and how strongly do my hands have to grasp it?

Even though I am hardly ever conscious of it, without this sense, purposeful movement would be impossible. The medical term for the sense of movement is bathyesthesia or deep sensibility, otherwise known as proprioception. It supplies information about the position of the body, the state of tension in the muscles and the tendons and how they are moving. This latter is also called kinaesthesia from the Greek *kinein*, 'to move', and *aisthēsis*, meaning 'sensation' or 'perception'. Meaningful movement is only possible when the sense of movement is intact. Without this, a movement would not get past the first stage or it would break down into single, uncoordinated jerks and spasms. We know such disorders from curative education. Our surroundings provide greatly varying conditions for our bodies and our movements – soft or hard floor, firm ground or water – and it is our sense of movement that enables us to adapt the body to them.

Rudolf Steiner comments, 'By means of the lower senses [to which the sense of movement belongs], a person can immerse themselves in the physical body and feel themselves as part of the outer world.'[2]

The sense of movement is the tool with which the I-being carries out its movements over a lifetime, learning new ones and correcting habitual ones. This is how children improve their power of movement.

Developing the power of movement

During pregnancy

From approximately the eighteenth week onwards, mothers can usually feel the baby moving in the womb, and thanks to modern ultrasound scans, we can observe the child's movements even earlier. After seven to eight weeks, it is possible to recognise movements on the part of the embryo that are not simply reactive. We can assume that every living being that grows through an embryonal phase uses that phase to develop not only its physical body but also the power of movement.

Embryos experience space and movement in intimate interplay, and we will continue to encounter this interplay throughout childhood development.

Infancy

After birth, babies have to cope with a completely different set of conditions from those they experienced previously. Their surroundings are now airy instead of liquid, there are changing sensations such as warmth and light, and there is the force of gravity. At first we recognise movements previously observed when babies were still in the womb. The act of suckling, now at the breast, is accompanied by rhythmical movements of the body: arms and legs kick and jerk, and the post-natal reflexes are triggered by the babies' own movement. Babies – especially newborns – are like one large sensory organ, sensing all the changes in their new environment and adapting their movements to them.

At four to six weeks, a great change in the pattern of movements can be seen as a struggle against the force of gravity begins. Especially when lying on their stomach, babies begin to raise their heads. They begin to look around, focussing on objects and making contact with their parents. There is the first smile. In the following weeks and months, the individual movements become more independent and purposeful as they strive to prop themselves up and move about.

After three months, babies discover they have hands. They look at them with fascination, trying out what they can do, before finally and deliberately grasping strange objects and moving them about. From six months on, the will to be on the move emerges. Older babies want to get up close to touch what they can see. With every movement, they practise keeping their balance while changing their position. By the ninth month, they love to be upright: they watch what is going on around them, and they pull themselves up wherever they can. Initially, when they crawl, babies need to use their hands to maintain balance. Although crawling is the most common preliminary stage before getting up and toddling, it is not the only physical option. There are many individual as well as cultural variations.

After approximately twelve months, the process of getting up and balancing, as well as the development of the bones (in particular the pelvis and the spine), enable babies to take their first few steps. From now on, they will not be still as they move constantly from one thing to the next. Anyone who has watched this knows the joy and triumph young ones radiate in this phase.

In their second year, toddlers consolidate and improve the way they move. The more confidence they have in their lower limbs, the more they can free their hands for other activities, like playing for example.

Up to the age of three, balance and surefootedness improve further. Initially, leg movements were guided by the thigh, later by the knee and the lower leg, and by the third year, the foot has taken over. Hopping and skipping become possible. The hands for their part have become tools for all sorts of things that toddlers want to do. These skills continue to improve in their harmonious little bodies.

Ready for school

Children's bodies fill out in their first years and this is followed, between the ages of five and a half and seven, by a period of stretching and growing longer. In contrast to puberty, when children's arms and legs grow disproportionately from the periphery, the process at this time is constant and harmonious. Their limbs are longer and more slender, their bodies narrow, and their heads are smaller in proportion. Facial features are more distinctive and more individual, the baby face has disappeared. All this is accompanied by a more pronounced S-shaped curvature of the spine, a visible waistline and clearly defined joints on arms and legs. The loss of the milk teeth shows that infancy is over, and that the children have taken over the formation of their own bodies. The milk teeth have been sacrificed in favour of teeth that they have shaped themselves.

Children are now much more skilled in their movements; the separate parts of their body can move independently. For skipping, the arms are no longer needed for momentum. They can act at a distance from the torso for throwing and catching. There are fewer involuntary reflexes. Each leg can be moved independently, for balancing and hopping. The fingers can be used separately, and finer motor skills enable children to carry out specific, differentiated actions. Movements are purposeful and goal-oriented (for example, throwing a ball, balancing on a tree trunk, skipping) and generally appear to be joyful and light.

At the age of nine

From the age of nine and ten, children's bodies fill out for a second time. They are now sturdier, and their torsos lengthen and broaden. With the rhythmical coordination of the limbs, walking and running become movements of the greatest harmony. What is missing is strength: the muscles are still soft and weak at this stage. At this time, all children love movements which demand and improve skills and dexterity.

Puberty and adolescence

From the age of twelve to thirteen, the second phase of growth sets in, beginning at the periphery: hands and feet first, then lower legs and forearms, finally upper arms and thighs. Growth is

not quite so harmonious this time and movements are awkward, as if the limbs are out of control. When young teens have a slender build, their arm and leg muscles are more visible but they still lack full strength.

It is only when this burst of growth comes to an end that movement becomes harmonious once more. Some adolescents derive great pleasure from movement during this time and feel a strong urge to be active; with others it is the opposite. Each individual's distinctive way of moving becomes apparent and reaches its physiological zenith at the age of twenty-one.

Medical and pedagogical tasks

Motor skills develop at different ages. During an examination, a paediatrician is able to see whether children are developing in a healthy manner or whether there is any difficulty or one-sidedness in their movements. The reflexes typical in infancy also regress. If they do not, this signals to the paediatrician that something is wrong.

Although certain skills usually develop by certain ages, there is still scope for variation when assessing children's progress. This includes the speed and manner in which they acquire movement skills as well as their kinetic behaviour and the development of bodily awareness. Every child incarnates in their own special way, and care is necessary in differentiating between individual and pathological deviations from the norm.

For teachers and parents too, it's important to know which motor skills are developing and at which age in order to observe how they unfold and are expressed by the individual. The motor skills that children develop of their own accord and in their own time ought to be neither guided nor accelerated by adults. There is a saying: 'The grass grows no faster if you pull on it.' As early as the 1930s, the Hungarian paediatrician Emmi Pikler pointed out how important it is to create safe, age-appropriate surroundings in which children can move and play. This allows them to acquire their own individual skills and strengths. In

Waldorf kindergartens, free play is a part of the daily routine, and the Waldorf school curriculum provides age-appropriate movement and physical education, as well as catering for individual needs.

All Education is Self-Education

Lutz Gerding

The title of this essay is taken from a lecture Rudolf Steiner gave in Dornach, in 1923, in which he said:

> All education is self-education, and as teachers we can only provide the environment for children's self-education. We have to provide the most favourable conditions where, through our agency, children can educate themselves according to their own destinies.[1]

This is a bold claim. In the education of children, Steiner is saying, we, the teachers, can only play a supporting role, while the children educate themselves. It is the teacher's job to create the general framework within which each child can achieve their true potential, without moulding or shaping. But how does self-education work?

Steiner had devised a fundamentally new approach to teaching, which even today surprises many educators. According to this new method, the teacher should not force the pace, but instead provide the best possible environment in which the children can develop freely – and this does not mean the physical environment alone. One of the important findings of the remarkable Visible Learning study carried out by Professor John Hattie was reported in *Der Spiegel*:

> Even if it is raining through the roof or a class is bursting with forty students, one charismatic and competent teacher can work wonders.[2]

Waldorf teachers enter the classroom in the role of development workers. Their aim is to enable and stimulate self-education by creating a space in which children can develop healthily and find a path towards inner, spiritual freedom, but it is the young people themselves who must take the necessary steps along this path. Education is about strengthening young people's ability to take responsibility for what they do.

In effect, they are continually teaching themselves, whether we like it or not. The question is 'simply' which role models they encounter and in which moments they experience their own progress.

This idea of self-education requires teachers to focus on the needs of each individual student, which is why we must individualise the learning process. Just as we can all only motivate ourselves, similarly we can only learn for ourselves. If the responsibility for what to learn, how and why is taken out of students' hands, learning is heteronomous and there is a danger that they become unmotivated. The technical term for this is extrinsic learning, which places emphasis on results.

Ready-made lesson units fit into this learning approach, as do exercise drills in P.E. and learning lists of historical dates. Instead, we need meaningful content – literally, content full of meaning – that reaches the hearts of children and adolescents and furthers their development. We hear how children are captivated by a fairy-tale world during P.E. lessons in the Lower School. These images endow an ordinary obstacle course with new meaning, and each child uses their own imagination and finds their own special place in the story. In the Middle School, a simple balancing exercise on an upturned long bench can become a real challenge and provide plenty of opportunity for individualised learning. For example, two students, one at each end of the bench, have to cross in the middle without putting a foot on the ground. How many different ways can they find to get past each other? It is exciting to watch how much fun they have and how creative they are in discovering ways of doing this, some of which surprise even experienced P.E. teachers. What teachers observe here often leads them to see individual students in a completely new way.

Although self-motivated working and self-motivated learning are similar to each other, they should not be confused. Self-motivated working is a precondition for self-motivated learning. Young people must also develop other qualities before they can become responsible for themselves and before they can cope with setbacks and disappointments without becoming demoralised. Feelings of self-confidence, social confidence, body confidence and confidence in using the gym equipment all play a large part. It is essential that P.E. teachers avoid making any excessive demands on students while they are building their confidence, especially during puberty, when it can be particularly fragile, and it is important to find both appropriate teaching methods and content.

There is really no other school subject in which this approach to self-motivated work and learning can be so easily implemented as in P.E. In P.E. lessons in Waldorf schools, the percentage of time the children spend being active is very high, and if the tasks they are set are difficult (while still being age-appropriate) then every single student will do their best. When the various exercises are expanded on or approached from a different angle, then the children's skills are further improved. Furthermore, if the teacher allows the students greater scope in how they approach the tasks, then each student can adapt the level of difficulty to their particular ability. In this way, they find their own learning rhythm: they progress at their own pace in a way that matches their individual needs, and this makes the work more fun to do. When the children return to the changing rooms after a lesson, red-faced and perspiring, they feel a sense of achievement in what they have been able to do. If P.E. teachers repeatedly manage to integrate moments like these into their lessons, then the experiment in educating towards freedom, at the heart of Waldorf education, has a good chance of succeeding.

Self-motivated working and learning takes time. But when students really get to grips with a task and are absorbed by it, then everything else takes a back seat. The work at hand becomes all-important. This can be clearly seen in lessons where students in the Upper School are working with students in the Middle School on the school circus project (see pp. 263f). When the older students take on responsibility for teaching the younger ones, helping them to learn and perfect special skills, a learning process is set in motion that is unequalled in normal school life. The keen observer might ask, 'Who is learning more in this moment: the younger student who wants to learn something new, or the older, more experienced student who has taken on the role of instructor?'

Precious moments like this make possible a form of learning which draws close to the words spoken by Rudolf Steiner at the start of this essay and which describe one of the aims of Waldorf education: all education is self-education and it is the responsibility of the teacher to provide the right setting in which this can take place. This is possible in all subjects and with all age groups, but with the special opportunities it offers, P.E. can lead the way.

Part Two
Physical Education from Class 1 to Class 12

Introductory Remarks

Gerlinde Idler

This part of the book provides sample physical education lessons for each school class, with examples of suitable games and exercises. It also describes how different age groups tend to respond to P.E. In describing pupils of various ages, we have considered the corresponding stage of development according to Waldorf teaching principles, though we are aware that in different countries children start school at different ages – some are not yet six; others are already seven and a half. As well as the age of the individual child, the unique composition of the group must also be taken into account, such as the ratio of boys to girls and the number of firstborn and only children in the class. Many diverse factors will play a significant part in how a particular group responds to planned lessons.

In describing the age groups, we also make reference to the content and themes of other school subjects taught in the corresponding class, and outline important motor skills developing at that stage.

The lesson material we cover is designed as a progression from Class 1 to Class 12. The examples we have chosen are not meant to be seen as recipes for copying, but rather as illustrations gathered by P.E. teachers with more than twenty-five years' experience of teaching in Waldorf schools. Most of them are designed for classes with up to forty pupils but can easily be adapted to smaller classes or carried out with less equipment in less space. The most important thing is always the pupils and their particular needs, combined with the strengths and capabilities of the P.E. teacher.

When it comes to planning lessons, a yearly planner showing all of the school's events and festivals for that year is very helpful. This is particularly true for those lessons involving project work, as the projects take place over a period of several weeks, and ideally these are not interrupted. A yearly planner provides a good picture of whether project work is viable or not and when pupils will get the most from the experience. Planning lessons on an annual basis also gives pupils and teachers a chance to show what they have accomplished during the various events and festivals that the school holds, for example, the St Michael festival in late September.

Class 1:
From Imitating to Following – Teaching Through Images and Stories

Class 1 pupils

Children come to their first physical education lesson full of expectation and an eagerness to take part. They are all the more enthusiastic when games and exercises are embedded in an imaginative framework. That is why Jochem Nietzold recommends that 'after the games they have enjoyed in kindergarten, in their first two school years children need imaginative, rhythmical, musical games'.[1]

In Class 1, children thrive on the ordered movements of roundelays: group games accompanied by songs that involve walking, running, dancing and marching. Pentatonic music (thought to represent an early stage in humanity's musical development) is just right for children of this age. Pentatonic music creates an atmosphere which is vibrant yet comforting and where possible it should be used in all Class 1 P.E. lessons.

Sophia Meyer-Fischer describes the Class 1 stage:

> In their first school year, children are in the process of losing their milk teeth. This does not just affect the body but signifies a metamorphosis of the whole being. Certain etheric forces, which have previously worked on shaping and organising the physical body, are now set free and become spiritual.[2]

The children of Class 1 need to feel rhythm and measured time within themselves, and everything we offer them works best when structured in a measured and rhythmical way.[3]

Approaches to teaching Class 1

In the first school year, for P.E. lessons with the whole class, it is important that the P.E. teacher leads the lesson, even though the children are accompanied by their class teacher. This avoids confusing the children over who they should pay attention to during the lesson and allows the theme of 'from imitating to following' to impress itself upon them more effectively.

Nevertheless, the two teachers must work closely together. Ideally, the P.E. teacher visits the class during the main lesson to see how the class teacher works with the children. This gives the P.E. teacher the chance to see which signs and gestures the children are accustomed to and where they are in their development.

Each P.E. lesson begins with the P.E. teacher collecting the children from the classroom and ends with bringing them back. There is a fixed ritual at the beginning; for example, the children enter the P.E. hall in a long line accompanied by a short poem or a song. After that, a game might be played in a circle.[4] These rhythmical, repetitive elements give the children a sense of security, as does content that is appropriate for their age group. Everything in the lesson is cloaked in imaginative pictures and stories, similar to the fairy tales and other stories heard in Class 1. At this age, children live in a world of pictures. As Rudolf Kischnik writes:

> Often [children] cannot differentiate between fantasy and reality, because what they feel and experience inwardly is stronger than outward appearances. In this situation, you cannot do them a bigger favour than giving them a chance, with their entire body, to live out the forms and figures of their imagination.[5]

The circle is another element of the lessons that gives children a feeling of warmth and safety. Games are played over many weeks, and this also enhances the sense of familiarity and continuity.

Main aspects of the lessons

With their imaginative abilities, Class 1 children thrive on stimulating, age-appropriate games. Pictures from the stories they hear are taken up and intensified, and the sheer joy of shared activities heightens the experience. Children also learn new forms of movement and social interplay.

Suggested activities for Class 1

- Roundelays: games with singing and skipping.
- Role-playing games.
- Games of catch and tag.
- Clapping and stamping games using rhymes.
- Finger games, for example, cat's cradle.
- Running, jumping, balancing, skipping games.
- Ball games.
- Simple, easy exercises with hand apparatus and other materials, such as hoop, rope, ball, balloons, feathers, cloths.
- Simple obstacle courses. Indoors, in the absence of any proper apparatus, this might make use of classroom furniture. Outdoors, obstacles can include anything in the playground, such as tree trunks or small boulders.
- Swinging.
- Climbing.
- Free imaginative play.

Additional activities for Class 1

- Hiking trips.
- Games in water as a preparation for swimming lessons.
- Ice skating.
- Skiing (introductory steps).

Information on sample lessons

Two sample lessons have been provided for Class 1: one for indoors and one for outdoors, though either could be adapted to suit the space available in a particular school. Both are suitable for large classes as well as smaller ones.

Sample Lesson: Dwarves. Duration: 45 mins			
Time	**Sequence of activities**	**Formation**	**Material used**
c. 5 mins.	The P.E. teacher asks the children to put on their P.E. shoes and go to the toilet if they need to. The P.E. teacher then leads the children in a line to the hall or the outdoor space where the lesson will take place.	An orderly walk.	None.
c. 5 mins.	The children enter the hall as the Giant Snake (see p. 211). They form a circle and exchange greetings.	Circle.	None.
c. 10 mins.	Game: The Pointy Hat. 1. The children form a circle. One child steps inside it and holds their hands on their head in the shape of the pointy hat. 2. To the tune of 'Here We Go Round the Mulberry Bush' (or adapting any similar song with a good walking beat), the children hold hands and walk round in a circle singing: Here we go round the pointy hat Pointy hat, pointy hat Here we go round the pointy hat In a bold and happy circle! The pointy hat child walks the other way. 3. When the teacher says, 'Stop!' the pointy hat child turns to the child facing them in the circle. They take hands and jump up, knees bent, kicking their feet behind them. 4. The song begins again, but now there are two children walking inside the circle with pointy hats. 5. The game continues until all children are 'wearing' a pointy hat.	Circular game.	None.
c. 10 mins.	A short obstacle course. 1. The teacher tells a story that incorporates the various obstacles and challenges in an imaginative way. For example: a dwarf with a pointed hat dares to go into a magic forest. He climbs over rocks and fallen tree trunks and jumps over little streams. When the bell rings, he finds his way back home. 2. The children are now allowed into the 'forest', returning to stand in the circle whenever the teacher rings a small bell. 3. The story continues and the children are given tasks to carry out, such as collecting precious stones together (coloured balls), rolling boulders (medicine balls) to the river bank (rolled-up mat) or they must find a store of chestnuts, and bring them back as fodder for the animals in winter.	Circular and free movement.	Benches, mats, hoops, plus small items such as balls or chestnuts for the finding task.

Time	Sequence of activities	Formation	Material used
c. 7 mins.	Game: King Big Ears. 1. All sit in a circle. The teacher tells the children about a special dwarf called King Big Ears who can hear everything. 2. One child is picked to be King Big Ears and sits in front of the teacher with their eyes closed. The teacher then points at several children, who get up and sit down quietly in a line behind King Big Ears. 3. The teacher asks, 'King Big Ears, how many children are sitting behind you?' and the child guesses. If there is time, repeat the game with another child as King Big Ears.	Circle.	None.
c. 5 mins.	End of the lesson. The children stand in a circle and chant: *[stamping loudly]* We're stamping, we're stamping, one, two, three! *[on tiptoe]* We're creeping, we're creeping, you can't hear me. *[standing quietly]* We're standing, we're standing, as still as can be. After a few moments of silence, the P.E. teacher and the children exchange farewells.	Circle.	None.
c. 3 mins.	The children leave the hall, walk back to the classroom together in an orderly fashion, and change into their school shoes.	An orderly walk.	None.

Sample Lesson: Fun in circles. Duration: 45 mins			
Time	**Sequence of activities**	**Formation**	**Material used**
c. 5 mins.	The P.E. teacher asks the children to put on their P.E. shoes and go to the toilet if they need to. The P.E. teacher then leads the children in a line to the outdoor area where the lesson will take place.	–	None.
c. 5 mins.	The children leave the building as the Giant Snake. The children form a circle and exchange greetings.	Long line into a circle.	None.
c. 5 mins.	Musical game: The Rover. 1. The children hold hands in a circle. The teacher picks one child to be the 'wanderer'. To the tune of 'The Gypsy Rover' (or a similar wandering song), the others all sing: The wand'ring traveller came over the hill, Bound for the green plains belo-ow, She clapped and she sang, And she stamped round again, Till she waved at a friend to come o-o-over. 2. The wanderer child walks around the outside of the circle until they get to the 'green plains' in the song. At this point, two children create a gap in the circle and let the child in. 3. The wanderer child claps as the song says, then stamps around until they wave at one of the children in the circle. This child dances around with the wanderer in the middle while the song is repeated, then becomes the new wanderer.	Circle.	None.
c. 10 mins.	Game: Good Morning, Dear Neighbour, and How Do You Do? 1. The children stand in a circle, holding hands. The teacher picks one child to run around the outside of the circle. At some point the child taps a classmate on the back. 2. This child runs the other way around the outside of the circle until the two children meet. They stop, shake hands, and the second child says, 'Good morning, dear neighbour, and how do you do? Goodbye!' 3. Both children then run on their separate ways, trying to get back to the gap left in the circle by the second child. The slower child must then run on, tapping someone else on the back. Note: This game can be played repeatedly. If some children are picked more than others, then children who have had their turn sit to the side and watch.	Circle.	None.

Time	Sequence of activities	Formation	Material used
c. 10 mins.	Game of tag: Three Blind Mice. 1. The teacher sets up a circle of rope inside the circle of children to represent the 'pot', chooses one child to walk outside the children's circle, then begins the game with the first few notes of the song. 2. The circle moves round singing the song once while the outside child walks in the opposite direction. 3. When the song starts again, the outside child taps three classmates and they step outside too. This is repeated until there is only one left in the circle. This last child is the 'farmer's wife'. 4. The children run around the farmer's wife singing the song again. The farmer's wife tries to tap the others lightly with their 'knife' (a small stick or baton will do). Any child tapped has to go into the rope 'pot' in the centre of the circle. The farmer's wife does not need to catch more than five. Note: This game can be repeated once or twice.	Game of tag.	One stick or baton; a rope circle.
c. 5 mins.	End of the lesson. The children stand in a circle and exchange farewells. The class teacher leads them out of the room in a long line, chanting, See the wave rolling past, Not too slow and not too fast, Happy in the wind and weather, That we've had this time together.	Holding hands in a line.	None.
c. 5 mins.	The children leave the hall, walk back to the classroom together in an orderly fashion, and change into their school shoes.	An orderly walk.	None.

Class 2:
Games and Discoveries – Fables, Legends and Tales of the Natural World

Class 2 pupils

At this stage children are completely at home in the world of pictures, and they are discovering the boundaries between right and wrong. With game rules, as with social interplay, they like to see how far they can go. They are also learning to concentrate on a given task for longer periods. Socially, as well as spatially, they are more independent and better orientated.

In Class 2, children show greater personal commitment in all they do. This is particularly evident in games involving calling and answering: reciting the words and rhymes is important to them. Everything is practised and worked on within the group, until the children begin to take on individual roles and tasks. They enjoy repeating the games and exercises in all sorts of variations, acting out the different roles.

Sophia Meyer-Fischer comments, 'Children slip into any role dealing with conflicts among animals and mythical creatures, acting out physically that which later becomes the spiritual ability of balancing and compensating.'[1]

Approaches to teaching Class 2

At most Waldorf schools, the combination of games and exercises continues into Class 2, with the class teacher and the P.E. teacher together giving one or two weekly lessons to the whole class. What was learned in Class 1 is now developed further. A bridge between outer movement and inner experience is formed through traditional roundelays, singing and skipping, as well as

various imaginative tasks cloaked in pictures and stories. Games remain at the forefront, because children at this stage learn best through the medium of play.

The element of call and response incorporated into these games is just right for this age group, and children love to take on the roles of the animals and mythical creatures. They often continue to play these games in the playground at break time.

It is possible to play simple games of tag that break up the circle, although, to ensure a positive experience for all participants, it is advisable that clear limits and instructions are laid down first (see games like 'Octopus' or 'The Magic Forest' as described in the sample lessons for Class 2 below).

Main aspects of the lessons

As in Class 1, the children are led through a world of imaginative pictures and stories. The experience of playing together, of running and jumping about, is an intense one: they are learning new forms of social interaction and developing new motor skills. Through this activity, children absorb pictures from the stories more intensely.

Suggested activities for Class 2

- Roundelays: games with singing and skipping.
- Role-playing games, games of catch and tag.
- Rhymes for clapping and stamping games.
- Finger games, for example, cat's cradle.
- Running, jumping, balancing, skipping, simple exercises with the long rope, stilts, exercises with a ball and other skills.
- First steps with hand apparatus (hoop, rope, ball) and other material (balloons, feathers, cloths).

- Simple obstacle courses, for example, Hengstenberg apparatus and classroom furniture or obstacles in the playground, such as tree trunks and small boulders.
- Swinging, climbing.
- Free play.

Additional activities for Class 2

- Hiking trips.
- Games in water as a preparation for swimming lessons.
- Ice skating.
- Skiing (introductory steps).

Information on sample lessons

For Class 2, three different sample lessons have been set out: one games lesson, one with skipping ropes and one with a parachute (or a large, circular, multi-coloured cloth). Each lesson can take place either in the sports hall or outdoors.

The aim is for these lessons to be repeated over a period of weeks, with the separate exercises being constantly varied. After a period of time spent introducing new themes, the content of past projects can be revived and developed – for example, short artistic tricks with the skipping rope, or playing 'Cat and Mouse' with the variation that the gate is quicker to close when the cat or mouse has to run through it.

The children of Class 2 also have lots of fun with adventure landscapes and exciting stories that lead them to feats of courage and the fulfilling of dangerous tasks – a continuation and development of the stories and games from Class 1.

As regards the parachute or cloth, the desired size and colours can be made from the silk used for lining garments. This comes in all colours, is easy to clean and much cheaper than real parachute silk (the only drawback being that games in 'the igloo' are not as satisfying because the thermal qualities enable real parachute silk to form an igloo in which the children play). For a class of roughly thirty-six children, a size of between 5 m x 5 m (16 ft x 16 ft) and 7 m x 7 m (23 ft x 23 ft) is recommended. But take the size of the room into account.

Sample Lesson: Games. Duration: 45 mins			
Time	Sequence of activities	Formation	Material used
c. 2 mins.	The children are led into the hall, hand in hand, in a long line. The P.E. teacher, class teacher and children form a circle and exchange greetings.	Standing in a circle.	None.
c. 10 mins.	Game: Cat and Mouse. 1. The P.E. teacher tells the children, 'In today's lesson, we are going to meet lots of different animals starting with a cat and a mouse.' The teacher then chooses two children, one to be the cat and the other the mouse. 2. All the children stand in a big circle and hold hands, except the 'mouse' is inside the circle while the 'cat' is on the outside. 3. A call and response begins the game: **Cat: 'Mousey, mousey, come on out. I'll give you a piece of sugar.'** *Mouse: 'Don't like sugar.'* **Cat 'Mousey, mousey, come on out. I'll give you a piece of bacon.'** *Mouse: 'Don't like bacon.'* **Cat: 'Mousey, mousey, come on out. Or I'll scratch your eyes out.'** *Mouse: 'Why don't you try!'* 4. The mouse can go through every gap in the circle, but the cat is prevented by the class, who continue holding hands. If the cat manages to touch the mouse, then the mouse is a prisoner. If not, then two other children are chosen and the game starts again. When the game is over, the P.E. teacher calls, 'Three, two, one, game is done,' signalling to the children to return to the original circle.	Circle.	None.
c. 10 mins.	Game of tag: The Beast Down in the Hole. 1. The P.E. teacher marks out the area in which the game is to be played, either on the field or in a suitable space (we suggest an area of around 20 m x 30 m – just larger than 65 ft x 100 ft). The children are divided into two equal lines facing each other, and the teacher picks a child to be the 'beast' who stands in the middle between the two lines. 2. The verse for this game goes: There is a beast down in the hole, It isn't a mole, It isn't a vole. It's looking around for something to munch, Run away quick, or you'll be its lunch!	Game of tag.	None.

Time	Sequence of activities	Formation	Material used
Cont.	3. With each line of the verse, the two rows march four steps backwards and forwards, while the beast crouches in the middle, growling and looking fierce. As soon as the verse ends, it jumps up and tries to tag as many children as possible. The children are safe beyond the area marked out for the game. The beast runs after the rest, until no one is left in the field. Once a child leaves the field, they cannot come back on. When the game is over, the P.E. teacher calls, 'Three, two, one, game is done,' and the children return to the circle.	Game of tag.	None.
c. 10 mins.	Running game: The Octopus. 1. The P.E. teacher chooses one child to be the 'octopus'. 2. The children are all little 'fish' standing on one side of the playing area. The octopus waits on the other side. 3. A call and response begins the game: **Fish: 'Look over there! Is that the octopus?'** *Octopus: 'Mmm. So many little fishies and I'm sooo hungry!'* **Fish: 'Catch us if you can!'** The fish swim through the water to the other side of the hall. Every time a fish is caught by the octopus, it becomes a tentacle and helps the octopus catch other fishes from the place where it was caught. This goes on until no fish are left or the time is up.	Game of tag.	None.
c. 10 mins.	Circle game: The Conductor. 1. The P.E. teacher chooses one child, who is sent out of the room to wait until they are called back. The other children, sitting in a circle, decide who the conductor of their 'orchestra' will be. The conductor will perform various discrete movements that the other children will have to copy. 2. The child waiting outside is called back in and they must work out who the conductor is from watching the actions of all the children. They have three guesses. If there is time, the game can be repeated with a different child sent briefly from the room while a new conductor is chosen.	Circle.	None.
c. 3 mins.	End of the Lesson. The children stand in a circle and exchange farewells with the teacher, then they walk back to the classroom together.	Standing in a circle.	None.

Sample Lesson: Skipping ropes. Duration: 45 mins			
Time	**Sequence of activities**	**Formation**	**Material used**
c. 5 mins.	The children are led into the hall where they form a circle and exchange greetings. The P.E. teacher announces, 'Today, we are going on a trip to the circus.'	Standing in a circle.	None.
c. 20 mins.	1. The P.E. teacher gives each child a skipping rope. They place it on the ground in a straight line from their feet pointing towards the middle of the circle. 2. The P.E. teacher tells them an exciting story about the circus. 'The circus is in town, children! They have pitched the Big Top and the show is about to begin! Let's head off for the fairground.' 3. The children run around the outside of the rope circle several times before returning to their places. 4. The P.E. teacher turned ringmaster then tells them all about the sensational acts waiting to perform, calling out the various animals and performers as they enter the ring one after another. As they speak, the teacher moves around the outside of the circle in a clockwise direction, tapping individual children on the shoulder as a sign for them to enter the circle. 5. The children then become the animals and the performers: horses prancing over the ropes, goats jumping, elephants marching, tightrope walkers performing tricks on the skipping ropes lying on the ground, and so on. 6. At the end of the performance, the children return to their original positions in the circle, moving in an anti-clockwise direction, and the skipping ropes are collected in.	Circle.	Skipping ropes (made from hemp if possible).
c. 5 mins.	Changeover. A short running game: Whirlwind. 1. Depending on the size of the group, the P.E. teacher chooses between three and five children who stand in the middle of the circle each wearing a blue ribbon. The remaining children stand around them with their eyes closed. 2. The children in the middle – the 'whirlwinds' – begin to howl eerily and when they stop, the other children open their eyes and run off. Anyone caught by a 'whirlwind' waits on the side until the next game begins. If there is time, the game can be repeated with a new group of whirlwinds. 3. When the game is finished, the teacher calls the children back to the circle by saying, 'Three, two, one, game is done!	Running game.	Blue ribbons.

Time	Sequence of activities	Formation	Material used
c. 10 mins.	Game: Dog and Bone. 1. The children lie face down pretending to be sleeping dogs with their eyes shut. In front of each one, there is a shoe – this is their 'bone'. In the middle, there sits a big, hungry dog – initially this is the teacher, although it can also be one of the children. The hungry dog has no bone. 2. The teacher tries to creep up and pinch one of the sleeping dogs' 'bones'. If they are successful, they say, 'Mmm, look what I've found.' The children look up and the child whose bone is missing is out of the game. 3. If one of the children sense that their 'bone' is about to be stolen, they bark. If they are right, they keep their bone and remain in the game. If not, they too are out and have to sit and watch.	Lying in a circle.	Single shoes.
c. 5 mins.	End of Lesson. The children stand in a circle and exchange farewells with the teacher, then they walk back to the classroom in line together.	Standing in a circle.	None.

Sample Lesson: Parachutes. Duration: 45 mins			
Time	Sequence of activities	Formation	Material used
c. 2 mins.	The children are led into the hall, where they form a circle and exchange greetings. The P.E. teacher announces, 'Today we are all going on a trip to the magic forest.'	Line becomes a circle.	None.
c. 7 mins.	Game: The Magic Forest. 1. Everyone sits in a circle. The parachute cloth is spread out in the middle. 2. The P.E. teacher tells a story about the Magic Forest. Each time a colour is mentioned that matches part of the cloth, the children sit on that segment. 3. The children take on the roles of the animals in the story: galloping, creeping, jumping or crawling along. Every time another colour appears in the story, the teacher also mentions a new animal for the children to perform. 4. At the end of the story the P.E. teacher calls out, 'Three, two, one, game is done.'	Running in a circle.	Multi-coloured parachute cloth (see Information on sample lessons, above).
c. 1 mins.	Changeover. The children are split into two lines and sit opposite each other with the parachute cloth between them.	Two rows.	Parachute.
c. 10 mins.	Free movement: running and jumping about bound up in story form. 1. The P.E. teacher tells the children about a frozen lake, which they can cross if they are careful and succeed in carrying out a particular activity. Every time they succeed in one activity, they return to their places and wait for the next one. 2. The various activities might be: ▸ Swimming underneath the ice: the children wriggle along the ground under the parachute. ▸ Leaping over the stream: the cloth is rolled up, held at both ends and swung to and fro. The stream gets wider and the waves get higher. ▸ A fallen tree blocks the way and the children must wriggle underneath it: the cloth is rolled up and held taut and low down. 3. At the end of the story, the children balance over a narrow footbridge (the rolled-up cloth is held taut along the ground) and sit back down in a circle.	Free movement.	Parachute.
c. 2 mins.	Changeover: The Storm. The P.E. teacher says, 'A big storm is coming!' *The children all drum on the cloth with their fingertips.* 'The wind is getting stronger.' *The children blow and howl.* 'The thunder rolls.' *They drum on the floor with their fists.* 'And the storm gets louder.' *They hammer their heels on the floor.*	Circle.	Parachute.

Time	Sequence of activities	Formation	Material used
Cont.	'The wind raises huge waves,' *First sitting, then standing, they all hold the cloth and raise and lower it to make big waves.* 'Then, finally, the storm slowly abates.' *They sit back down and the cloth comes to rest.* 'Only a few raindrops can be heard.' *They tap quietly on the cloth.* 'At last the storm is over.'		
c. 7 mins.	Game of tag: The Fishermen and the Fish. 1. The P.E. teacher tells the class they are sitting around a pond (the parachute). 2. The P.E. teacher picks between five and seven children, depending on the size of the class. These children turn away from the pond and wait. 3. The P.E. teacher picks between five and ten children to be fish, who then slip into the water (under the cloth). The remaining children help to make waves, so that the fishermen do not catch all the fish at once. 4. The remaining children call out, 'Take care! Take care! The fishermen are there.' This is the sign for all the fishermen (the children who turned away) to turn back and crawl onto the cloth on hands and knees, and catch the fish underneath. 5. Every fish caught goes back to their place in the circle. When every fish has been caught, or the time is up, the teacher calls, 'Three, two, one, game is done.'	Game of tag.	Parachute.
c. 7 mins.	Game of tag: The Crocodile in the River. 1. The P.E. teacher tells the children that they are sitting by a pool in a river. 2. The children sit in a circle around the pool. Every second child puts their feet in the water (under the cloth). No one is allowed to peek under the cloth. 3. A hungry crocodile is chosen who slides into the water (under the cloth). The children meanwhile flap the cloth to simulate waves. 4. The crocodile now tags the toes of one child after another, who, having been 'eaten', cry out once and disappear into the water (under the cloth). 5. When all the children with their feet in the water have been eaten, the game is over and they return to their places in the circle. 6. When the game is repeated, the other children put their feet in the water and a new crocodile is chosen.	Game of tag.	Parachute.
c. 2 mins.	Changeover: The Storm. Repeat the story of the storm until silence descends.	Circle.	Parachute.
c. 5 mins.	End of the lesson. The children stand in a circle and exchange farewells with the P.E. teacher, then they walk back to the classroom together.	Standing in a circle.	None.

Class 3:
Being Active in the World – Crossing the Rubicon

Class 3 pupils

At the beginning of the third school year, we are met with individuals who are curious, trusting and ready for anything. They have found their place in the class community and hopefully feel at home there. In most cases, the children have become more coordinated in their movements and feel more self-assured; they feel their way into the environment around them and into all their activities. They are clothed in a certain warmth, in the broadest sense, which offers comfort despite their impending apprehension of the end of childhood. Tonnie Brounts and Helga Daniel characterise the situation in the following way:

> Up to the age of nine or thereabouts, children see the world and people around them just as they experience these things inwardly with all their imaginative power. But now they become aware of the difference between their inner experience and the real world outside themeselves. This can lead to a feeling of rejection and loneliness. Children begin to sense that other people experience the world differently and therefore cannot really understand what they feel like inside. This is also the stage at which the children realise they are able to put themselves in someone else's place, though this realisation tends to make life harder rather than easier.[1]

In Waldorf education, this point is called the 'Rubicon'. The word compares a child's development with the moment when Julius Caesar crossed the River Rubicon and committed himself

to war with the Roman senate. It marks a point of no return. For the individual child this means there can be no return to that earlier time when they felt more seamlessly joined to the world around them. Instead they begin to experience themselves as an increasingly separate, self-contained individual. This moment represents a serious crisis that all children must deal with. As Brounts and Daniel go on to say:

> It is important to mention that this crisis goes hand in hand with a change in the breathing rhythm. The relationship between pulse rate and breathing changes and becomes that of adults, i.e. one breath for four heartbeats.[2]

Fear and insecurity tend to arise when there is a change in the heartbeat and circulatory system. In Class 3, the main lesson stories are taken mostly from the Old Testament. The story of Adam and Eve and their banishment from Eden in particular reflects the emotional state of children of this age. What can help them overcome this period of insecurity is meaningful, manual activity. When children engage in free play, they immerse themselves in activity and in accompanying mental imagery. The customary pattern of their active free play is to wear themselves out and then stop 'for a breather'. This helps their bodies establish 'correct breathing', in a physical sense, and also in the sense of alternating between strenuous and relaxing activity, between excitement and calm. This play is important for healthy development.

As the physical act of breathing becomes freer, the children become more focused and present in all they do. Towards the end of Class 3, they are hopefully more self-assured, more self-confident and more alert.

Approaches to teaching Class 3

From Class 3 onwards, the P.E. teacher takes over the lesson entirely. Usually there is one double lesson or two single lessons a week. For the children, this represents something new: they are no longer 'just playing games'; rather they are taking part in their first 'proper' P.E. lessons. Getting changed into their P.E. kit helps to instil this feeling. In the classroom there are P.E. bags, each containing shorts, a shirt and eurythmy shoes. The pupils are led from the classroom to the changing rooms and then into the hall (or wherever the lesson is to be held).

In the first lesson, the class and P.E. teacher form a circle (see sample lessons below and the description of 'our circle') in which each child has their own special place. This remains the same throughout the school year. This is where every lesson begins and ends, and when something new is introduced or something is explained, the children return to the same place in the circle.

At the beginning of Class 3, certain customs are introduced that are retained in the following years; this helps create a feeling of security. For example, there is the 'treasure chest', in which valuables (jewellery, watches and so on) are collected and kept until the end of the lesson. There might also be a 'hair bobble bowl', containing bands that children with long hair can borrow during the lesson, and a lost and found box, full of useful garments for children who have forgotten to bring their P.E. kit or in which they might later find their own lost belongings.

Children at this age love to take on special tasks. One popular role is to be the 'treasurer', responsible for the treasure chest at the start and the end of lessons; another is helping to set up and dismantle the gymnastic apparatus. The more consistently these habits and customs are introduced, the more organised and effective the children will be all the way through to the higher classes.

Everything that is regular and rhythmical gives children the confidence to try something new. The call and response element of a game or a special verse provide safe ground before the adventure begins. Meaningful pictures and images are taken up with great enthusiasm. Language and rhythm are also at the heart of the Bothmer exercises. The children soon get to know and enjoy the long sequence of movements as they move together in a common rhythm. The main aim is that the children learn to work wholeheartedly together at all the activities, especially those involving manual equipment and obstacle courses.

Main aspects of the lessons

The circle is at the heart of P.E. lessons, with its emphasis on the communal experience. Children love accomplishing tasks that enable them to experience the world and test their own abilities. Some of the topics dealt with in the main lesson are taken up in P.E., employing pictures and images that are both emotive and imaginative.

Suggested activities for Class 3

- Games in the circle, games of catch and tag.
- Clapping and stamping games, rhymes and verses.
- Finger games, for example, cat's cradle.
- Bothmer exercises: the first roundelay.
- Running, hopping, balancing, skipping, stilts.
- Games with a ball: throwing and catching, bouncing, rebounding off the wall.
- Games for learning basic skills with manual equipment, such as hoops, ropes, balls and other things like balloons, feathers and cloths.
- Simple obstacle courses.
- Swinging.

- Climbing.
- Tumbling, forward rolls.
- Free imaginative play.

Additional activities for Class 3

- Hiking trips.
- Games in water as a preparation for swimming lessons.
- Ice skating.
- Skiing (introductory steps).

Information on sample lessons

There is a wealth of material for this age group. It would be great for the children's development if we could have P.E. lessons every day, but as this is usually not possible, it is important that what P.E. tachers do in the time they have meets the demands of the children's particular stage of development. This requires close observation. For example, are the children ready to tackle an obstacle course? What about a skipping exercise or a team game?

The sample lessons below show how important rituals and habits are. The first one is best carried out in a sports hall, whereas the games lesson with the manual equipment can use any indoor or outdoor space.

It is a good idea to make the same equipment used during the P.E. lessons, such as balls and ropes, available at break time and in the after-school care group. This has a positive effect on the playground atmosphere and allows children to continue movements they have been exploring.

All P.E. teachers are encouraged to try their hand at Bothmer exercises and introduce them with Class 3 pupils. If you are unsure, find an expert to show you how to carry them out, then practise until you feel confident enough to try them with the children.

Beginning the lesson with the first Bothmer exercise and the accompanying verse can be a satisfying experience. It is lovely to see how the children get into the swing of it, and enjoy the rhythm and the images. Gradually, over the course of the year, more and more is added, until the children know the entire sequence. As with all rituals, when the children know this exercise forms part of every lesson, it gives them a feeling of security.

Occasionally, when games take place outdoors or when lessons are shortened by the extensive setting up and dismantling of equipment, the Bothmer exercise can be set aside for a while. When it is revived, the children take real pleasure in performing it in small groups and then learning the next segment.

Sample Lesson: The first 'proper' P.E. lesson. Duration: 90 mins

Time	Sequence of activities	Formation	Material used
c. 5 mins.	The P.E. teacher collects the children from the classroom or the playground and accompanies them to the changing rooms. After changing, they form a line and the P.E. teacher leads them into the hall.	In a line.	None.
c. 10 mins.	The P.E. teacher calls out the children's names one after another. Each child then takes their place in the circle that is beginning to form in the middle of the hall. This continues until all the children are sitting in the circle. The P.E. teacher then asks the children to memorise where they are in the circle – for example, who they are standing next to and what the markings on the floor look like if there are any. From then on it is known as 'our circle' and the children keep their particular places throughout the year. The P.E. teacher also has a particular place, perhaps between children who benefit from staying close to an adult.	A circle takes shape.	Class register.
c. 4 mins.	The children exchange greetings. The P.E. teacher selects one child to be the 'treasurer', who will be responsible for the 'treasure chest'. This can be any type of container. The treasurer places it in the middle of the circle and all the children put their valuables into it. The treasurer puts the container safely to one side or in the equipment room. The teacher offers hairbands to those with long hair.	Circle.	Treasure chest container, hairbands.
c. 5 mins.	A colour is called out. The children wearing clothing of that colour run one lap around the circle in a given direction before returning to their places. The teacher tells a short story in which various colours appear. Every time the children hear one of the colours on their clothing mentioned, they run one lap.	Circle.	None.
c. 5 mins.	In the next variation, animals appear in the story. Now the children must not only listen out for colours, but also for the different animals. They then move around the circle in the manner of that animal – for example, slinking like a cat, galloping like a horse and so on.	Circle.	None.
c. 7 mins.	Game of tag: The Autumn Wind. 1. The P.E. teacher tells a story about the autumn wind, which gets stronger and colder as it blows. 2. Depending on the size of the class, the teacher chooses between three and five children to be the autumn wind. They are given coloured team bands and stand in the middle of the circle. The children standing around the circle close their eyes. 3. The children in the middle take a deep breath and blow loudly, which signals the beginning of the game of tag and the moment for the others to open their eyes and run. The autumn wind children chase, blowing. Rather than tagging by touching, any running children who feel the cold wind pretend to be frozen stiff, standing still with their legs apart. They can only be released if another running child stops to crawl between their legs.	Game of tag.	Three to five team bands of the same colour.

Time	Sequence of activities	Formation	Material used
Cont.	4. After a while, the teacher calls out, 'Three, two, one, game is done.' All the children return to their places in 'our circle'. The game can be repeated with new children as the autumn wind.		
c. 10 mins.	The first Bothmer exercise. 1. Everyone kneels down, facing inwards. 2. The teacher provides the rhythm for the opening lines of the verse (no words as yet) by slapping their thighs. The children join in. 3. Once the rhythm has been established, the teacher picks between five and seven children who run, skip and jump around the circle, trying to keep in time with the clapping. They turn and repeat the exercise in the other direction. 4. The children return to their places and then it is the turn of another group. If possible, every child should have a turn. 5. Finish with everyone sitting in the circle.	Circle.	None.
c. 7 mins.	Obstacle course: A Trip to the Mountains – Part 1. 1. The apparatus is set up to represent a mountain range with a route through it that avoids touching the floor. 2. The children are divided into groups of three or four, and each group is given a different colour of team band. One child in each group is picked to be the mountain guide. 3. The teacher tells the class about a trip to the mountains, describing rocks and streams, ravines and narrow paths, ridges and rope bridges. The teacher explains how important it is that the teams stay together and that they keep to the path to avoid getting their feet wet. 4. One group after another sets off along the path over the mountains, following their team guide. The children can climb from one piece of equipment to the next or use the gymnastic hoops on the ground as stepping-stones. They must avoid touching the floor, which would mean getting their feet wet. 5. After a time, the teacher calls, 'Three, two, one, game is done' and the children return to their places in the circle.	Begin in a circle, then in groups on the obstacle course.	Various apparatus (e.g. benches, vaulting box), hoops, team bands.

Time	Sequence of activities	Formation	Material used
c. 7 mins.	Obstacle course: A Trip to the Mountains – Part 2. 1. Each group gets a new mountain guide and they set off again. 2. Any children who get their feet 'wet' must stop by one of the teachers and get them dried (the teacher gives their feet a quick rub.) before they carry on climbing.	As above.	As above.
c. 7 mins.	Obstacle course: A Trip to the Mountains – Part 3. 1. The P.E. teacher tells the children about a mighty eagle that lives in the mountains. The eagle is enjoying its midday nap and must not be disturbed. 2. If the children get too loud the teacher blows a loud whistle to signal that the eagle has woken up. The children must hide among the apparatus – the rocks and caves – until the eagle returns to its eyrie, as signalled by the teacher blowing the whistle a second time. 3. After a while, the teacher calls out, 'Three, two, one, game is done.' The children return to their places in the circle.	As above.	As above.
c. 5 mins.	Clearing the equipment away. If possible, two teachers supervise. One goes into the equipment room and waits for the other to send the children through with the various items. Instructions must be exact, for example: 'Yellow team, collect the stepping-stones [the hoops] and take them to the teacher, then come back to your places.' The teachers put away the larger pieces of equipment afterwards.	None.	None.
c. 8 mins.	Game: Sleepyhead. 1. The P.E. teacher yawns and says to the children, 'After all these adventures, we are very tired. Everybody look for a place to have a snooze.' 2. The children spread out and lie down on the floor, not too close to each other or too near to the wall. They close their eyes and pretend to fall asleep. 3. The teacher taps two children on the shoulder. They wake up and are then allowed to wake others up. Those who are awakened get up and wait. When there are only two children left, everyone calls out, 'Sleepyheads!' These two last children must now catch the others. 4. The ones that are caught sit at the side until the next round, which begins with two new 'awakeners'.	All spread out.	None.
c. 10 mins.	End of the lesson. The treasurer brings out the treasure chest and the children collect their valuables. They exchange farewells and, in an orderly line, they go to the changing rooms. When everybody is ready, the children return to the classroom. The P.E. teacher gives each one a handshake.	Circle.	Treasure chest.

Sample Lesson: Ball games. Duration: 45 mins			
Time	**Sequence of activities**	**Formation**	**Material used**
c. 3 mins.	The P.E. teacher collects the children from the classroom or the playground and accompanies them to the changing rooms. After changing, they form a line and the P.E. teacher leads them into the hall.	Standing in a line.	None.
c. 2 mins.	The children take up their places in 'our circle' and exchange greetings. The treasurer brings in the treasure chest and the children place their valuables in it.	Circle.	Treasure chest.
c. 5 mins.	Game of tag: Bobble Robin. 1. The children sit in a circle. The P.E. teacher puts on a bobble hat and becomes Bobble Robin. 2. The children point at the P.E. teacher and call out, 'Look who's there! It's Bobble Robin! He's going to tell us a story.' 3. The teacher makes up a story featuring a dragon or a monster who lives in the wood. They describe its ferocious appearance – its sharp teeth and long claws, its big scary eyes. Finally, the teacher says, 'Now I'm going to show you how it would *eat you all up!*' 4. The children run away. Anyone the teacher catches is out and waits at the side until a new game begins. 5. When the game is finished, the P.E. teacher calls out, 'Three, two, one, game is done!' and the children return to the circle.	Game of tag.	A bobble hat.
c. 8 mins.	Game: The Clock. 1. The children stand in a small circle and the P.E. teacher stands in the middle. (Form two circles if there are two teachers.) 2. Turning in a clockwise direction, the teacher throws a softball to each child and the child throws it back. When the teacher throws the ball, everyone says 'tick', and when the child throws it back, everyone says 'tock'. This can be repeated with numerous variations, for example: ▸ the clock goes backwards – throwing and catching anticlockwise; ▸ the clock has fallen off the wall and is broken – throwing in no fixed order; ▸ the clock goes wild – the ball is rolled, bounced or thrown between legs, and must be returned the same way; ▸ the clockmaker comes to repair the clock – the children hold out their hands palms up and the ball rolls from one hand to the next around the circle; or ▸ use a different kind of ball. Note: With the throwing and catching, children who have caught and returned the ball three times sit down.	Circle.	A selection of balls: softballs, tennis balls, juggling balls.

Time	Sequence of activities	Formation	Material used
c. 2 mins.	Changeover. The children return to their places in 'our circle'. The teacher tells them of talented performers who can balance a ball on one fingertip and who have learned to juggle with several balls. The children are going to get a chance to do some simple exercises.	Circle.	A bouncy ball for every child.
c. 5 mins.	Simple exercises with a ball. Every child is given a ball and finds space to try out some exercises. At the end of each exercise, the teacher beats a tambourine or a gong. At the sound, the children stand still, holding their ball in both hands, while the teacher describes the next exercise. The exercises could include: ▸ bouncing the ball with one hand and then with the other; ▸ throwing the ball up into the air and catching it; ▸ rolling the ball to the wall so that it stops just before it touches the wall; or ▸ bouncing the ball, spinning round and catching it again.	Spread out.	A bouncy ball for every child; a gong, bell or tambourine for the teacher.
c. 8 mins.	Ball game: Ten Ball, Nine Ball. 1. Each child finds a space where they can throw their ball at the wall. The game consists of ten steps. Once each step has been accomplished, the children move on to the next one. The teacher stands in the middle, reminding them what comes next. 2. The ten steps: ▸ 10 times – throw the ball at the wall and catch it on the rebound. ▸ 9 times – throw the ball and clap once before catching. ▸ 8 times – throw the ball and clap twice before catching. ▸ 7 times – throw the ball and clap three times before catching. ▸ 6 times – throw ball and clap once behind your back before catching. ▸ 5 times – throw the ball and clap once, front and behind, before catching. ▸ 4 times – throw the ball under one leg at the wall and catch it. ▸ 3 times – throw the ball under the other leg and catch it. ▸ 2 times – children turn their backs to the wall, throw the ball over their heads, turn and catch it. ▸ 1 time – throw the ball at the wall, spin round and catch it.	Lined up in front of the wall.	As above.

Time	Sequence of activities	Formation	Material used
c. 2 mins.	Changeover. The teacher calls out, 'Three, two, one, game is done,' and the children return to the circle. The balls are collected in.	Circle.	A basket for the balls.
c. 8 mins.	The first Bothmer exercise 1. Everyone kneels down, facing inwards. 2. The teacher provides the rhythm for the opening lines of the verse (no words as yet) by slapping their thighs. The children join in. 3. Once the rhythm has been established, the teacher picks between five and seven children who run, skip and jump around the circle, trying to keep in time with the clapping. They turn and repeat the exercise in the other direction. 4. The children return to their places and then it is the turn of another group. If possible, every child should have a turn. 5. Finish with everyone sitting in the circle.'	Circle.	None.
c. 2 mins.	End of the lesson. The treasurer brings out the treasure chest and the children collect their valuables. They exchange farewells and, in an orderly line, go to the changing rooms. When everybody is ready, the children return to the classroom. The P.E. teacher gives each one a handshake.	Circle.	Treasure chest.

Class 4:
Face to Face – Meeting Each Other

Class 4 pupils

For the children of Class 4, encountering another individual is an important experience. Wide awake and alert, the children look at the teacher as if to say, 'Do you see me? Do you know who I am and what I can do?' During this phase it is important for the teacher to have short moments of personal contact with each child. This can be a word of praise or encouragement, a friendly hello or a farewell handshake, or simple eye contact. The children have taken a big step forward. They want to test themselves and their boundaries. They enjoy seeing how the teacher responds to a particularly weak handshake or a very firm one. 'I dare you,' is part of the world they live in.

Tonnie Brounts and Helga Daniel describe the situation of the children in Class 4 as follows:

> After the Rubicon has been crossed, the procedure is reversed. For three years, the children have been encouraged into action by their teacher; they have become one with the various exercises they have been practising. The effect of this has been to enable the children to immerse themselves in pictures, images and the general mood of the lessons. But now … they have their own inner pictures, which, of their own accord, they carry into the outside world.[1]

This means that the children perform the various exercises much more consciously when working on them. They are more self-reliant and want to find their own answers. They want to discover what the world is about and to move around in it, but they are also aware of themselves as being separate from the world. This allows them to become more inwardly aware of their own actions. They experience themselves as being in the centre of any given space, and as such they can keep to a line when running, while others are crisscrossing around them. They are self-aware and concentrated in their movements, yet can still remain in harmony with the group (this can be observed during the second Bothmer exercise).

The children are growing taller and they are keen to test their physical strength with others. In this phase, the middle senses of sight, smell, taste and warmth undergo a tremendous development, which leads to the world being experienced anew.

Approaches to teaching Class 4

At the beginning of Class 4, a couple of the old rituals are changed to take account of the children's further development. The children are no longer collected from the classroom but instead walk proudly to the hall of their own accord. They change then wait in line, in order to enter the hall together. The lesson begins in a different formation: in contrast to the circle, the children stand side by side in one long line facing the teacher for the greeting. This constitutes a new form of encounter, a new 'me and you'. During this phase, children like to test limits and quibble about instructions. For example, they will stand on a different blue line to the one the teacher meant, and maintain: 'You said "blue line"!' At such times, the teacher needs patience, presence of mind, a healthy sense of humour, and a calm manner.

Standing in a long line is not just useful for the greeting but also crops up in various gymnastic exercises such as 'Ringing the Bell' and the first exercises in rhythmical jumping. Similarly, in the classic game 'Ball Over the Rope', the children play facing each other – this will be the first time they change positions on a field, moving forwards and backwards, to left and right.

The virtues of chivalry (courage, honesty and determination) and the legends of the gods feature heavily in the other subjects for this age group, and these can be adapted for P.E. lessons.

Another recurring motif of Class 4 is the 'crossover'. This is explored in other subjects through symmetry in form drawing, with cross-stitch in needlework, and in many eurythmy forms. This element of mirroring and crossing-over can be introduced into P.E. lessons in various ways. For example, in running symmetrical paths over benches and ropes (see the sample lesson below), in clapping games with a partner where the hands and feet cross, swapping places on a narrow bridge or beam, or stepping out intricate forms marked on the ground using skipping ropes, as well as in folk dances.

In dealing with Class 4 children, it is important to find a new approach to the three soul forces of thinking, feeling and willing. From now on, the element of thinking gains importance: clear instructions are given without resorting to images from fairy tales. The will is strengthened by practising and repeating exercises, albeit for relatively short periods at this age. And feeling, the force of mediation between thinking and willing, should not be neglected here either. Through healthy feeling the children are able to participate 'heart and soul' in all the different tasks and challenges that the teachers set them. In the course of the fourth school year, it becomes increasingly important for the children to realise what they are capable of and what they can learn.

Main aspects of the lessons

The communal experience of 'we' has been replaced by a more self-aware perspective of 'me and you'. The children now see themselves and their potential in a new light and they deliberately seek out encounters with other individuals. Courage and zest for action are what motivate the children to test their abilities and practise them for short periods.

Suggested activities for Class 4

- Games with clapping and stamping, rhymes and rhythms.
- Finger games, for example, cat's cradle.
- The second Bothmer exercise.
- Simple exercises in rhythmical jumping with variations.
- Running and tag games, short relay races.
- Running, jumping, balancing, skipping, practising ball skills.
- Practising basic skills with manual apparatus such as baton, hoop, rope, ball, as well as other materials like balloons, feathers and cloths.
- Selected exercises on combinations of gym apparatus.
- First exercises on climbing ropes and rings.
- Climbing.
- Floor exercises: forward roll, backward roll, a series of rolls, cartwheel, headstand, shoulder stand.
- Folk dances.
- Free play.

Additional activities for Class 4

- Hiking trips.
- Games in water as a preparation for swimming lessons.
- Ice skating.
- Skiing (introductory steps).

Information on sample lessons

The following sample lessons cover the three options for P.E. lessons in Class 4. They include one double lesson of ninety minutes, indoors; one single lesson of forty-five minutes, indoors; and one single lesson of forty-five minutes, outdoors

Running and games of tag, which call for daring and commitment, are suitable for the beginning of the lessons. While the children are playing, teachers have the opportunity to assess the general mood of the class and to observe how individual children are tackling the various tasks and roles.

Following on from that, the second Bothmer exercise helps to concentrate the children's minds and calm them down. It can be beneficial to do this exercise not just once but several times, with a new element introduced each time. For example, 'Today we'll swing strongly despite the stiff breeze,' or 'Today we'll ring the bells in unison!' This exercise can also be used to conclude the lesson.

Concerning the various activities, children need to be given time to try things out and see what they can achieve. The lesson must therefore provide for such moments. It is wonderful to see how inventive children can be when they apply themselves to a particular tricky task.

Sample Lesson: Gymnastic apparatus. Duration: 90 mins

Time	Sequence of activities	Formation	Material used
c. 2 mins.	The children enter the hall and form a straight line. They exchange greetings and place their valuables in the treasure chest.	In a line.	None.
c. 12 mins.	Game: Guards and Robbers. 1. An area roughly the size of a volleyball court is marked out to serve as the 'forest'. A padded box large enough for a child to stand on is placed at each corner. These are the four towers. 2. The P.E. teacher picks four pupils to be the guardians of the towers. They are given coloured team bands and each steps up onto one of the towers. Three to four robbers are chosen, who take their places in the middle wearing team bands of a different colour. All the other children spread out in the forest. The teacher calls out, 'The robbers are in the forest!' and the game begins. 3. The robbers try to catch the children in the forest as quickly as possible. Once tagged by a robber, a child sits down. They can only be freed if they are tagged by one of the tower guardians. Once freed they can then re-join the game. 4. A guardian can also be tagged by one of the robbers and must wait to be freed in the same way. Standing on their towers, the guardians are safe. They can change towers and even share a tower. If all the guardians are caught, then the robbers have won. 5. The game can be played again with new guardians and robbers. Then the boxes are cleared away and everyone returns to the circle.	Game of tag.	Four boxes large enough for a child to stand on, coloured team bands.
c. 8 mins.	If the P.E. teacher or a specialist teacher is trained in Bothmer exercises, this is a good time to introduce the second Bothmer exercise. The teacher recites the verse aloud ('I'm standing, I'm walking…') and does the exercise with the children.	Circle.	None.
c. 15 mins.	Skipping. The children form a line. The teacher rotates a long rope for skipping – the other end can be tied to a post or a child can rotate with the teacher. The children in the line take turns to run through the turning rope. If there are two teachers, there can be two ropes – one in each half of the hall – and the children can form two equal lines, queuing for each rope. After running through one rope, they can join the queue for the other one.Repeating exercises is recommended so that the children get into a rhythm. There are several skipping variations, including: ▸ run through; ▸ run in, jump and run out; ▸ run through in pairs; ▸ run in together, jump and run out; (cont.)	A line for each turning rope.	Two long skipping ropes.

Time	Sequence of activities	Formation	Material used
Cont.	▸ use counting for rhythm: a number is chosen (for example, 70) and the teacher counts out loud every time the rope is swung and one child runs through. Every time there is a break in the rhythm (if no child runs through, or if two go at once or the rope touches somebody) the counting begins again. The number can be increased in the following lessons and the rope can be swung in the other direction.		
c. 8 mins.	Setting up equipment for balancing. The children sit in a circle in the middle of the hall. The P.E. teacher gives small groups of children instructions about where to set up apparatus to construct a balancing obstacle course: for example, a long bench and a bar, followed by a box set at a slant, leading up to two bars lying parallel between two boxes. Then come the asymmetrical bars (with the bars set crossed) framed by two vaulting boxes at half height. As soon as the teams have accomplished the set-up, they return to the circle and sit down. Depending on the size of the class and what equipment is available, more than one course can be set up, which will allow for team games.	Circle.	Long benches, boxes, wooden rods, balance beam, mats, parallel and uneven bars.
c. 30 mins.	Balancing. 1. The P.E. teacher introduces the exercise with a short story about a trip to the countryside, where there are lots of wobbly bridges to be crossed. The children should understand from the story that the task is to balance carefully, not to be fastest around the course. 2. After the first few tries, the course can be made more difficult. Children can be given objects to carry across, representing parcels that need to be delivered or fodder for animals.	One to three groups waiting in line.	As above.
c. 5 mins.	Clearing the equipment away. As with the setting up, the P.E. teacher gives instructions for each piece of equipment to be put away. Groups of children carry out the various tasks and sit back down in the circle.	Circle.	None.
c. 8 mins.	Final game: Pantomime. 1. The children sit in two groups, each group in a half circle that is apart from the other group. One group decides upon an object that can be imitated or dramatised, for example, a circus tent, a teapot or a candlestick. (cont.)	Two half-circles apart from each other.	None.

Time	Sequence of activities	Formation	Material used
Cont.	2. A child from the other group comes over and the object is whispered in their ear. They return to the front of their own half circle group and act out the object without speaking, as in a game of charades, until someone from their group guesses it. 3. It is then the other group's turn. If there is time, the game can be repeated.		
c. 2 mins.	End of the lesson. The children stand in a line and exchange farewells with the P.E. teacher. They recover their valuables from the treasure chest and leave the hall.	Straight line.	None.

Sample Lesson: Games. Duration: 45 mins			
Time	**Sequence of activities**	**Formation**	**Material used**
c. 2 mins	The children enter the hall and form a straight line. They exchange greetings and place their valuables in the treasure chest.	Standing in a line.	None.
c. 10 mins.	Game of tag: Red and Blue. 1. The children sit in pairs facing each other, their legs outstretched, their toes not touching, either side of the centre line or a long rope. One side is the red group, the other the blue group. There are baselines identified five to ten paces behind each group. (There must be enough space behind the line to stop safely.) 2. The teacher stands on the centre line and begins to tell a story. If the word 'red' appears in the story, all the children leap up and members of the red group try to catch the blue child opposite before the blue child reaches the baseline behind them. 3. If one catches the other, it is recorded and they both go back to their starting positions; likewise if the chased child manages to reach the baseline safely. 4. As soon as the children sit back near the centre line, the story continues. When 'blue' is mentioned, the roles are reversed. For example: 'This morning, when I looked out of the window, I saw a red-bellied parrot!' *Everybody leaps up, reds are chasing.* 'Its wings were pink.' *Some may run by mistake.* 'And its head was blue.' *Everybody starts running again, blues chasing.'*	Game of tag, two rows.	Centre line marking or long rope.
c. 7 mins.	Long benches and winding roads. 1. Three to four long benches are placed in a line down the middle of the space. Half the class lines up behind the P.E. teacher on one side of the benches. This is Group A. The rest of the children line up, mirroring this on the other side. This is group B. 2. The teacher leads Group A, running along a fairly simple path to the other side of the hall. Group B must run a mirror image of the path, thus reaching the other side of the hall for them. (cont.) 3. The paths become increasingly complicated: jumping over the benches, running loops, even crisscrossing between the two groups. A practical tip: always to finish back at the starting point. 4. After a while, Group B leads off and Group A must mirror them. Children can also lead the groups.	Running in two groups.	Long benches.

Time	Sequence of activities	Formation	Material used
c. 2 mins.	Changeover. A new set-up. The children sit along one of the walls, waiting for the P.E. teacher to say who does what. The teacher asks a small group of children to set up three benches in one long line. If there is more than one teacher and plenty of equipment and space, there can be more than one set of balancing benches and the class can split into groups.	Sitting in a line.	Benches, balls, rings.
c. 15 mins.	Balancing. 1. The children are given various balancing tasks to perform – for example: ▸ walking forwards along the benches; ▸ then backwards; ▸ walking in pairs, holding hands, one forwards, the other backwards; ▸ rolling or carrying a ball over the benches; and ▸ walking in pairs with the ball held between stomachs – no hands allowed! 2. Obstacles are introduced on the benches, such as various balls held in rubber rings at points along the route. 3. Finally, all the children link hands and the whole class tries to walk, balancing, in a line across the benches.	Between one and four groups in single lines, depending on class size, supervision possible, benches available and space.	Long benches, various balls, rubber rings.
c. 2 mins.	Changeover. The children help to clear away the equipment then return to their places. Then they all form their circle.	Circle.	None.
c. 5 mins.	The second Bothmer exercise. The teacher recites the verse aloud ('I'm standing, I'm walking…') and does the exercise with the children.	Circle.	None.
c. 2 mins.	End of the lesson. The children stand in a line and exchange farewells with the P.E. teacher. They recover their valuables from the treasure chest, and leave to get changed and return to the classroom.	Straight line.	None.

Sample Lesson: Orienteering and outdoor games. Duration: 45 mins			
Time	**Sequence of activities**	**Formation**	**Material used**
c. 2 mins.	The children wait in line outside the changing rooms. They have already changed and, after exchanging greetings and placing their valuables in the treasure chest, they are ready to begin.	Standing in a line.	Outdoor shoes.
c. 2 mins.	To the playground/sports field in an orderly march.	Straight line.	None.
c. 10 mins.	Game: Scarecrow. 1. The children join hands in a circle. In the middle there is a frame (for example, a hurdle, goal, high-jump stand) with an old hat on it. The children pull and tug each other, resisting being pulled towards the frame themselves but trying to pull others close to it, until one of them is dragged into contact with it. This child then puts on the hat and becomes the scarecrow. 2. The scarecrow runs after the other children and tries to tag as many of them as possible. Once tagged, children are frozen unless they can touch the frame. 3. As long as the scarecrow is touching the frame, no one else can return to it. When the scarecrow leaves it, others can run back and rescue themselves by touching it. 4. When all the players have either been tagged or rescued, a new game can begin.	Game of tag.	Simple frame, such as hurdle or high-jump stand.
c. 20 mins.	Orienteering. 1. The children are divided into groups of three. The teacher provides each group with a pencil and a sheet of paper with an outline of the school grounds on it. 2. The teacher has earlier identified ten special features in the school grounds – for example, a particular tree or a gate – and created a list of them. The children have to find these features and draw them in on their sheet of paper, creating a map as accurately as possible. 3. In addition, at each feature there is a piece of card with a letter written on it. Once all the letters have been found, they can be arranged to form a key word. 4. The groups of three set off at staggered times (this is a challenge, not a race).	Moving freely in small groups.	Outline of the school grounds. A list of particular features to be found and drawn. Pencil and paper. Cards with letters on placed at the features.

Time	Sequence of activities	Formation	Material used
c. 5 mins.	The solution. 1. After the agreed time, the groups assemble at the starting point with their maps and answers. 2. Who has found all ten features? How well have they been drawn in? Who has solved the puzzle? 3. The solution might be a ten-letter word pointing to where the next orienteering game will take place.	Assemble at the starting point.	As above.
c. 5 mins.	End of the lesson. The children return indoors and get changed. They exchange farewells and retrieve their valuables from the treasure chest. They form a line to head indoors to change and return to the classroom.	Straight line.	None.

Class 5:
Light and Heavy – Harmony in Rhythmical Movement

Class 5 pupils

At this age, children will throw themselves into anything involving movement. They adore all things rhythmical. By observing them in the playground it can be seen how keenly children take up any game that swings back and forth between the elements of 'heavy' and 'light', or that involves balancing, or running in long, looping curves – just think of them with their arms out to the sides like the wings of an aeroplane, pretending to fly as they swoop around the playground. In small groups, they like to play with balls and ropes, continually developing and refining new skills. They are in their element with any sort of physical exercise, which makes this the perfect time to consider which games and activities will fully involve them.

It is best to try out a variety of activities during break time to see which ones children prefer. Consultations between parents, trainers and the P.E. teacher can help find the games or activities that offer the most. A child will frequently choose the same activities as their friends, which means that all too often the particular needs of individual children are neglected. P.E. lessons are a chance to let them explore. Also, in many schools extracurricular activities such as circus skills, ball games or gymnastics are on offer. Try providing an assortment of equipment during break time, so that children can keep trying a variety of movements.

Approaches to teaching Class 5

Around this time, children begin to find out about the world for themselves in their own individual way. The accumulation of knowledge now is not just an emotional experience but part of a genuine, developing understanding. One special subject in Class 5 is local history and geography, where children learn about their own immediate surroundings. The first botany project also deals with the natural world around them. In the animal kingdom, animals such as the eagle, bull and lion are portrayed, culminating in an age-appropriate study of the human being. In history lessons, children hear about ancient cultures and take a journey into Greek mythology.

The children of this age group are like miniature Greek athletes, elegant and graceful in their movements. This is the ideal time to introduce some of the traditional athletic disciplines into the P.E. lessons. But whether it be running, throwing the javelin or high jump, the emphasis is on the aesthetic aspect. This is what appeals to the children, and it does not take long for them to learn the new techniques. They have no real interest in how fast they run or how far they jump, so there is no call for a stopwatch and tape measure. On the contrary, what the teacher tries to create is an aesthetic feeling for the beauty of the actions and movements.

The children feel the need to test their strength and abilities, and the athletic disciplines provide them with a wealth of challenges. The children willingly identify themselves with age-appropriate images and stories concerning willpower, stamina and courage. For the first time, activities such as swimming and athletic disciplines are taught, which set every child more or less demanding challenges, depending on their individual strengths and weaknesses.

It is important, however, to continue the rituals and customs that the children have grown used to. In this sense, the customary greetings and farewells as well as the treasure chest, which was introduced in Class 3 for the safekeeping of the children's valuables during the lesson, are welcome rituals that still convey a feeling of security. Depending on local conditions, available equipment and the general teaching situation, it may be helpful to have a period of free play before the proper lesson begins.

The sample lessons in this section are always described as beginning in a circle, as this has generally been successful for most classes in the past. However, Waldorf education is not dogmatic, and P.E. teachers should always feel free to devise other ways of commencing and structuring the lessons, depending on the situation and the needs of the children.

Main aspects of the lessons

One motif of Class 5 is the path the children take from free play to specific exercises – exercises which are, however, still introduced pictorially rather than intellectually.

The main aim in P.E. lessons at this stage is free, imaginative movement. The contents of the lessons are clothed in pictures and stories that invest the children's actions with meaning and emotional relevance. Setting challenges for children, either singly or in small groups, ensures healthy progress in the process of individualisation, although care must be taken to remain age-appropriate and not to demand too much of them. The themes of the main lessons continue to be adapted for use in P.E. lessons. The motif of 'heavy and light' is an important part of the games they play.

Suggested activities for Class 5

- Bothmer exercises: the third exercise, Light Beat/Heavy Beat, which explores the phenomenon of light and heavy in rhythmical movement.
- Rhythmical body percussion.
- Variations on rhythmical jumping and running.
- Running and tag games, short races including relays.
- Running, hopping, balancing, skipping.
- Further games for learning basic skills with manual apparatus: balls, ropes, hoops, rods, juggling balls, cloths.
- Games with simple rules, passing, throwing and catching.
- Floorball and dodgeball in a simplified form.
- Exercises on combinations of gymnastics apparatus.
- Swinging on the ropes and rings.
- Floor gymnastics: forward roll, backward roll, cartwheel, headstand, acrobatics, exercises in pairs.
- Introducing athletics disciplines: sprints, relays, long jump, first attempts at javelin and maybe discus and wrestling.
- Olympic Games, where possible in cooperation with other schools.
- Folk dancing, for example Greek dances in an open circle with cross-step.

Additional activities for Class 5

- Swimming lessons: practising floating in the water as the basis for all swimming styles; getting used to being in water and underwater; simple games of skill; short relay races; jumping into the water forwards and backwards.
- Hiking trips.
- Ice skating.
- Skiing.

Information on sample lessons

Swimming

Before swimming lessons begin in Class 5, it is valuable to hold a parents' evening towards the end of Class 4 to give parents an idea of what their child can expect. After a brief discussion about the stage the children have reached in their development and why swimming now appears on the Waldorf curriculum, give a summary of what is taught: for example, learning the right position in the water, moving in and under the water, learning through play within the framework of pictures and images. The parents can be reminded of the importance of ensuring that their child has something to eat and drink in the break after swimming. The parents are also asked to give the teachers written information on any medical issues their child might have, such as asthma or epilepsy, as well as any traumatic experiences they may have had in connection with water.

A practice swimming session at the end of Class 4 is also a good idea. A trip to the swimming pool gives the teacher a chance to assess the children and, if necessary, to recommend that parents enrol their child on a swimming course over the summer holidays. Should there be children with disabilities in the class, a class assistant or a child escort with the appropriate swimming safety certificate ought to be present. Children who have forgotten to bring swimwear should still accompany the others to the pool. There are always tasks they can carry out. In this way, they still participate in the lesson and, knowing what has taken place, it is easier for them to join in the lessons to come.

Athletics

The first athletics lesson picks up on the history lesson given by the class teacher. For the P.E. teacher, it is worthwhile finding out how Greek mythology and the Olympic Games have been introduced and discussed. Building on this, they can then organise and carry out their own 'Olympic Games', something that is now common in many schools. As in ancient Greece, it is the beauty and elegance of the performance that counts and not measuring times and distances. The elements of fair play and the pure joy experienced in one's own skills are paramount.

Manual apparatus and games

The sample lesson that begins with the game The Indian Club Thief gives the teacher an opportunity to observe each child in motion as well as seeing how the class behaves as a social unit. The best way to introduce new games is still to explain them pictorially so that the children get into the game quickly. In the case of this particular game, this involves describing the roles of the guard with their Indian clubs and thief who tries to steal them.

There is much value to be found in the third Bothmer exercise, with its theme of 'heavy and light'. It is worth repeating this exercise over the weeks and months, and when it is no longer necessary for the teacher to accompany them, the children can invent and practise their own variations. These can be in staggered time, as with a musical canon, in small groups and in differing formations.

When doing relay races, try and arrange for evenly matched teams and make sure the mood remains amicable. Introducing an element of chance into the relays can help offset an overly competitive mood, when otherwise only speed and skill would count. When it comes to devising new forms of relay race, the children themselves often have the best ideas.

After a series of orderly relay races, during which the children have waited and queued for their turn, it is good to have something which allows more freedom, allowing the children to go about their business without feeling they are in the limelight. At the end of the lesson, a circle is formed. Outwardly the children calm down, while inwardly the excitement of a lively lesson lingers on.

For the children, it is important to finish the lesson with a strong feeling of having accomplished something. This does not need to be articulated. Nevertheless, the result is that they look forward to the next lesson, ready to try out new exercises as well as continuing to practise more familiar ones.

Sample Lesson: Swimming. Duration: 70 mins		
Time	Sequence of activities	Material used
	The P.E. teacher collects the children from the classroom. Before setting off, the teacher tells them how they are expected to behave on the way to the pool. When they arrive, the teacher tells the children the rules that apply in the pool. The children then change and shower before assembling by the side of the pool with towels and swimming goggles. The teacher's towel serves as the treasure chest if the children have no access to lockers.	Swimwear, towels, goggles.
c. 10 mins.	Trial run. The pupils stand in line and enter the water one by one. They swim one length, thus giving the teacher an opportunity to assess individual swimming ability.	
c. 5 mins.	Game of swimming tag: Strange Fish (in waist-depth pool). 1. The children enter the water on one side of the pool. 2. The teacher tells a story about some fish that have a strange attribute. If they touch you, you freeze and cannot move until another fish dives and swims between your legs. 3. Depending on the size of the group, three or four children are chosen to be the fish and put on swimming caps. 4. The children chosen to be fish then chase after the other children. Essentially this is a game of tag but played in the water. Note: The game may be repeated with other children donning the swimming caps.	Swimming caps.
c. 5 mins.	Exercises. The children are in the water on one side of the pool and are given various tasks: ▸ Holding onto the edge of the pool, each child goes underwater and exhales firmly. This can be repeated several times. ▸ In pairs, the children submerge themselves and exhale while showing a certain number of fingers. On surfacing, each partner says how many fingers they saw. ▸ Still in pairs, one child carries out one or two movements underwater while the other child watches. On resurfacing, the watching child says what they have seen.	
c. 5 mins.	Exercise: Treasure Hunt. 1. Each child is given a diving ring, which they throw into the pool wherever they want. They then swim and fetch it.	Diving ring for each child.

Time	Sequence of activities	Material used
Cont.	2. This can also be done in pairs, with one child throwing the ring into the pool and their partner diving in to retrieve it. The aim should be to retrieve it on the first dive without having to come up for air. The children take it in turns.	
c. 5 mins.	Game: Two Dogs and a Bone. 1. The children are divided into two equal groups and stand on opposite sides of the pool. The children on each team are numbered, so that there are two number one children, one on each side of the pool; two number two children, one on each side of the pool, and so on, 2. The teacher throws a diving ring (the bone) into the middle of the pool and calls out a number. The corresponding child from each team tries to get to and grab the ring as fast as possible. The one that gets to it first takes it back to their team's side. 3. At the end of the game, the rings are counted to see which team has won. Note: The game may be repeated.	Diving rings.
c. 5 mins.	Introducing floats. Each child is given a float or kickboard with which to try out a number of tricks. ▸ Can they sit on it and move forwards? ▸ Can anyone stand on it? ▸ Can they balance it on their head? ▸ Can anyone balance it on their head, sink under water so that it floats, then come up underneath it so that it balances once more on their head without using their hands? ▸ Who can move it around with one foot? Now the other one. ▸ Finally, can anyone push it to the other side of the pool using only their head?	Swimming floats or kickboards.
c. 5 mins.	These exercises with floats or kickboards practise a good swimming position in the water. The children swim across the pool then back again: ▸ lying on the float; ▸ holding the float upright like a shark fin between the ankles; ▸ stretching arms forwards on the float while kicking feet; ▸ resting back and shoulders on the float while kicking feet; ▸ one-armed swimming with the other arm resting on the float. (Repeat this one with a change of hands.)	As above.

Time	Sequence of activities	Material used
c. 5 mins.	Exercise: jumping in from the edge. The children stand in a line at the edge of the pool and are alternately numbered one and two. At the teacher's sign, the ones enter the water, followed by the twos when the ones have climbed out. They enter the water in the following ways: ▸ running into the water forwards and continuing to run on in the water; ▸ running into the water backwards and continuing to run backwards in the water; ▸ holding hands together (all the ones, then later all the twos) and stepping in. Tell them beforehand that they are to let go as soon as they are in the water; ▸ holding hands and stepping backwards; ▸ doing an individual standing jump forwards; ▸ doing an individual standing jump backwards; ▸ doing a running jump forwards; ▸ doing an running jump backwards; ▸ crouching on the edge, hands holding shins, then rolling forward into the water; ▸ standing on the edge, facing away from water, bending to clasp ankles, then toppling backwards into the water; and ▸ the same, but this time holding their neighbour's ankle and all the ones (then later all the twos) toppling in together in a row.	
c. 25 mins.	End of the lesson. Children clear away the equipment then go to shower and get changed. Time for their snacks.	Snack, drinks.
	Return to school, where the children say farewell to the P.E. teacher.	

Sample Lesson: Athletics. Duration: 90 mins			
Time	Sequence of activities	Formation	Material used
c. 5 mins.	The children collect twigs, stones or even leaves that catch their eye on the way to the playing field. These will be used later for marking distances at the long-jump pit.	None.	Twigs, stones and leaves
c. 2 mins.	At the field, the children form a circle and exchange greetings. They put their valuables in the treasure chest.	Standing in a circle.	None.
c. 10 mins.	Warm-up game: Bears and Hares. 1. The children spread out over the playing field and crouch down. 2. One child is chosen to be the bear and one is chosen to be the hare. The other children remain crouching. 3. The bear must try to catch the hare. 4. If the bear succeeds, then the hare becomes the new bear and a new hare is chosen. 5. But if the hare jumps over a stone (a crouching classmate), the hare has escaped and can crouch down. Then the stone takes on the role of the bear. The old bear now becomes the hare. Note: a variation on the same game can be played, this time with several bears and hares in pairs. Each bear is only allowed to catch their hare.	Game of tag.	None.
c. 20 mins.	With the help of pictures from Greek history, the P.E. teacher gets the children to cross the field in a variety of ways including: ▸ walking forwards; ▸ walking backwards; ▸ creeping; ▸ trotting; ▸ hopping; ▸ running; ▸ jumping forwards with feet together; ▸ jumping backwards with feet together; ▸ skipping; and ▸ galloping.	None.	None.

Time	Sequence of activities	Formation	Material used
c. 3 mins.	The children place the twigs, stones and leaves they collected on their walk to the playing field next to the long-jump pit. These will serve as their personal markers.	None.	Twigs, stones and leaves that the children have found.
c. 5 mins.	Standing jumps. Beginning with standing jumps from the edge of the long-jump pit, the children practise landing and the correct way to leave the pit.	In a line.	Long-jump pit.
c. 15 mins.	Running jumps. The children form a queue (two queues, if the pit is large enough). One by one they run up and jump into the long-jump pit, gradually accelerating during the run-up. The take-off point, as yet unimportant, is from somewhere in the jumping zone.	In a line.	Long-jump pit.
c. 25 mins.	Now each child practises run-up, take-off and landing three times. Each pupil places their own personal marker at the side of the long-jump pit to show how far they have jumped. It remains there until they manage to jump further. This emphasises individual progress over competition. The teacher is quick to praise an elegant run-up or a successful jump and landing.	In a line.	Long-jump pit.
c. 5 mins.	End of the lesson. The third Bothmer exercise, Light Beat/Heavy Beat, is accompanied by the teacher reciting the appropriate lines. The children retrieve their valuables from the treasure chest.	Circle.	None.

Sample Lesson: Manual apparatus. Duration: 85 mins			
Time	**Sequence of activities**	**Formation**	**Material used**
c. 2 mins.	The children form a circle and exchange greetings. They put valuables in the treasure chest.	Circle.	Treasure chest.
c. 8 mins.	Game: The Indian Club Thief. 1. The children spread out over the playing field, each with an Indian club between their feet. They close their eyes. 2. Quietly, the teacher takes clubs away from some children and places them at the feet of others. When the teacher gives the word, the children open their eyes again. 3. Every player, regardless of how many clubs they now have, may try to steal clubs from the other players and put them with their own store. 4. A player can prevent a thief from stealing a club by tagging them, but only if the thief has already touched the club. If the player tags the thief before the thief has laid hands on a club, then the thief may take them all. 5. The game ends after a few minutes and may be repeated, with each child having one club. Note: When this game is played for the first time, it is recommended that the teacher redistributes the clubs before the children open their eyes. The teacher can then arrange things so that the more reticent children get two clubs and can concentrate on guarding them rather than having to run off straight away, whereas other children who seek a challenge may be left with no club at all.	Game played in a large space.	Indian clubs, at least one per child.
c. 10 mins.	Learning skills with Indian clubs. As a preparation, the teacher tells a story featuring magic clubs for doing all sorts of tricks. These can include: ▸ balancing it on the palm of first one hand then the other; ▸ balancing it on one hand while standing and then while walking; ▸ balancing it on one hand while sitting down and getting up again; ▸ balancing it on one finger; ▸ balancing it on one foot; and ▸ balancing it on the head.	Forming a circle.	One club per child.

Time	Sequence of activities	Formation	Material used
Cont.	Other activities with the clubs could include: ▸ setting the clubs up and jumping over them; ▸ laying them down and trying out different jumps; ▸ holding a club at both ends and jumping over it; ▸ swinging the club with an outstretched arm (then the other arm); ▸ rotating the club from the wrist, then changing hands in a single, smooth motion; and ▸ drawing a figure-of-eight in the air with the club.		
c. 10 mins.	The third Bothmer exercise: Light Beat/Heavy Beat. The exercise is accompanied by the teacher reciting the appropriate lines.	Circle.	None.
c. 20 mins.	Team relay races using manual apparatus. The children are divided into equal groups (minimum of four per group, maximum of ten). They form into rows and are given tasks. For example: ▸ using the club to roll a ball to a fixed point, around it and back again, before passing the club and ball to the next waiting teammate; ▸ using two clubs, one in each hand, to propel a third club along the floor to the turning point and back again; ▸ placing the clubs standing on the edge of a frame or box. The children bounce a ball as they approach and bend or crouch through the frame without upsetting any clubs. They continue to bounce the ball all the way to the turning point then return the same way. Any clubs knocked down must be replaced before continuing. The first team to finish the race and sit down is the winner.	Groups assembled on one side of the playing area.	Apparatus that can be set up as a low frame for bending underneath, one ball and three clubs per group.
c. 13 mins.	Game: Skittles. 1. The box sections are placed in the middle of the playing field with ten clubs set up on top. 2. The groups, standing at both ends of the field, throw balls to knock the clubs off. One option is to count how many clubs each group hits. 3. The game can be repeated with each player using their other hand to throw.	Two to four groups depending on class size.	Box sections, ten clubs, one ball per child.

Time	Sequence of activities	Formation	Material used
c. 15 mins.	Game: Dodgeball with Clubs. 1. In this version of the game, each child has a club, which they must protect. 2. Ball throwers aim at the clubs, not other children. 3. When a club falls, that child leaves the playing field and lays the club down on the sideline.	Game played in a large space, ideally 18 m x 9 m (59 ft x 30 ft) with 2 m (6 ft) to spare all around.	One club per player; one ball.
c. 5 mins.	Game: Wall of Clubs. 1. The clubs are set up next to each other at one end of the playing area to form a wall. 2. With the greatest care, each player rolls their ball so that it stops as close to the wall as possible. The winner is the one who gets closest without knocking a club over.	Children stand in a line parallel to the wall of clubs.	All of the clubs, one ball per child.
c. 2 mins.	End of the lesson. The children form a circle and exchange farewells. They recover their valuables from the treasure chest and return to the classroom.	Circle.	Treasure chest.

NYC
WAYS

Class 6:
Accuracy and Geometry – the Emergence of Rules and Laws

Class 6 pupils

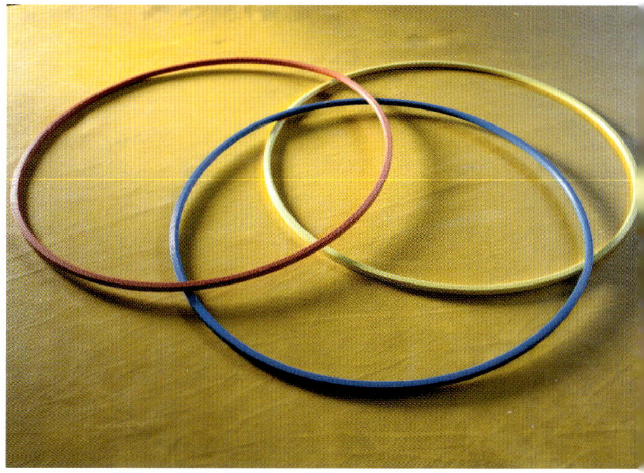

By the time the sixth school year begins, the period of childhood is on the wane for most of the children and the stormy times of puberty are setting in. The way the children move, which until now has been visibly harmonious, begins to change. There is a shift in their physical proportions: a stretching and lengthening. Emotionally, the young people are approaching new lands. As Rudolf Kischnik describes it, 'Previously, the individual's total experience of psyche and physis was undivided. From this point on, it becomes permeated by an awareness of the human ability to stand erect.'[1]

The way the children see the world changes too. They become more conscious of their physical proportions, they begin to compare themselves with their contemporaries, and there are special moments when they discover their own talents and strengths. By the same token, they develop the capacity to appreciate the skills of others while accepting that there are things they cannot do themselves – yet. They see this as an incentive to practise and take pleasure in the progress they make.

Where the children once immersed themselves in the subject matter of lessons through the element of play, there is now a real sense of working to achieve specific aims. According to Kischnik, 'there is now a greater emphasis on accuracy and a path leading to physical mastery. Performing particular movements correctly becomes important and constitutes a step towards individualization.'[2]

This is an exciting period. There are now children in the class who are already true specialists in one area or another, for example, in music lessons, where some children are mastering instruments at a level beyond the music teacher's ability to teach. In P.E. too, there are some children who have found their special niche and have already achieved great prowess. If we can give these children due recognition, and give them an opportunity in lessons to show what they can do, it means a lot to them. It also benefits the social group.

Here are two examples. One of the quieter girls in her year group brought her waveboard* to school and amazed her classmates with a demonstration after the P.E. lesson had ended. The classmates asked for more and for the last ten minutes of the following lesson, the girl went through the basic moves. It was not long before many of her classmates had learned their first tricks from her on borrowed waveboards.

One young boy, almost blind, used to play cat's cradle with great skill while waiting for the bus. His classmates asked him to show them what he could do. All were impressed, particularly with his answer to the question how he remembered it all: 'I have inner pictures,' he said. Within a week, all the girls and a few of the boys had got string and were learning tricks. Some were even trying it with their eyes closed, using their own 'inner pictures'.

Approaches to teaching Class 6

The way the children see themselves and the way they connect with the world around them does not simply mean putting intense effort into P.E. lessons. It also means learning how to move and train more purposefully. This has a lot to do with how the children learn to call up their powers of the will – something that will occupy the young people and their teachers in the coming years. The foremost task of the P.E. teacher is to prepare lessons that are so full of attractive ideas for the children that they take up the physical and sporting challenge wholeheartedly. Emotionally, there

* A waveboard is similar to a skateboard. It has two wheels and rotates in the middle, which helps the rider power it along and creates the wave-like motion that gives it its name.

are many subtle connections between each child's newly awakening inner life and their experience of the outside world. This is why it is important for the P.E. teacher to find out from their colleagues teaching the other subjects how they see the children and which lesson content best meets their needs.

The cognitive powers of the young people begin increasingly to seek out law and order in the surrounding world. In P.E. lessons, it comes as no surprise that sticking to the rules in all games becomes incredibly important. At the same time, it is 'cool' to question the referee's decisions. A certain amount of friction and resistance is necessary in young people's development and providing this is one of the adult's roles at this time, even if it leads to conflict. But rules should not be an end in themselves. There is no reason why they may not be discussed in the group and changed if need be. New rules can make games more exciting and set the children greater challenges.

The way the children see the teacher is also changing. They have a keen, not to say critical, eye on their integrity. Is the teacher honest with themselves? Do they really stand by their convictions?

In Class 6, the main theme of the history lesson, the Romans, illustrates how important rules can be in ordering the world. This is also reflected in the maths lesson. In geometry the children are taught geometric laws and learn how to draw with accuracy and precision using a ruler and compasses for the first time. In arithmetic they learn about percentages and how to calculate simple interest. This produces clear results that can then be checked and verified. In the craft lesson and woodworking, the children make objects that not only look good but are designed to serve a clear, useful purpose.

This is the year when the children take their first real measurements. In running, jumping, throwing and swimming, distances and seconds count a great deal. Yet it is important at this stage not to let the competitive spirit take the upper hand. The experience of being part of a group is still paramount, and the children derive great emotional benefit from it. But this need not conflict with the process of each child becoming more and more individual: in all races, everything depends on the performance of the individual, but the group wins or loses together. Training and practising with clear aims in view helps the children develop strongly.

Carrying out careful, controlled movements, as well as practising the different games and activities, enhances the powers of the will. The repetitive element inherent in practice is of great significance too. With each attempt to perform any given exercise as skilfully as possible, each child takes another step on the way to becoming an individual. The emphasis on exactitude and order also has a positive influence on children's cognitive powers.

Lesson content is designed to lend constructive support to the individualisation process, in which outer and inner mobility and agility go hand in hand. For orientation, the children in Class 6 rely increasingly on themselves and not so much on where they are.[3] Because of the different ways boys and girls are developing, it may be useful to separate them now and again for certain exercises. Still, they should be able to observe each other from a distance and also get a chance to perform for each other, demonstrating to each other what they have learned.

The Bothmer exercises in the sample lessons concentrate on the human achievement of standing upright and the awareness of 'above' and 'below'. Spatial awareness and measuring one's own proportions also begin to play a part. Regardless of how separate the movements of the exercise are, the emphasis is on experiencing them as one connected whole.

Main aspects of the lessons

The element of practice is now genuinely important. It becomes a means of individualisation through the engagement of the will. An initial experience of walking and standing straight takes place. The motifs of honesty and fair-mindedness, of measurement and assessment, and of orientation are also important. In the social sense, the feeling 'I am part of a group, the group supports me and my contribution matters' plays a significant part too.

Suggested activities for Class 6

- Bothmer exercises: The Triangle, Triangle with Stave, variations on Light Beat/Heavy Beat from Class 5.
- Rhythmical body percussion.
- Variations of rhythmical jumping and running.
- Running and tag games, relay races.
- Running, hopping, balancing, skipping.
- Further practice with manual apparatus such as rod, hoop, rope, ball, juggling balls and cloths, and exercises with a partner or in a small group, simple choreographic arrangements.
- Games: short sporting games with simple rules, passing, throwing, catching.
- Floorball, dodgeball, German rounders, obstacle rounders, prisoner, netball.
- Floor gymnastics: forward and backward rolls, bridge, hand- and headstands, cartwheels, small diving rolls, simple exercises with partner, small pyramids.
- Gym equipment: uneven bars, various vaulting exercises.
- Parallel bars: light kip exercises, pike, swinging, turning, straddling.
- Beam: mounting, balancing, with ball, easy variations on dismounting.
- Horizontal bar: various swinging exercises (up, under, around, from hip, knee), pull-up, swinging along hand over hand, balancing, knee hang, tuck, turn, side, straddle.
- Rings: swinging, swinging with half and full turn, hanging bent at waist and head down from standing position.
- Vaulting box: kneeling, squatting, straddling.
- Athletics: rounders, sprinting (50 m–75 m), long jump, standing jump from crouch, high jump, running, long-distance running
- Swimming: distances, against the clock, swimming techniques, especially back- and breaststroke, swimming underwater, diving (1 m and 3 m), water polo, swimming badge where possible.
- Dancing: dances that begin in a circle, dances requiring presence of mind and awareness of surroundings – 'Where should I be? Where are the others?'

Additional activities for Class 6

- Class trip with sporting theme.
- Hiking trips.
- Ice skating.
- Skiing.
- Roller skating.
- Orienteering.

Information on sample lessons

The sample lessons, in project form, are designed to cover one theme over a period of four to six weeks. They take place within the framework of already established patterns and rituals. At this age, because children have a tendency to overexert themselves, it is worth allowing the lessons themselves to breathe: balancing phases that are more strenuous and exhausting, emphasising inhaling, with phases that are freer and more relaxed, emphasising exhaling. Similarly, towards the end of the lesson, the children need to calm down in order to arrive at the following class lesson in a fit state.

Children at this stage also like to understand what the basic concepts of the various exercises are and their overall aim. This can be discussed with them in the form of a short, age-appropriate overview of the course.

Acrobatics with a partner, and games

This sample lesson begins in the usual way with an exchange of greetings. Then there is a tag game, Three Nations. During this phase, the teacher has an opportunity to observe the children in motion to see how alert and active they are. They are also able to assess the mood of individuals as well as the class as a whole.

In the Bothmer exercise, The Triangle, the class progress from simply doing it together to carrying it out it with greater awareness, performing the movements as precisely as possible. They might also do the exercise with a partner. Performing this exercise, or parts of it, as consciously and as accurately as possible is important in Class 6. After this, there is a moment in which the class acts together, standing in a circle or performing the exercise in staggered time, like in a musical round. When practised over several weeks in all sorts of variations, the Triangle is an exercise that gives the individual child as well as the whole class a great chance to progress.

Working on acrobatic skills in small groups requires concentration, courage and accuracy. It is a wonderful opportunity for social learning. However, the teacher must have a good sense of which children work well together in a group in order to ensure the lessons are safe. Health and safety is important, and the children must learn how to cooperate and support each other to avoid injury. The teacher will enjoy many special moments in which the children take on mutual responsibility and learn to trust and appreciate each other. Over a few weeks working in groups (which are changed around from time to time), the children come to devise wonderfully imaginative short choreographies, perfect for demonstration at any upcoming school festival. The children of Class 6 place great value on performing for others.

The game Prisoner is a popular game used as a preparation for learning volleyball. Once the children feel confident, they love trying out different versions. This is one of those games that, years later, students in the Upper School still remember fondly and ask to play.

Games and ball skills

A project which consists of playing games and improving ball skills is something the children enjoy a lot. The game Mr Jungle sets the pupils appropriate challenges. Alertness to what is going on, personal initiative, teamwork and first steps in tactical know-how make a great combination, being an age-appropriate preparation for the classical sports as well as furthering the children's development in general. Each player can take on a specialist role – for example, rescuing or acting as a decoy – but teamwork is the overall key to success.

The way ball skills are practised, as described, provides a good opportunity to correct technique. The children are intensely committed, while having to adjust to their respective partners. The children themselves come up with lots of good, creative ideas for practice. After a certain time, a change to free practice is important, so that the children learn to move with the ball, improve their awareness of the space around them and hone their passing skills.

In German rounders, instead of using a bat, the player throws the ball as far as they can. They then proceed to run round the bases marked out while the opposing team attempts to field the ball. In order to get the player out before they complete their run, the opposing team must throw the ball into a hoop in the middle of the field. Only the 'kingpin', a player specially selected for this task, can do this. This a great game for developing a sense of tactics. Once the teams have been picked, there is a short consultation: 'Who goes first? Who is a strong thrower? In the field, who feeds the kingpin? Who has a safe pair of hands?' If the game goes well, you can progress to simple variations of obstacle rounders or even begin using a club or baseball bat. At half-time, the teams change round.

Athletics: the crouch start

There are several different relay races that can help children practise the basic techniques of the crouch start, whether the races take place in a hall without starting blocks or outside on the running track. Inviting questions and providing positive feedback help the children improve their technique and encourages a willingness to train hard. Keeping to the rules is expected: a foul is a foul, and a false start means one more chance – but only one.

As soon as the pupils have realised that they have learned one thing, they look forward to tackling the next, more challenging exercise. There are those that train with great stamina and even at home, when they have grasped the point of the exercise. Finally, when the stopwatch shows that their work has been worthwhile, there are beaming faces, even from those at the back, who have nevertheless improved on their times.

Sample Lesson: Acrobatics with a partner, and games. Duration: 105 mins			
Time	**Sequence of activities**	**Formation**	**Material used**
c. 2mins.	The children form a circle and exchange greetings. The treasure chest is brought out and the children place their valuables in it.	Standing in a circle.	Treasure chest.
c. 20 mins.	Game of tag: Three Countries. 1. The children are divided into three teams of the same size. Coloured bands are given out to show which 'country' each team belongs to. 2. The countries are gym mats, which are arranged in a large triangle. Members of the three countries stand together on the appropriate mat. 3. The game begins when the teacher calls out, 'Blue hunts yellow, yellow hunts red, red hunts blue!' The players then leave the mats to tag those with the corresponding colours. It is especially entertaining when the hunters realise that they are being hunted! 4. When a member of one team is tagged by a member of another team, they are then taken prisoner back to that team member's mat. The prisoner then stands with one foot on the mat, waiting for one of their team members to take them by the hand back to their own country. 5. If several players of the same colour are prisoners, the last one to be caught stands with one foot on the mat and they all form a chain by joining hands and wait to be led back.	Game of tag.	Three mats, team bands.
c. 3 mins.	Changeover. The team bands are collected in. More mats are brought out and set in a circle so that two children share a mat.	None.	Small mats for children working in pairs.
c. 10 mins.	Bothmer exercise: The Triangle. 1. In carrying out the exercise together, focus can be placed on one particular aspect, for example, measuring the baseline of the triangle at the toes with the fingertips and then projecting it as accurately as possible up above the head with open arms. 2. The work can be continued in pairs. Each child can evaluate how well their partner manages to take the measurement from the baseline to above their head without faltering. They can also explore how standing with their feet closer together or further apart affects the exercise. Is there an ideal distance that makes it easier to carry out?	Standing around a circle of mats.	Mats.

Time	Sequence of activities	Formation	Material used
Cont.	3. Next, every second child takes a step into the circle, creating an inner and an outer circle. Now the exercise is repeated three times in a row in staggered time, like a round: first, the inner circle begins, then the outer circle joins in and vice versa. 4. Finally, the ones standing in the inner circle turn to face outwards and the round is repeated one more time.		
c. 15 mins.	Warm-up exercise. 1. The children sit in a circle on the mats. One child gets up and runs around the circle, followed by their neighbour and, one by one, by the rest of the children. The teacher calls out a variety of running and jumping exercises for each circuit they make. 2. Next, the children crouch on the edge of the mats, facing inwards, for 'rocking chair' practice. With their knees up to their chin they roll backwards and then forwards back onto their feet in a crouching position. They repeat the movement, this time rising to a standing position. Then in pairs, facing each other, they touch fingertips when coming into standing position. 3. Finally, doing the exercise alternately: while coming up, one child joins hands with the other, supporting them so that, when they reach the standing position, they can push off and gain impetus for a jump.	As above.	As above.
c. 25 mins.	Simple acrobatics exercises. 1. The mats are placed together in threes to form large rectangles. Groups of three now practise simple exercises on them with pupils forming bridges by getting down on their hands and knees. These can include one bridge on top of another bridge, one pupil standing on one bridge, then on two bridges side by side. Safety precautions are vital: 'Where can I place my feet on my partner and where is it out of the question?' 2. There should be some time for the pupils to devise their own tricks, which can then be performed for and tried out by the other groups.	As above.	As above.
c. 2 mins.	Changeover. The mats are cleared away and a volleyball net, or a cord, is set up.	None.	Volleyball net or cord, one volleyball.

Time	Sequence of activities	Formation	Material used
c. 25 mins.	Game: Prisoner. 1. The children who were in the inner circle during the Bothmer exercise stand on one side of the net, and the childen who were in the outer circle stand on the other side. 2. The aim of the game is to take all the members of one team prisoner. The name of one of the opposing team is called out and the ball is thrown over the net. If the ball hits the ground, the player whose name was called out leaves the field as a prisoner. If someone catches the ball, it's their turn to call out a name from the opposing team and throw the ball back at the same time. 3. If a player calls out 'Prisoner!' and the opposing team fail to catch the ball, then the prisoner who has been sitting out the longest returns to the game. If the ball is caught, the game continues as before. 4. As in volleyball, the ball can be thrown and caught three times on one side of the net. 5. If a player throws the ball into the net, or out of the field of play, or they calls someone's name who is already a prisoner, then they must leave the field as a prisoner and wait to be set free. The same penalty applies when a player calls 'Prisoner!', but all of their team is on the field. 6. Once the children are getting on well with the game, a second ball can be introduced. In this case, it is useful to have a second referee.	Two teams stand in a line on either side of the net.	As above.
c. 3 mins.	End of the lesson. The children form a circle and take a few moments to look back over the lesson. They retrieve their valuables from the treasure chest and exchange farewells.	Standing in a circle.	Treasure chest.

Sample Lesson: Games and ball skills. Duration: 90 mins

Time	Sequence of activities	Formation	Material used
c. 2 mins.	The children form a circle and exchange greetings. The treasure chest is brought out and the children place their valuables in it. The teacher gives the children a preview of the lesson and instructions on setting up equipment.	Standing in a circle.	Treasure chest.
c. 3 mins.	Set-up: Treasure Thieves. A large mat is placed on the sideline of the hall and the balls are placed on the mat. This is the strongroom with its store of treasure. The small mat and the second large mat are placed at opposite ends. These are the pirates' treasure chest and the jail respectively. The hoops, or 'magic stones', are spread around the hall.	Orderly set-up: each child is given a task and sits on the sideline when completed.	Two large mats and one small one; five hoops; thirty to forty juggling or tennis balls.
c. 20 mins.	Game: Treasure Thieves. 1. Three to five guards are chosen and given coloured team bands. The guards have the task of guarding the treasure in the strongroom, although they are not allowed to set foot in it. The guards can capture every pirate (the rest of the class) by tagging them. 2. Captured pirates put their hands on their heads and go to jail (the second large mat). They can be set free when pirates who have not been captured and are not carrying treasure lead them by the hand back to the pirates' treasure chest (the small mat). From there, they are free to rejoin the game. 3. The pirates must steal the treasure from the strongroom to take to their treasure chest, but they can only carry one piece of treasure at a time. If they are caught on their way back, they have to return the treasure to the guards, then proceed to jail with their hands on their heads. 4. Any pirate who manages to get into the strongroom cannot be captured. 5. The magic stones (the hoops) are places where the pirates are safe, but only for one pirate at a time. If two pirates land on one magic stone, they can both be taken prisoner. 6. The magic stones can be used whether or not a pirate is carrying treasure. Note: If there is time for a second game, new guards are chosen.	Game of tag.	As above.

Time	Sequence of activities	Formation	Material used
c. 2 mins.	Changeover. The children clear away the mats, balls and hoops.	Clearing away equipment.	–
c. 10 mins.	Practising ball skills. Working in pairs and moving freely around the hall, the children perform the following exercises: ▸ hold hands and bounce the ball from one to the other, then change hands; ▸ repeat the exercise while walking backwards, then change hands again; ▸ the same again, but without holding hands; and ▸ change partners and repeat the sequence.	Working in pairs.	One ball per pair.
c. 20 mins.	Various throwing and passing exercises for ball games. The children stand in two rows roughly 6 m (20 ft) apart and perform the following exercises: ▸ passing to partner as accurately as possible; ▸ changing hands from throw to throw; ▸ increasing the tempo; ▸ direct two-handed pass at chest height; ▸ two-handed overhead pass; ▸ pass with one bounce; ▸ pass with two bounces; ▸ pass with as many bounces as possible; ▸ change hands; and ▸ holding the ball behind their back, they throw it overhead to their partner. Once the pupils have got used to this formation, a change of partners can be introduced by shifting the rows along. Where the rows overhang, one child can run round to join the other end of their row. Depending on how the class progresses, the distance between the two rows can be increased.	Working in pairs, standing in two rows.	As above.
c. 8 mins.	Working in groups of three, the children move freely around the hall passing the ball to each other: first with one bounce, then a normal pass at chest height. This exercise can be intensified by counting the successful passes and going back to the beginning when something goes wrong. The highest number reached is the one that counts.	Moving freely in groups of three.	One ball per group.

Time	Sequence of activities	Formation	Material used
c. 3 mins.	Preparation for German rounders. The balls are collected in and the children help to set up the playing area. An easy way to pick the teams is to have the class form a line and then hand out blue and yellow team bands alternately.	Orderly set-up.	One hoop, one volleyball, five small mats, team bands.
c. 20 mins.	Game: German Rounders. 1. The mats are placed around the outside of the volleyball field at three corners and on both sidelines in the middle. The hoop is placed on the field about 5 m (16 ft) from the baseline. One team, blue, spreads out around the volleyball field, the other team, yellow, waits behind the baseline at the fourth corner. 2. The first player on the yellow team stands at the corner and throws the ball as far as they can. They run to the first mat, and further if possible. The player must be safe on one of the mats before the other team can bounce the ball into the hoop. 3. Only one player on the blue team – the kingpin – may bounce the ball in the hoop. The others have the job of retrieving the ball and passing it to them as quickly as possible. 4. If a runner does not reach a mat in time, they leave the field and sit on the sideline. 5. A runner that gets round all five mats wins a point for their team and remains in the game. If they manage to get round in one go, touching each mat with at least one foot, it counts as five points. 6. When all the players on the yellow team have taken their turn, points are counted up and the teams change places. The team with the most points wins.	Game of rounders.	As above.
c. 2 mins.	End of the lesson. The equipment is cleared away. The children form a circle and take a few moments to reflect on the lesson. They retrieve their valuables from the treasure chest and exchange farewells.	Standing in a circle.	Treasure chest.

Sample Lesson: Athletics – the crouch start. Duration: 95 mins			
Time	**Sequence of activities**	**Formation**	**Material used**
c. 2 mins.	The children form a circle and exchange greetings. The treasure chest is brought out and the children place their valuables in it. The teacher gives the children a preview of the lesson and what to expect.	Standing in a circle.	Treasure chest.
c. 25 mins.	Warm-up game: Apes and Panthers. 1. Four children are chosen to be the apes and go to stand at the foot of the climbing frame. The rest of the class are divided into four rows and stand back somewhere near the centre line. 2. When the teacher says, 'Go!', the apes start climbing and the first four panthers from each row sprint towards the climbing frames in the hope of catching one of the apes before they climb to safety. The winner of each of these contests gets a point. 3. The panthers that have just run become the next apes. The apes join the end of one of the four queues and become panthers. 4. When every pupil has had a turn, the starting position can be changed. For example, instead of standing, the children can sit cross-legged or lie down, facing forwards or facing away.	Four rows on centre line.	Two small mats, climbing frame.
c. 10 mins.	First exercises for learning the crouch start. 1. Position of the hands: the fingers are kept together with thumb and forefinger spread to form a 'bridge'. The 'bridge' is placed on the starting line, the hands at least as far apart as shoulders. Alternatively, to relieve pressure on the fingers, fold them into fists with thumbs out to form the bridge. 2. Position of the feet: feet should be around 30–40 cm (1–1½ ft) apart. The front foot should be 60 cm (2 ft) behind the starting line, the back foot at least 90 cm (3 ft) behind it. Allow children time to try out various distances.	In a line.	None.
c. 10 mins.	Getting to know the starting blocks. The front block is set less steeply than the back one. If there are no starting blocks, then in pairs the children can take it in turns using their feet as blocks for their partner to practise against.	As above.	Starting blocks (or partner's feet).
c. 10 mins.	Settling into blocks: backing in, knees bent, toes touching the track.	In groups.	As above.

Time	Sequence of activities	Formation	Material used
c. 10 mins.	The starting orders. 1. Phase 1: 'On your marks!' – adjust the blocks and step back into them, then place hands on the line and crouch down on back heel. Head down, listen carefully. 2. Phase 2: 'Get set!' – buttocks rise above shoulder height, back slopes forward and with shoulders just over starting line. Front leg bent at 90°, back leg almost straight. 3. Phase 3: 'Go!' – push off strongly with both legs, upper body stays low, short steps at speed.	As above.	As above.
	These three phases can be practised several times, with the option of moving over onto a hard surface or onto grass.		
c. 25 mins.	Competition. Each member of the class takes part in a series of sprints over 30 m (100 ft). Their position in the race decides the 'league' they run in in the following race. In this way, a winner in each league is established. Finally, all the league winners run against each other to find the quickest runner in the class.	As above.	Starting blocks (or partner's feet).
c. 3 mins.	End of the lesson. The equipment is cleared away. The children form a circle and take a few moments to reflect on the lesson. They retrieve their valuables from the treasure chest and exchange farewells.	Standing in a circle.	Treasure chest.

Class 7:
Inner and Outer Limits – Inventors and Explorers

Class 7 pupils

In Class 7, the children are keen to explore new horizons. It is no coincidence that history lessons in Waldorf schools deal with explorers and inventors during this school year: like Columbus, the children are keen to go beyond limits, to set foot on unexplored territory and act purposefully. This is a wonderful age when children feel there is nothing they cannot understand and master. They search for ideals and for beauty; a sense of aesthetic value develops which can become the benchmark for their own actions. In chemistry lessons, attempts are made to grasp 'objective reality'. In art lessons, aesthetics and handicraft are taught alongside perspective drawing and the golden section (also known as the golden ratio or golden mean).

This is also the beginning of puberty, when all sorts of new possibilities begin to present themselves. Once again, teachers face the challenge of finding the right material, the right images and topics, to answer the many questions and encourage the growing aspirations new adolescents will have.

In classes 7 and 8, physical education in particular can provide a good counterweight to the young people's hypercritical view of the world around them. The games, which are becoming more and more complicated, serve as a distraction from all the problems and doubts that typically plague them at this time. Their rapid physical growth indicates that previous limitations can now be overcome, and there is a greater turn outwards to the world around them, which means they can be more objective in discussions and arguments. This is an important element when dealing with young

people at this time. Acrobatics can be a great help here. As Rudolf Kischnik writes: 'Acrobatic artistry should be practised, so that the pleasure which the young people experience in performing graceful, aesthetic movement comes to full expression.'[1]

Approaches to teaching Class 7

Rudolf Kischnik points out a further peculiarity:

> They (the young people) should be in a state of inner tension. Their whole being demands this. This inner tension can only be triggered by an emotional impulse, for example, joy, enthusiasm or pride. The child yearns for inner quality in order to show the outside world that they are here, that they are somebody.[2]

'Sinew' is what symbolises the children of Class 7. Sinew connects bone with muscle. It possesses great elasticity and resilience and plays a major part in transporting energy, but it can also tear. These qualities equally apply to the overall physical state of the boys and girls in Class 7. Physically, they are taut and tensed and the way they move is generally skilled and nimble; their elasticity is conspicuous. Now that they are getting taller, the old ways of moving need to be adapted to new circumstances. A lot of practice and stamina is required for this, something that is not easy to come by at this age. It is therefore more important than ever that students continue to enjoy the work at hand.

Where it is felt to be necessary, boys and girls are separated during P.E. lessons.

Main aspects of the lessons

The basic theme of P.E. lessons in Class 7 is exploring and overcoming the contrast between wide and narrow. Experiencing beauty, order, strength and agility is a basic aim behind all performance. The leitmotifs are found in inner tension, in joyful and elated release, and in a yearning for inner quality in order to show outwardly both skill and competence. Jumping and swinging exercises are the movements young people need to explore this experience.

Suggested Activities for Class 7

- Bothmer exercises: Jump to Middle Point, The Rhythm, Strong Triangle, Sideways Circling.
- Gymnastics: practising exercises from Class 6.
- Floor gymnastics: rolls (running and jumping start), handstand, wheels, headstand, forward somersault, cartwheel, jumping (with and without rotation), rhythmical step sequences.
- Uneven bars: swinging up (various styles), push-up exercises, swinging off from lower bar.
- Parallel bars: push-up exercises, swinging, swinging and straddling at front and behind, turning.
- Beam: mounting with run-up, with a jump (also using springboard), jumping and balancing exercises, easy combinations, dismounting with emphasis on landing.
- Horizontal bar: repetition of mounting and swinging round, leaving the bar using a roll, one-legged rotation, one-legged start.
- Rings: repetition of swing with turn and half-turn, from swinging gently into hanging bent at waist, various rolls from standing start.
- Box: vaulting on into squat, vaulting over with knees up, vaulting on in straddle, vaulting feet first, rolling onto and over lengthwise and across, vaulting feet first.
- In principle, combinations of the above can be developed into a short routine for performing in front of the class.
- Athletics: 80 m sprint, rounders and slingball, long jump, standing jump, long-distance running.
- Games: volleyball (practising basic skills), basketball (preliminary exercises), rounders, baseball, games with vortex and frisbee.
- Artistry: further practice with clubs and ropes.
- Acrobatics: in pairs, figurehead (as in *Titanic*), chair, Superman, plank, pyramids in small groups. Aesthetic appeal, lightness and grace are important
- Swimming: front crawl technique, swimming underwater, against the clock, diving (1 m and 3 m), basic dives forwards and backwards, somersault, cartwheel.
- Dancing: first dances for pairs, square dancing, line dancing, maybe even waltz.

Additional activities for Class 7

- Class trip with sporting emphasis.
- Hiking trips.
- Ice skating.
- Skiing.
- Roller skating.
- Orienteering.
- Climbing.

Information on sample lessons

Climbing

The climbing sample lesson is one unit of a climbing project. In the previous two weeks, the children should prepare for it by climbing over obstacle courses as well as on wall bars. Top-rope climbing is the next step and, if possible, a visit to a climbing wall or an outdoor climbing facility. It is essential to observe the regulations concerning who can teach climbing. If the P.E. teacher is not qualified to do so, then a professional climbing instructor must be used.

The children are keen to put into practice what they have learned in preliminary climbing exercises in the gym. They are familiar with some simple knots and safety measures, and they are eager to begin training in an indoor climbing or bouldering centre. They understand why safety measures and set rules are important and they are ready to take responsibility for themselves and each other. In the sample lesson below, climbing offers the pupils many ways of testing how far they can go, of exploring their potential. Teams that have been picked by the teachers with insight and empathy make good vehicles for social learning. It is really something special when experienced climbers help the novices overcome their anxiety. What better way to finish a climbing project than to take the whole class (and, if possible, the class teacher too) on a trip to a natural climbing wall or rockface in the countryside or to a nearby outdoor climbing facility.

Apparatus gymnastics

The sample lesson given begins with a game for the whole class. Once again, this is primarily to give the teacher a chance to see what mood the children are in when they arrive and how they function as a social unit. Playing All or Nothing is always a hit with this age group. What counts is the action of the individual within the context of the team. Each player gets to show what they can do and how far they dare go.

Whatever takes place in the warm-up phase must meet three criteria: it must be varied, it must give the pupils purposeful tasks and it must set them a challenge. The benches are very good for this. A simple exercise such as the turning jump from the crouching position provides such a challenge. The children often have their own ideas of varying the exercise, which can be put to good use.

The Bothmer exercise Jump to Middle Point can be applied with the main focus changing from one phase to another, for example, from contraction just prior to the jump through to the release.

The gymnastics lesson is perfectly structured to meet the needs of children in Class 7. Self-assessment, courage, trust and balance are important factors. In some places, cooperation and teamwork are called for where the individual plays their special part in helping the team succeed in the set task. The general aim is healthy development. In addition, these exercises are good practice for working on apparatus gymnastics (sprint approach, take-off, push-off, landing).

In every class, there should be tasks set for various levels of competence and skill so that children learn to work on their own and gain more experience. This also has the effect of reducing waiting times at the various pieces of equipment (especially with large classes).

To finish the lesson, the whole class joins together in one last exercise. It should be something slow, calm and rhythmical, for example, the opening Bothmer exercise.

Handball

A game of Spaceball begins the lesson. Some children may already be familiar with it and it isn't long before they are ready for a more complicated version of the game: the Secret Two. In this version, each team secretly choses one player, and whenever the ball is passed to that player the team scores double points. It is exciting to see how the teams' tactics evolve as they attempt to work out who the secret player on the other team is, while at the same time trying to keep their own secret player hidden. The teacher should allow some time for initial team talks about tactics.

Variety and methodical diversity are important for honing ball skills. Once the pupils recognise the purpose of the exercises and note the progress they are making, there is no stopping them. Their willingness to work and practise is enormous.

Another favourite game is Mat Handball, often requested later in the Upper School or organised by the pupils themselves in free lessons. As ever, putting well-balanced teams together is half the battle. The children are now of an age when this aspect can be discussed with them. Are the teams well-matched? Can we look forward to a tight game?

To conclude the lesson, there is the Bothmer exercise The Rhythm. This has a calming effect, which, after all the excitement and activity, serves to bring the children together into one class unit. It ends with a moment of quiet.

Sample Lesson: Climbing. Duration: 95 mins		
Time (Times for each exercise vary according to skill, class size and local conditions.)	**Sequence of activities**	**Material used**
–	See Information on sample lessons to understand where this lesson fits into a sequence on climbing.	–
–	The students assess the bouldering wall with the climbing instructor. The instructor discusses health and safety and the correct behaviour while on and around the wall.	–
–	Practice session in circle. The class is split into two equal groups. Group A practises putting on their climbing harnesses and making sure they are fastened properly. They practise tying the knots needed for top-rope climbing. The climbing instructor checks that the harnesses have been put on correctly and that the children have mastered the knots. Group B practises on the bouldering wall, moving from one side to the other, climbing no higher than 1½ m (5 ft) from the ground. For a variation on The Floor is Lava, two climbers start on opposite sides of the wall and must get past each other without touching the floor, which has become burning-hot lava. Groups change places.	Harness and ropes.
–	Further activities for the bouldering wall: ▸ Climbers can only use handholds with particular colours to scale the course. ▸ The climber carries a carabiner in one hand while climbing across. ▸ Crossing three-legged: the climber uses one hand and both feet to get across.	Carabiner.
–	End of the lesson. The instructor once again goes through the main points concerning health and safety, putting on the climbing harness, and tying the knots for the top-rope climbing.	–

Sample Lesson: Apparatus gymnastics. Duration: 90 mins

Time	Sequence of activities	Formation	Material used
c. 3 mins	The students form a circle and exchange greetings. The teacher gives the student a preview of the lesson and what to expect.	Standing in a circle.	None.
c. 15 mins.	Game: All or Nothing. 1. Teams A and B line up facing each other on the baselines of a playing area roughly the size of a volleyball court. In Team A's half, there is a wooden club 3 m (10 ft) from the baseline. Team B must steal it and bring it back behind their baseline to win the game. 2. Both teams can send several players onto the court, but although players from Team B can run back and forth from their baseline, when a player from team A runs onto the court they are not allowed to return until they have tagged a player from the opposing team – it is all or nothing for them! 3. If the player from Team A fails to tag a member of the opposing team and they make it back to their baseline, then the player from Team A loses their 'life' and they must go and sit on the sideline. If a player from Team B is caught, they are also out and whoever tagged them returns to Team A's baseline. 4. Several players from Team B can be on the field at any one time. If one of them gets the club, they have to carry it back behind their own baseline. The player may not give it or throw it to another teammate. 5. If the game cannot be decided after a certain time, changing round is a good idea, so that everyone gets to experience attacking and defending tactics.	Game on a volleyball court.	Wooden club, team bands.
c. 10 mins.	Warm-up exercise. Between six to eight benches are placed parallel to each other 2 m (6 ft) apart. The children stand in line behind one of the benches and, one after another, they perform various tasks in zigzagging over the benches, for example, running, moving on all fours (knees not touching benches), in a squat turning left then right using hands alternately a) backwards, b) facing down forwards, c) with knees drawn up and using arms to pull along.	Orderly running, various exercises on benches.	Six to eight benches.
c. 8 mins.	Bothmer exercise: Jump to Middle Point.	The students form rows between benches.	As above.

Time	Sequence of activities	Formation	Material used
c. 25 mins.	Apparatus gymnastics. The students are divided into two groups; one group will begin with the horizontal bars, the other with the vaulting box. At half-time, they swap over. **Horizontal bars.** Three bars are set up. The group working with them is divided into three smaller, mixed groups. The teacher explains the exercise for each bar and the students then have seven minutes to carry them out before moving onto the next one. **First bar:** set at hip height with mats on the floor beneath it. The students carry out the following exercises:	Practise in small groups on gym equipment.	Three bars, six small mats, one large mat (high-jump mat if possible).
	▸ balancing over the bar forwards; ▸ balancing over the bar backwards; ▸ forwards with their eyes shut; ▸ backwards with their eyes shut; ▸ in pairs doing variations: for example, one moving forwards, the other backwards; ▸ the students' own ideas. **Second bar:** bar set at shoulder height with mats on the floor beneath it. Two students stand at opposite ends of the bar and must cross to the other side without touching the floor. This task requires a degree of inventiveness in coming up with workable methods.		
	Third bar: set at a height of 2 m (6 ft) with a large, soft mat underneath. The group (at least 5 students) stand at one side of the bar and try to get over the bar to the other side without touching the two posts. They can help each other, as long as they are on the same side of the bar (similar to clambering over a high wall).		
	When this half of the class is finished, the students sit down to watch their classmates and see how cleverly they have coped with the tasks that have been set for them.		

Time	Sequence of activities	Formation	Material used
c. 23 mins.	**Vaulting Box.** The students practise on the vaulting box with a number of exercises: 1. The students begin their warm-up by vaulting over a low box with the teacher supporting at the side. Those students who feel confident can move to another box of the same height and practise on their own. 2. The height of the box is gradually increased and the students must decide when they have reached their limit and can go no higher. 3. Further option: the students get into groups of four, with three crouched down in a line leading up to the vaulting box. The fourth group member leapfrogs over them, landing two-footed at the end and leaping over the vaulting box in one movement. The distance between the pupils and the height of the box can be varied.	Practise on gym equipment.	Two boxes, two springboards, two large mats.
c. 3 mins.	Changeover. The equipment is cleared away.	Orderly working.	None.
c. 3 mins.	End of the lesson. The students form a circle and take a few moments to reflect on the lesson and look forward to the next one. Lesson concludes with the first Bothmer exercise, then the students exchange farewells.	Standing in a circle.	None.

Sample Lesson: Handball. Duration: 100 mins			
Time	Sequence of activities	Formation	Material used
c. 3 mins	The students form a circle and exchange greetings. The teacher gives the students a preview of the lesson and what to expect.	Standing in a circle.	None.
c. 12 mins.	Game: Spaceball. 1. Two well-matched teams are given coloured team bands. The players of one team try to pass a ball from one to another ten times without the other team taking the ball from them. If they are successful, they get a point and the other team gets the ball. 2. The opponents must keep at least an arm's length from the person who has the ball.	Team ball game.	One handball, team bands.
	3. Return passes are not allowed; the penalty for this is losing possession of the ball. 4. A pass can bounce only once. The game is played on an area roughly the size of a handball court. Depending on the size of the class, teams can be between five and twelve players. If there are more players, then make four teams and play on two smaller pitches.		
c. 15 mins.	Game: The Secret Two (a variation of Spaceball). 1. Each team secretly nominates one player to be their secret player. Every pass this player catches will count for double points. The referee is told who the two players are. 2. The rules are the same as for Spaceball. When a point is won, the ball changes teams.	Team ball game.	As above.
	3. After about ten minutes, the referee calls a halt and the teams hold a private discussion. The team in front has one guess as to who the opposing secret player is, then the other team guesses.		
	4. The team that guesses correctly, wins, because a right guess counts more than points won. If both teams are right (or wrong), the team with more points wins. 5. After the game, a talk about tactics is something the children benefit from.		
c. 10 mins.	Training with ball. The pupils move across the playing area, each with a ball. When the whistle blows, they stop, hold the ball still and listen for instructions, which could include:	Ball game.	A ball for each player.
	▸ bouncing the ball forwards, backwards and sideways, using first one hand and then both; (cont.)		

Time	Sequence of activities	Formation	Material used
Cont.	▸ bouncing the ball against the wall; ▸ catching and bouncing; ▸ trying to intercept another ball; ▸ bouncing the ball without touching the floor markings; ▸ bouncing the ball, tapping another player's back (or shoulder) while protecting one's own back; ▸ allowing for any ideas the pupils contribute.		
c. 7 mins.	Exercises in pairs. The students stand on the goal line at one end of the field in two rows 4 m (13 ft) apart. In pairs, the students cross the field to the other goal line while carrying out the various exercises below, then they run back along the sideline: ▸ running while bouncing the ball between them, first left-handed, then right-handed, then alternating from one hand to the next; ▸ direct pass from chest height; ▸ alternate between direct pass and a pass with a bounce; ▸ avoiding obstacles (cones or benches) while passing; and ▸ spinning round once after each pass.	Two lines.	One ball between two, cones, benches.
c. 2 mins.	Changeover. Equipment is reset for the next activity.	None.	See below.
c. 18 mins.	Depending on the size of the class, the students are divided into three small groups (six if the class is larger). The teacher explains the rules and regulations of the game and the lines that mark out the court. The groups then take up positions in different places on the court and spends six minutes on each of the following tasks: ▸ throwing at goal; ▸ throwing from the 7m spot, changing goalkeepers each time; and ▸ from a distance of 5–6 m (16–20 ft) the children try to hit cones or clubs that are set up in line along the wall 20 cm (8 in) apart.	Three small groups (six if class is larger).	Two handball goals, cones or clubs if possible, one ball per pupil. (Mats placed against the wall can be used instead of goals, adhesive tape can be used to mark out the area.)

Time	Sequence of activities	Formation	Material used
c. 3 mins.	Orderly changeover. The students sit in pairs facing each other along the centre line. One team puts on coloured team bands, then the teacher counts off down the line so that each pair receives a number. The teams then sit at the edge of the court.	Two lines facing each other.	One handball, team bands.
c. 20 mins.	Game: Handball on mats. 1. Two large mats are set down where the handball goals would normally be. A goal is awarded when a team lands the ball on the mat immediately after one bounce. 2. Running with the ball is not allowed. 3. If a team commits a foul, they lose possession of the ball. 4. Diving onto the mat to whisk the ball away is allowed. 5. At the start the referee calls out five numbers, denoting the ten players who take the field. Every two minutes or after a goal, the referee calls out five new numbers.	Ball game with running changes.	As above but with two large mats.
c. 7 mins.	Bothmer exercise: The Great Rhythm. The students gather in a circle and perform the exercise. The slow rhythm helps the students calm down after their previous exertions and brings them together.	Standing in a circle.	None.
c. 3 mins.	End of the lesson. Still in a circle, the students take a few moments to reflect on the lesson and look forward to the next one. They exchange farewells.	Standing in a circle.	None.

NG

ERHARD SPORT

molten

Class 8:
Beauty and Agility – Resistance and Strength

Pupils of Class 8

At the end of the previous school year, a significant change in the young people became noticeable, notably in their bearing and gesture and the way they moved. Now, in Class 8, the children themselves are aware of it: they no longer feel at ease with themselves; arms and legs have grown longer, but the muscular strength is missing; their bones sometimes hurt and general aches and pains are common. Everything is out of proportion, and the well-built athlete is a distant memory. Now they move awkwardly, constantly bumping into things, and, figuratively speaking, this also applies to their thought processes. They keep having little accidents. It is a time of cuts and bruises. But these collisions cannot be avoided and clearly belong to a process of development characteristic of the way the individual encounters other people and the world in general. It is a case of engaging with others, competing with them, of becoming aware of oneself during such encounters. Such observations made in sports lessons occur in equal measure in the cognitive and artistic subjects.

Childhood finally comes to an end in Class 8. An era is left behind, shaken off, sometimes vehemently rejected. This transformation, which is seldom painless, comes with many opportunities as well as many dangers. But, for the adolescents, the purpose of this transformation is not yet clear – which simply increases the feeling of insecurity. Young people of this age are constantly searching for ideals and role models. As a rule, they are very interested in social topics. They are quick to recognise an injustice and just as quick to pass judgement and condemn. History lessons take this up, by discussing topics such as the Industrial Revolution as well as the way the world around us is changing today. Working on biographies (potential role models such as great scientists, Nobel prize winners and political idealists) is of immense pedagogical value.

Approaches to teaching Class 8

In the science subjects, the pupils work on basic principles that form the framework for the subject matter to come. In biology, this framework is of course the skeleton. In physics, it is mechanics. As in previous years, the pupils of Class 8 should be given an opportunity to come to their own conclusions based on how they see the various phenomena. One of the biggest challenges for teachers dealing with adolescents is helping them to form judgements that are critical but nevertheless well-founded. Adults, however, with their set ways and fixed ideas, often succeed in making life more difficult for younger people. A healthy sense of humour is essential for getting along with them (for both the young people *and* the adults), as is showing that you believe in them. It will come as no surprise to the attentive teacher that, in times of outward disorder, which can even degenerate into total chaos, a well-structured lesson with clearly defined aims and well-expressed methodical procedures can be a godsend to the young people. The aim is to help the pupils feel secure in what they do and give them a sense of understanding of the world in which they are growing up.

As in Class 7, the boys and girls are separated in physical education (P.E.) lessons where it is felt to be necessary or appropriate. But this ought not to be automatic and the whole class should begin and end the lessons together. Warm-up games, many exercises and even entire projects are ideal for mixed groups. They help girls and boys to overcome a bit of the natural timidity and bashfulness which is part of the baggage of puberty. What is more, teachers of either sex should frequently teach both boys and girls, giving both an opportunity to experience the diverging development of the sexes.

Gravity presents the biggest challenge for many of the boys in Class 8, with their long, gangling arms and legs are barely capable of controlled movement. The girls also struggle with the way their bodies are changing. Boys and girls alike are preoccupied with many things which are light years away from P.E. lessons. To combat this, the teacher needs strong arguments! What helps a lot is when the teacher – or even better, the teaching team – already knows the class and can fall back on old rituals and customs. It is useful to take further steps in the athletic disciplines: shot put, sprint and wrestling. Stamina, already an important quality in the previous year, is developed and trained more intensively. This creates a basis for healthy movement and provides children's rapidly growing bodies with the necessary musculature. This is particularly important for the lower back and for the feet.

But P.E. lessons are not carried out simply to compensate for all the sitting done in many of the other subjects. On the contrary, they have much more to do with experiencing movement in all its facets and variations. A pupil might have aching muscles, but alleviating them is not an end in itself. In Class 8 too, and then in the Upper School, the main thing is to take pleasure in all activity and movement, to improve one's appreciation and awareness of movement, and to gain in confidence in everything one does.

Main aspects of the lessons

Differentiation and individualisation in lesson content now come to the forefront. For the pupil, becoming aware of and working on their posture, as well as developing their stamina further, are two of the principle aims.

Suggested activities for Class 8

- Bothmer exercises: The Fall into Space and The Frontal Walk, intensifying exercises with rod.
- Gymnastics: exercises with rope and rod, and rhythmic gymnastics with ribbon, hoop, ball and clubs.
- Artistry: continuing work with balls, clubs, hoops and rods.
- Games: running and team games, relays, mat handball, rugby basics, fistball, prellball (a distant relation of volleyball), games with simple rules e.g. basketball, volleyball, handball, floorball.
- Floor gymnastics: simple combinations of rolls, headstands, handstands, forward somersaults, cartwheels.
- Uneven bars: push-up and swinging exercises, upward circle, ways of mounting and dismounting, combinations of movements.
- Parallel bars: push-up and swinging, strength exercises, rolls.
- Horizontal bar: push-up and strength exercises, upward circle, chin-ups, squat through, under swing.
- Rings: swinging with half and full rotation, swinging with arms at sides, gently swinging then bending/falling, various ways of swinging on and off in combination with trapeze.
- Vaulting box: squat, turn, vaulting feet first.
- Large trampoline: basic jumps, coordinated and rhythmical jumps, simple combinations.

- Athletics: 100 m and 200 m sprints, 2,000 m and cross-country, long jump, high jump.
- Swimming: practising technique, including turns; introduce butterfly stroke, rescue procedure, swimming longer distances.
- Dancing: in pairs, perhaps a first look at ballroom dancing.

Further ideas for activities

- Class trip with a sporting emphasis.
- Hiking trips.
- Climbing.
- Ice skating.
- Skiing.
- Roller skating.
- Orienteering.

Information on sample lessons

Apparatus gymnastics

The focus now is on the pupils experiencing the moment of falling – something that has a lot to do with letting go and then regaining control, with being ready to face a new situation.

As usual, at the start of the lesson, the pupils stand in a circle. They generally arrive after group lessons in other subjects, or after the midday break, and it is helpful to have them gather like this so that they can see and take notice of each other before starting an exercise or game together. This has a positive effect on maintaining a healthy, close-knit social unit.

The game Stage Run is a hit with every class from Class 7 on. It is particularly well-suited for pupils of varying abilities because each player can decide how much they want to be involved while still remaining part of the team and contributing to the collective effort. After the game it is useful to look back at the tactical aspects as well as mentioning particularly good moves during the play. For the team in the field, guessing who the hidden player is (this is another game with a secret player) has an additional appeal and certainly teaches them to keep a watchful eye on what is going on.

During the warm-up session in the circle, now a long-standing tradition, individual pupils can often contribute. Anyone whose name is called out must be on their toes to lead the next exercise.

The group exercises that deal with body tension, falling and mutual trust are especially effective when practised over a period of several weeks with constantly changing groups. And while the Bothmer exercise Fall into Space seems rather too easy for this age group, when the pupils are asked to concentrate on a particular aspect – for example: how long can they prolong the fall? How does the length of their stride affect the fall? How do they experience the fall when their eyes are closed? – they are soon immersed in serious practice.

When it is time for work on the gym equipment, it makes sense for the teams to stay together for the duration of the course. When the team members reassemble after a week's interval, they are immediately able to start where they left off. Whether they are in mixed or unisex groups depends on the disposition of the class. If it is possible for boys and girls to work together, each pupil makes progress not only in what they do, but also in how they experience it.

When it comes to practising falling from the vaulting box, on the other hand, it is best at the beginning if the boys and girls practise separately. This provides the teacher and the pupils with the opportunity to talk about the various parts of the body and how and where one may, or may not, be touched and supported.

As usual, the lesson concludes with a look back on the various activities and a few moments of quiet.

Athletics: the high jump

In this sample lesson, the game and exercises that follow the customary greeting at the beginning are designed as preparation for learning the high-jump technique.

The circuit set-up gives the pupils a chance to practise this technique in a variety of ways. After the circuit work, they are led step by step towards the actual high jump. It can be useful to split the class into groups based on ability, especially if it is a large class. The teacher then gets the chance to look at all of them and give quick corrections where necessary. It also halves the time that pupils stand in a queue waiting for their turn.

For the pupils, it is essential that they get involved in all the various games and activities with great commitment, which also means becoming acquainted with the appropriate sporting jargon. There will be pupils who are members of sports clubs and thus in a position to bring specialist knowledge to the school sports lessons. They can help classmates in practising skills and learning technique and can be responsible for setting up equipment. This of course applies to athletics in general.

The lesson ends quietly and calmly with a look back on the lesson and forward to the next one.

Volleyball and Digging Tennis

Mastering basic ball skills is a precondition for enjoying well-known ball games. Before starting a project on one of these games, it is worthwhile taking stock of the class (including assessing pupils who are new to the class). Beginning the lesson with interval training in pairs motivates everyone to take part wholeheartedly from the word go.

The Bothmer exercise The Strong Triangle is a development of The Triangle, which the pupils already know from Class 6. Having formed groups of four, the pupils are quick to begin practising, especially with the focus on some special part of the exercise.

During the phase in which the pupils are working on ball skills, the teacher can take a good look at them and assess exactly where they are and what the next step should be. To keep the young people focused and engaged, the exercises need to be as varied as possible.

When the games phase begins, it is worthwhile occasionally picking teams according to ability, so that the more gifted players have an opportunity to develop good, flowing moves together.

The opening Bothmer exercise is always good for finishing the lesson, as it also has a useful calming effect.

After this project, the game of Digging Tennis can be used in later P.E. lessons as part of the games phase.

Sample Lesson: Apparatus gymnasics. Duration: 91 mins			
Time	Sequence of activities	Formation	Material used
c. 2 mins.	The teacher and students form a circle and exchange greetings. The teacher gives them all a preview of the lesson and what to expect.	Standing in a circle.	None.
c. 15 mins.	Game: Stage Run. 1. Mats are placed at each corner of the volleyball court to create the four stages. 2. The class is then divided into two teams and given coloured team bands. Team A gathers on one of the mats, which becomes their home base. Team B are given three softballs and spread out over the court. They are not allowed to step on any of the mats.	Ball game.	Four mats, three softballs, coloured team bands.
	3. During the game, players from Team A run from one mat to the next, completing a circuit as often as possible. Each completed circuit counts as one point. The referee stands at home base and counts the points. Players from Team B try to hit them with the softballs. Team A are safe on the mats. 4. Although players from Team B can move all over the court, when they have one of the softballs, they may only take three steps before passing it to one of their teammates. 5. Each player from Team A has three lives. Once they have been hit three times, they leave the game and sit on the sideline. A hit must be a direct hit: if the ball bounces first it does not count. 6. If a player from Team A catches the ball thrown at them it does not count as a hit. They place it on the ground and continue running. 7. After seven minutes, the teams change round.		
	8. An added difficulty is introducing a Hidden Five: this is a player secretly nominated by their team who gets five points for every completed round. It is then necessary for the team to discuss tactics and protect this player.		
c. 2 mins.	Changeover. The students sit in a circle and final score is announced. They review the games and particularly good moves are pointed out. The coloured team bands are collected in.	Sitting in a circle.	None.
c. 5 mins.	Warm-up session. In large circle, the teacher begins with one exercise then calls out a student's name, who then begins the next one and so on.	Circle.	None.

Sample Lesson: Apparatus gymnasics. Duration: 90 mins			
Time	**Sequence of activities**	**Formation**	**Material used**
c. 10 mins.	The class is divided into groups of three. 1. One student stands in between the other two. They tip themselves towards the student in front, who catches them by the shoulders and pushes them back up. The student then tips backward to be caught by the other student, who also pushes them upright (see pictures below). 2. This can be repeated several times before they change places. It is important that the feet of the student in the middle remain firmly on the ground. 3. The exercise can be repeated, but this time the student in the middle keeps their eyes closed. 4. After a while, the groups are changed around.	Working in groups of threes.	None.
c. 4 mins.	Bothmer exercise: The Fall into Space. The students perform the exercise in a large circle.	Circle.	None.
c. 2 mins.	Changeover. The students are tasked with setting up the equipment for the next part of the lesson. They are divided into three groups.	None.	Various equipment.
c. 40 mins.	The class is divided into three groups. The gymnastic equipment is set up in three different areas so that the groups can move easily from one to the next. Stage 1: several mats are laid out together, including one placed against the wall. The pupils then perform the following tasks: (cont.)		Stage 1: one large mat, two small ones.

Below: the Bothmer exercise The Fall into Space.

Time	Sequence of activities	Formation	Material used
Cont.	1. Standing at the edge of the mat then falling forwards with hands out to arrest the fall. 2. Go into a handstand, supported by classmate, then roll forwards onto the mat. 3. Perform a handstand against the wall, with support if necessary. Then a handstand away from the wall and without support if possible. Stage 2: several mats are laid out together and the students practise the crab or bridge position by leaning backwards and supporting themselves on their hands and feet with their back arched. If necessary, a teammate can also support them.		Stage 2: mats, low bar. Stage 3: vaulting box, large mat.
	One of the mats can be draped over the low bar and the students can practise moving from the crab or bridge position into a handstand, supporting each other where necessary. Stage 3: a large mat is placed on the floor behind the vaulting box. The students stand on the mat in two rows facing each other and hold out their arms to form a cradle with which to catch the students who falls from the box (see photo on p. 136). The students take it in turns to fall forward, then backward, then with their eyes closed. Important safety precaution: the P.E. teacher should stand in the middle of one of the rows. The stronger student should also stand close to the middle. The teacher should make the students aware of the risks of this exercise if they do not take it seriously. No student should be forced to take part. Each stage should take ten to fifteen minutes.		
c. 3 mins.	Changeover. The students from each group dismantle the apparatus and clear it away, then they stand in a circle.	Clearing away; standing in a circle.	None.
c. 5 mins.	Game of trust and coordination. Standing close together in their circle, the students face in one direction then slowly sink to sit on the knees of the person behind them. If this works, the whole class finds itself sitting in one large circle.	Circle.	None.
c. 2 mins.	End of the lesson. The students take a few moments to reflect on the lesson and look forward to the next one. They exchange farewells.	Circle.	None.

Sample Lesson: Athletics – the high-jump. Duration: 90 mins

Time	Sequence of activities	Formation	Material used
c. 2 mins.	The teacher and students form a circle and exchange greetings. The teacher gives them all a preview of the lesson and what to expect.	Standing in a circle.	None.
c. 5 mins.	Warm-up: Hop Tag. Several players, hopping on one leg, try to tag the rest of the class. The area in which this is played need not be too big.	Game of tag.	None.
c. 8 mins.	Exercises can include: ▸ straddle hopping; ▸ swinging arms backwards and forwards overhead; and ▸ hop/skip run across gym, forward then backward; Preparatory jumping exercises: ▸ practising run-up; and ▸ running with leaping strides through the gym.	Moving freely around the hall.	None.
c. 20 mins.	High-jump technique. A variety of equipment is set up in a circuit, for example, a vaulting box, horizontal bar, boxes, mat trolley, benches set up at an angle against wall bars. The students move around the circuit, practising 180° turning jumps as they go.	Circuit work.	A variety of gym equipment.
c. 45 mins.	The high-jump. The technique described here is known as the straddle jump: the athlete twists and rolls their body sideways over the bar, in contrast to the Fosbury Flop, in which the athlete turns and arches backwards over it. 1. From a standing position, the student swings their outside leg over the low bar, placing their foot and the corresponding hand on the mat, and rolling sideways over it. 2. The exercise is repeated, but with the focus now on turning the inside leg during the jump. 3. Next the students practise marching up to the bar, learning to measure their stride and working out which is their take-off or leading leg. 4. The students stand in two lines, according to their take-off leg, and jump over the bar, beginning with three strides and then later on five. The final stride is the longest.	Practise run-ups.	Soft mat and high-jump stand.
c. 5 mins.	Changeover. The students clear away the equipment.	Clearing away equipment.	None.
c. 5 mins.	End of the lesson. The students take a few moments to reflect on the lesson and look forward to the next one. They exchange farewells.	Standing in a circle.	None.

Sample Lesson: Volleyball and Digging Tennis. Duration: 90 mins

Time	Sequence of activities	Formation	Material used
c. 2 mins.	The teacher and pupils form a circle and exchange greetings. The teacher gives them all a preview of the lesson and what to expect.	Standing in a circle.	None.
c. 13 mins.	Warm-up session. Interval training in pairs: one student runs round the volleyball court while the other times them with a stopwatch and counts the laps.	Working in pairs.	Stopwatch.
c. 10 mins.	Bothmer exercise: The Strong Triangle. To begin with the students do the exercise together. Then they are divided into groups of four and practise the exercise standing square on to each other. Next, two of the students face each other and perform the exercise, while the other two offer suggestions for improvement. Finally, all return to the large circle and repeat the exercise together.	Standing in a circle; groups of four.	None.
c. 20 mins.	Volleyball: basic ball skills. 1. Each student gets a volleyball. The teacher demonstrates the dig. This is a basic move in volleyball and the key to a successful defence. The player must get under the ball to prevent it from hitting the ground when the opposing team knocks it down from above the net. 2. The students spread out and practise on their own, while the teacher offers advice. Next, the students throw the ball into the air, let it bounce, then practise the dig. 3. Working in pairs, the students place a hoop on the ground between them. One student slams the ball into the centre of the hoop, bouncing it to their partner who digs it up into the air, returning the pass if possible. After a while, they swap places.	Alone and in pairs.	Volleyballs, hoops.
c. 30 mins.	Game: Digging Tennis. The class is divided into teams of two. Depending on the size of the hall, several smaller courts are set up with two benches placed on top of one another to serve as tennis nets. The teams then play tennis with a volleyball using the digging technique. After fifteen minutes, the benches can be replaced by a cord set at a height of 2 m (6 ft). The teacher offers the teams advice.	Team games on small areas in gym.	Benches, rope, volleyballs.
c. 5 mins.	Changeover. The pupils clear the equipment away, then gather in a circle. They consider ideas and possible rule changes for coming lessons.	Clearing away; standing in a circle.	None.
c. 5 mins.	The students perform the opening Bothmer exercise.	Standing in a circle.	None.
c. 5 mins.	End of the lesson. The pupils take a few moments to reflect on the lesson and look forward to the next one. They exchange farewells.	Standing in a circle.	None.

Class 9:
Tension and Release – the Turbulent Years

Class 9 pupils

With the arrival of Class 9, nobody can fail to see that the children have become young adults. They scrutinise the teacher, wanting to know who they are and what they stand for, observing them closely to see if the teacher's words and actions mirror their innermost convictions. Pupils at this age can be provocative and demanding, but this should not obscure the fact that they are vulnerable and very insecure. Indeed, emotionally, Class 9 pupils may be the most vulnerable of all the age groups. The teacher must treat them with great understanding but also with firmness.

Around the age of fifteen, young people begin to search for their place in the world. Discussions become more earnest, great issues are debated, and high ideals dominate arguments that often take place, it has to be admitted, for their own sake. This is characteristic of an age group in which young people are trying to find their own personal standpoint. Putting high ideals into practice, however, is anything but easy. Puberty, particularly in Class 9 and Class 10, is characterised by a lack of 'get up and go'. It takes an enormous amount of effort to turn thoughts and ideas, which often appear so clear and vivid, into realities, and the further away these ideas are from real life, the more difficult it becomes. Young people sense this too. They are afraid of failing and begin to retreat into themselves. The resulting decline in performance, which the young people themselves are all too aware of, further underlines this fear. They risk developing a fixed mindset, one that demands perfection in everything they do yet is fearful of being able to achieve it. As a result, they have a tendency to give up too easily. 'I can't do it!' is a complaint frequently heard by teachers.

For the adults, it helps to be mindful of the changes taking place in the young people, especially in the structures of the brain. A great deal of composure is required to manage the lethargy and general apathy with an understanding smile – though never a pitying one.

Although this is period can be fraught with difficulties, do not forget that it is also a fantastic time of life. It is like a rebirth: painful at times, but awakening tremendous potential, especially if the young people have been developing healthily in the years before. This rebirth, which begins in Class 7, happens so quickly that the participants can hardly keep up – and often it is the adults who limp along furthest behind.

It can often happen at this age that young people develop completely new interests that point them in a new direction. They search for new role models; old friendships break down and new ones form that often last for years. Once they have found a topic that captures their interest, young people are able to digest enormous amounts of information in a short amount of time. The teacher must look for ways to nurture strong interests in their pupils that will awaken the power of their will and provide a firm foundation for a healthy attitude towards life.

Approaches to teaching Class 9

The guiding principle for the four years of Upper School is to find lesson material that speaks directly to the young people in their inmost selves. This will differ in different subjects, but the key question remains: 'What is it that moves this young person, this class?' For the teachers, the challenge lies in helping the young people find answers to questions bubbling up within them.

The teacher's focus is now clearly on the individual – a natural consequence of the development from child to adolescent to young adult. Increasingly, the topics and subjects of the school lessons are aimed at encouraging the young person's further development. They are topical and pertain to the world we live in; the Upper School has arrived in the present. The pupils are grateful to learn anything meaningful to do with the real world. Class 9 usually undertake a fortnight's work experience on a farm. This is their first time doing work experience but they'll do more in subsequent classes too. When the young people take on responsibility for some task, the farmer can generally be sure that there will be no disappointments. Getting up at five o'clock for milking? No problem. Even weeding endless rows up and down an enormous vegetable patch gets done – try that at home in the family garden!

In Class 9, as well as in Class 10, the lesson content aims to help young people understand their own individual situation. Because of their passion and conviction, young people often develop fixed and absolute opinions that narrow their horizons. There is a need to loosen them up and broaden their view. This shows most clearly in the English lesson, in which the pupils learn about humour and tragedy. Through laughter they experience inner freedom and in the study of humorous works they learn the importance of stepping back from themselves and seeing themselves more objectively. Through the experience of tragedy they develop empathy and compassion for the suffering of others and a deeper understanding for different points of view. In the swing between these opposites, pupils learn to see how 'phenomena in the world are held in the field of tension that unites … extremes.'[1] It provides them with the opportunity to temper their own absolutist opinions and bring them more down to earth.

Class 9 are keen to try out things for themselves and should be given opportunity to do so. Teachers are there to assist them in overcoming the sluggishness and heaviness typical in the time of puberty, and this is only possible if the young people take pleasure in physical activity. Due to the wide-ranging changes that have taken place in their bodies over the previous months and years, pupils often need to relearn many movements and actions. This requires time and patience. Team games which set age-appropriate challenges fit the bill, enabling young people to forget their self-consciousness and self-absorption, if only for a few minutes.

Central themes of P.E. lessons in Class 9 are building up strength and stamina and tackling challenging exercises. A lot of the work can be done in mixed groups, the general mood becomes relaxed. Not only strength but also technique is important. The shot put is a good example. Strength alone is not enough; rather a sophisticated sequence of movements (which incidentally have great aesthetic value) must be mastered.

Main aspects of the lessons

P.E. lessons are now concerned with life as it is experienced between two polarities: namely, learning to fall and then regaining one's balance. Movement is experienced as an expression of the human will, and the inner sense of space can be experienced anew. According to the developmental needs of boys and girls alike, differentiation and individualisation are factors to be considered. This requires the introduction of certain well-chosen activities into the lessons, which give the pupils opportunities to get to know each other better.

Suggested activities for Class 9

- Bothmer exercises: Fall to the Point, Fall into Space, The Strong Triangle, The Plunge. Earlier exercises are also repeated and developed, for example, Jump to Middle Point.
- Gymnastic exercises with and without hand apparatus.
- Circuit training, with elements for both strength and speed.

- Rhythmic gymnastics (not yet to music): basic skills using ribbon, hoop, rope, clubs and ball as well as simple choreographies in small groups.
- Floor gymnastics: continuing exercises from the Middle School, with emphasis on rolls (from standing and running), handstands (and rolling out), cartwheels and somersaults; practising combinations of the different exercises.
- Acrobatics: backbends and bridge, back handspring, flick-flack, backward somersault, pyramids, slow combinations of elements in pairs
- Parallel bars: straight-arm support, from support into swinging, straddle, twist, turn, roll, upper-arm stand (body straight, head down).
- Uneven bars: mounting, swinging over, swinging over sideways with legs together, simple combinations of elements in pairs.
- Beam: practising diverse balancing skills, short combinations of exercises when mounting and dismounting.
- Bar: swinging up from chin-up, swinging freely, rotating at waist, various leg raises.
- Rings: various swings, hanging and with straight-arm support, also with attached trapeze, hanging head-down, swinging with straight-arm support, straddle from standing position.
- High jump/long jump: continuing Middle School exercises with the emphasis on take-off; strong push-off and rhythmical run-up.
- Large trampoline/mini-trampoline: improving on basic jumps and preparing for forward and backward somersaults

- Obstacle course: pupils set up their own courses, intensifying rotating jumps, expeditions outdoors.
- Athletics: shot put, 100 m sprint, middle-distance running, Cooper test (pupils run as far as possible in twelve minutes), high jump (straddle, flop), long jump, hurdles.
- Games: handball, basketball, volleyball, tchoukball, baseball, badminton, variations of Spaceball (see p. 121 for description of the game) and relays.
- Swimming: further work on swimming technique, rescue, swimming longer distances and diving.
- Dancing: ballroom dancing, possibly jazz dance.

Additional activities for Class 9

- A class trip with sporting emphasis where possible.
- Hiking trips.
- Climbing.
- Skiing.
- Orienteering.

Information on sample lessons

Quidditch and apparatus gymnastics

As in previous years, the rituals at the beginning of the lessons help the pupils to feel at home. As such, the lesson which is presented begins with everyone standing in a circle. The pupils are told what to expect and hopefully feel motivated. Although many pupils may already be familiar with Quidditch, be aware that explaining the complex rules to newcomers will take up a lot of time during this first lesson. As regards the size of the playing field and the teams, a volleyball court is only big enough to cater for teams of twelve players maximum. With larger classes, a second playing field is needed, or else flying changes frequently take place. This game is a good choice for Class 9, as tactics play a part and every player gets a chance to take the field and show their qualities in their chosen role.

In the warm-up session the pupils are actively involved in choosing the exercises themselves. The Bothmer exercise Fall to the Point epitomises the theme of the lesson and is the perfect preparation for work on the rings, where the pupils will practise dropping down from a height. Some pupils are so keen that they not only practise dropping from the rings but also repeat the Bothmer exercise several times (see photos pp. 144–45).

For the work on the gymnastics equipment, each piece of apparatus sets the pupils a different challenge. It is important that the equipment remain the same over a period of several weeks, although the set tasks become increasingly difficult. What counts here is individual performance and the progress that each pupil makes. In the case of dropping from the rings, how each pupil experiences the height and the drop is the important aspect. While groups of pupils are watching or assisting, they often talk about how they themselves cope with falling and letting go, and discuss the elements of courage and fear.

After this strenuous, concentrated phase, a game of volleyball at the end of the lesson is a fine contrast. Finally, in the usual circle, there is a pause for reflection, but rather than looking back and summarising the whole lesson, the teacher can ask the pupils what the highlights were for them.

Athletics: shot put

During the pep talk at the beginning of the lesson, the teacher may wish to find out how much the pupils know about the various athletic disciplines, the athletes who have made a name for themselves in them and the records they hold. As in other subjects, the pupils find it helpful to learn a little about the lives of sporting personalities, some of whom might become role models for them.

Learning about the equipment leads to the pupils handling it with respect. There is also an overlap with other school subjects, in this case with physics and learning about the trajectory of an object in motion. Many pupils are intimidated by the weight of the shot. The first simple exercises and a light-hearted approach to the discipline help them overcome this.

As usual, how the teacher divides up the class will depend on the size of the class and its particular composition. The important thing, however, is that the pupils work hard at the basic techniques, get a feeling for the specific bodily movements, and experience satisfaction in making progress.

The game that follows at the end, in this case Boccia, offers the pupils a bit of relaxation after the concentrated work that has gone before.

Games, rhythmic gymnastics and wrestling

After the usual exchange of greetings and a preview of the lesson to come, there follows a version of the game Spaceball. This version is played with four teams, making it more complex and multi-layered. Another exciting variation on this is to have two games going on at the same time on the same pitch, with two referees and two different-coloured balls. The game begins with one referee calling out which two teams are to play each other (for example, 'Red plays Yellow!'), meaning the remaining two play each other simultaneously. This is a great challenge for every pupil, testing their passing skills, their presence of mind and their awareness of the whole playing area. In addition, a rule can be introduced that says that a point can only be awarded if the ball has been played in both halves of the field and that at the moment of gaining the point, at least two players of the team are in each half. The young people love this degree of complexity and, given the chance, will often play it in free lessons.

The pupils also enjoy interval training on the obstacle course, not least because they can choose their own pace. This obstacle course, with all its variations, gives each pupil a chance to see what they are capable of and develop their stamina. After several weeks the pupils can see they are making progress and are able to keep going for longer. In my experience, almost every class has asked for the time working on the obstacle course to be extended and for the intervals to be lengthened.

It is worth integrating the Bothmer exercise Fall to the Point into as many P.E. projects as possible. It is one of the more challenging exercises, as well as the longest, and the pupils need time to feel their way into it and discover the essence of it. What is more, they soon grow accustomed to the frequent repetitions and it becomes second nature for the pupils to practise it.

Traditionally, the class would be divided into single-sex groups at this point, the girls to do rhythmic gymnastics and the boys to do wrestling. However, there are girls who enjoy wrestling just as there are boys with an interest in rhythmic gymnastics, and both groups should be allowed to try their hand at either activity.

To start with, the pupils work on the basics of rhythmic gymnastics. The best approach is to practise with one of the pieces of hand apparatus, for example

the ribbon. The ribbon reproduces the flow of movement but also clarifies and magnifies it; it matches the mood of the pupils at this age as they search for the harmony they once knew when they were younger. The pupils can work together to create, practise and present choreographies using the various hand apparatus. At this stage the presentations are without musical accompaniment, focussing entirely on movement and rhythm. From Class 10 onwards, music, which the pupils may already be learning about with their music teacher, can be introduced. This gives the choreographic work an added dimension.

If they could, some pupils in Class 9 would no doubt do some wrestling in every lesson. Keeping to simple rules and learning the various holds, the pupils enjoy practising the moves on each other and, occasionally, even on the P.E. teacher!

A game of touchdown rugby, together or in separate groups, is a good way of winding down the lesson. Finally, the Bothmer exercise changes the mood from loud and hectic to calm and concentrated.

Below: the Bothmer exercise Fall to the Point.

Sample Lesson: Quidditch and apparatus gymnastics. Duration: 90 mins			
Time	**Sequence of activities**	**Formation**	**Material used**
c. 2 mins.	The students form a circle and exchange greetings. The teacher gives the students a preview of the lesson and what to expect.	Standing in a circle.	None.
c. 23 mins.	Game: Muggle Quidditch. The class is divided into two teams. One team puts on coloured team bands. The playing area is the entire hall, as a minimum the size of a volleyball court. Two hoops are tied together with rope and attached to the basketball baskets at either end of the court. These are the goals for the quaffle (handball). The game is played using three different balls: the quaffle (handball), the beater (softball) and the snitch (rubber ball). Before the game, each team nominates one of their players to be a seeker. It is their role to catch the snitch. **The quaffle.** With only a minimum of three passes, the team in possession of the quaffle tries to get near enough to the hoops to score a goal. Running with the ball is not allowed, although players are allowed to take a step when throwing. Back passes are allowed. After three passes, the team must try and score a goal in either of the two hoops hanging from the basketball baskets. A goal is worth ten points. The opposing team then gets the ball and the game continues. If the ball goes out of play or someone runs with it, they forfeit possession to the other team. **The beater.** Any player on either team can throw the beater at another player. If a player is hit, they must stand motionless with their feet apart until they are 'revived' by a teammate crawling between their legs. During this rescue, both can be hit by the beater and both must remain motionless. If an opposing player catches the beater, then the thrower must stand still. Even being hit by a teammate counts. Running with the beater is not allowed. **The snitch.** One of the referees throws the snitch onto the field of play. This may only be caught by one of the nominated seekers, who must return it to the referee. A player who does this without being hit by the beater wins thirty points for their team. The seekers wait on the baseline of their respective halves of the field, one foot touching the wall, until the snitch comes into play. A seeker gets one chance to catch the snitch then must make way for a teammate. It is good to have two referees and to change ends after ten minutes.	Team game.	Handball (the quaffle), softball (the beater), rubber ball (the snitch), coloured team bands, two hoops tied together, basketball baskets or posts for holding the hoops.
c. 15 mins.	Warm-up exercise. Standing in a circle, the students take it in turns to step forward and perform a brief warm-up exercise which the rest of the class participates in. Next, they perform the Bothmer exercise Fall to the Point. The focus is on the moment of falling. The students can explore how far they can stretch before falling becomes inevitable, how the fall may vary with the height and tension of the stretch, and how they recover themselves from the fall.	Standing in a circle.	None.

Time	Sequence of activities	Formation	Material used
c. 45 mins.	Group work. The two main exercises are 'dropping from the rings' and the 'horizontal ladder'. Secondary exercises can include 'circling the beam' and the 'bar through the rings'. **Dropping from the rings.** A large high-jump mat is placed beneath the rings. One student takes hold of the rings and the other pupils pull them up until they say stop. The student chooses for themselves when they will let go and drop down onto the mat. Tips for landing safely: keep the mouth closed and the knees relaxed. For those feeling confident, the height of the rings can be increased. **The horizontal ladder.** The students must cross hand over hand without letting their feet touch the ground. If the ladder is adjustable, one end can be raised to create the additional challenge of climbing upwards. When they reach the end, the student drops down onto the mats below. Only one student is allowed on the ladder at a time. **The beam.** This secondary exercise requires the student to hook their arms and legs around the beam and then manoeuvre themselves underneath and up over the other side without touching the mats on the floor. First, they go clockwise then anticlockwise. **Bar through the rings.** A wooden bar is placed through the rings. A student sets the rings swinging at a slow, steady pace. The students take it in turns to lie face down on the mats beneath them. They must time the swing so that they jump up and over the bar as it swings towards them, then lie down again before it swings back. Another student writes down how many jumps a classmate manages. Several attempts can be made. The students move from one stage to another at regular intervals.	Group work.	Beam, large and small mats, ropes, 4–5 m (13–16 ft) ladder, rings, wooden bar, uneven bars.
c. 2 mins.	Changeover. The students clear the equipment away.	Clearing away.	None.
c. 3 mins.	End of the lesson. The students take a few moments to reflect on the highlights of the lesson, before repeating the Bothmer exercise Fall to the Point. They exchange farewells.	Standing in a circle.	None.

Sample Lesson: Shot put. Duration: 90 mins			
Time	**Sequence of activities**	**Formation**	**Material used**
c. 2 mins.	The students form a circle and exchange greetings. The teacher gives the students a preview of the lesson and what to expect.	Standing in a circle.	None.
c. 3 mins.	The shot. The teacher gives each student a shot and provides them with information on this piece of sports equipment. Because the shot isn't thrown but *pushed,* we say it is putted, where 'putted' or 'putting' means to be pushed.	Standing in groups.	One shot per student.
c. 5 mins.	Warm-up exercise. Bending down with their feet apart, the students pass the shot between their legs in a figure-of-eight movement.	As above.	As above.
c. 5 mins.	How to hold the shot. The teacher shows the students how to hold the shot, cradled on the fingers with the thumb holding it in place.	Two students at a time.	As above.
c. 5 mins.	First steps. Taking it in turns, two at a time, the students stand with their legs apart, facing away from the putting direction. They swing the shot in both hands and, after two swings, hurl it backward over their heads, keeping their arms straight.	Standing in groups.	As above.
c. 5 mins.	Putting the shot. The students stand in a row at a safe distance from each other and try putting the shot facing forward. They bend their knees twice, then spring up and project the shot almost vertically.	Standing in a row (with the left-handers on the left). The shots are collected only when all are finished.	As above.
c. 20 mins.	The five stages of the sideways shot put technique (for left handers the positions are reversed): 1. the student points their left shoulder in putting direction; 2. stands with their weight on their right foot, knee bent, upper body bent downwards and backwards; 3. straightens their back leg; 4. swivels their hip to the frontal shot put position; and 5. straightens their putting arm diagonally upwards.	Standing in a row.	As above.

Time	Sequence of activities	Formation	Material used
c. 5 mins.	The next stage is to combine these five phases in one flowing movement.	In a row, alone or in pairs.	As above.
c. 5 mins.	The sideways turn. The students practise the sideways turn (without the shot at first), pivoting from their left foot to their right foot and back to their left, taking care not to lose contact with the ground.	As above.	As above.
c. 5 mins.	The sideways turn is practised again, but this time with the shot.	As above.	As above.
c. 15 mins.	The final step. The students put the various stages together, the sideways turn building momentum for putting the shot.	As above.	As above.
c. 10 mins.	Winding up the lesson. A game of Boccia is played using the shots as balls and one small weight as the jack.	Behind the line.	As above, plus one small weight.
c. 5 mins.	End of the lesson. The equipment is cleared away. Standing in a circle, the students take a few moments to reflect on the highlights of the lesson and look forward to the next one. They exchange farewells.	Clearing away. Standing in a circle.	None.

Sample Lesson: Games, rhythmic gymnastics and wrestling. Duration: 90 mins			
Time	**Sequence of activities**	**Formation**	**Material used**
c. 2 mins.	The students form a circle and exchange greetings. The teacher gives the students a preview of the lesson and what to expect.	Standing in a circle.	None.
c. 15 mins.	Game: Spaceball. 1. In this variation on the popular game, the class is divided into four teams and are given coloured team bands to wear. The players spread out around the gym (the game should be played in an area at least the size of a volleyball court). 2. The game begins with one referee calling out two of the teams who are to play each other (for example, 'Red plays Yellow!'). The remaining two teams play each other at the same time. 3. The usual rules of the game apply (see p. 121). In addition, a rule can be introduced that states a point can only be awarded if the ball has been played in both halves of the court and that at the moment the point is gained, at least two players of the team are in each half. 4. After around five minutes, there is a short break, then the referee calls out a different combination of team colours. The individual teams take their points with them into the new game. Teams change again after another five minutes.	Ball game.	Volleyball, coloured team bands.
c. 20 mins.	Changeover. The students sit in a circle and the team bands are collected in. The teacher then gives each student a specific task in setting up the obstacle course. Once they have completed the task, the students return to the circle and await instruction. Ideas for the different obstacles include: ▸ a wall of high vaulting boxes with mats either side for landing on; ▸ benches placed in a line for squat turns; ▸ benches set up against the uneven bars with a mat behind, for running up and jumping off; ▸ a row of small boxes set up as stepping-stones – the pupils hop across them; and ▸ a beam for crawling under. Each student decides where on the course they want to start. They then exercise for three periods of three minutes each with an interval of one minute in between. If one section is still in use, the students go on to the next part. This is not about counting completed laps but keeping going and finding one's ideal pace. At the end, the students cool down with a slow jog into a walk.	Warm-up on obstacle course.	Bars, beam, benches, large and small mats, large and small boxes.

Time	Sequence of activities	Formation	Material used
c. 10 mins.	Warm-up exercises. Standing in a circle, the students loosen up and stretch together before performing the Bothmer exercise Fall to the Point.	Standing in a circle.	None.
c. 2 mins.	Changeover. The obstacle course is cleared away. Mats are laid out in one half of the gym for wrestling; ribbons are placed in the other half for the rhythmic gymnastics.	None.	None.
c. 23 mins.	**Wrestling.** The teacher clearly sets out the rules and explains the various moves and holds, which the pupils then practise on each other, occasionally changing partners. Towards the end of the session they engage in free wrestling on the mats. **Rhythmic gymnastics.** The students practise basic exercises with the ribbons. The teacher can introduce new elements, for example, simple throws of the ribbon forward while jumping. Then, in groups of no more than five, the pupils work together on short choreographies, which they perform at the end of the session.	Group work in both halves of gym.	Thick mats; ribbons.
c. 15 mins.	Game: Touchdown Rugby. 1. The class is divided into two teams for touchdown rugby (not to be confused with touch rugby), a simplified form of rugby. Each team defends a mat, upon which the ball can be laid by the opposing team for one point. 2. When the player of one team has the ball, they can run. If they are forced to the ground by an opponent (a sitting position is enough), the ball changes hands. 3. The game can be played with mixed teams, although it is important that the teams are well-matched and the rules are clearly defined rules.	Ball game.	Two mats, one rugby ball, coloured team bands.
c. 3 mins.	End of the lesson. The equipment is cleared away. Standing in a circle, the students take a few moments to reflect on the highlights of the lesson and look forward to the next one. They exchange farewells.	Standing in a circle.	None.

Class 10:
From the Centre to the Periphery – the Discus

Class 10 pupils

At sixteen, young people are still trying to find out who they are. Their gaze turns inward, and for people who know them, it's as if they are shutting up shop. Anyone fortunate enough to glimpse inside this suit of armour finds a young person wrestling with grand issues such as responsibility and authenticity and trying to fathom the meaning of life. Their faculty of judgement is maturing and becoming a more reliable aid when discussing complex subjects. The pupils in Class 10 are ready to take on tasks beyond their immediate horizon and make a good job of them.

Especially important in this school year is the period set aside for work experience, something the previous school years have prepared the young people for. Ideally, the young people take up the challenge wholeheartedly and find themselves playing an active part in adult life. It is particularly rewarding for them when adults acknowledge their contributions and take their actions and opinions seriously, even learning from them.

It is a particular pleasure to see how young people's intellectual powers are developing at this time. They have honed their analytical capabilities and schooled their powers of judgement on specific problems and questions of quality. Observation and close study in the natural sciences and the humanities helps them gain a better understanding of the world they live in; they also find initial answers to questions concerning the future.

Emotionally, young people at this time are trying to find

a balance between their inner life and the world around them. This polarity is typical for the age group. Class 10 pupils inwardly identify with the various tasks they are set in P.E. lessons and do their best to execute them. There are parallels here with the way Class 7 pupils develop in their search for new limits and new experiences that deeply affect them. But the inner experiences of Class 10 pupils are far more intense. Young people are critical not only of society, but also of themselves. It is this conscious recognition of flaws and difficulties that leads to character development, often at a breath-taking, bewildering speed.

For P.E. lessons, Harald Geißler sums up the situation as follows:

> The aim is to mobilise the forces of the will in order to overcome the gravitational pull after the fall. In Class 10, the circumference of the circle (in the gymnastic exercises) ought to be performed with a bold, spirited, swinging motion, corresponding to the nature of the young person. Just as important is not losing one's self on the circumference but remaining in the centre. The will, working outwards, must be countered by the will working inwards. Movement must be given the corresponding forms, for example, in figures of eight, spirals and loops.[1]

Despite these observations, we should not forget that the crisis known as puberty is not yet over. There is an ever-present egocentrism, which occasionally overwhelms the young person.

Approaches to teaching Class 10

Two different periods of practical work experience stand out in Class 10. On the one hand, during two weeks' field surveying, the students chart their own map and fix their standpoint. This can be seen as a metaphor for the young people who are trying to find their place in the world. The work with compass and theodolite leads to fixing positions and charting the map, just as, inwardly, young people go through a similar process on the way to finding their true self. The pupils take pleasure in applied maths and geometry and they are given their first taste of the complex problems that crop up in Upper School maths.

Then there is the time spent working for an outside company that opens the door to the world of work. This is not intended as a time for pupils to find future jobs or professions, but it is designed to give them genuine hands-on experience of the work place and to experience being a useful part of the adult world. It also allows young people the chance to reassess their academic experience and consider what might be best for them.

In the light of these developments, discussions take place at many schools between pupils, teachers and parents, in which they look back at their time at school, assesses their strengths and weaknesses and articulate their aims for the near future. Hopefully, Class 10 pupils will show a readiness to take on more responsibility, knowing that they are supported by those around them.

This motif of taking on responsibility can easily be applied to P.E. lessons. Pupils often develop and perform variations on all of the exercises as well as introducing their own specialist skills to the group and taking over certain units of the lesson (see sample lesson below, p. 162).

When young people get the chance to use their own specialist skills and knowledge, which some of them will have gained outside of school in sports clubs, it not only strengthens their self-esteem but also encourages them to pursue their own particular activity more intensely.

Main aspects of the lessons

The main aspects of Class 10 P.E. lessons concern the centre and the periphery – the relation between within and without. All the skills the pupils have thus far acquired are intensified, diversified and further improved on. The growing interest in understanding and testing their own corporeality and physical ability is characteristic of this school year. The pupils take on more responsibility in practising their skills.

Suggested activities for Class 10

- Bothmer exercises: Three Circles, The Discus, Walking in the Horizontal, Double Eight (also called the Twofold Eight), Extending into the Width (sometimes referred to as The Lion); Extending into the Height (sometimes referred to as The Eagle).
- Gymnastics: further work with rod, ball, hoop and rope.
- Rhythmic sport gymnastics: practising technique in all disciplines; consolidating and choreographing work in one discipline (can also be set to music).
- Artistry: in pairs facing each other (3–6 balls), passing clubs, formations with apparatus, involving varying heights.
- Floor gymnastics: kips, somersaults, round-offs both sides.
- Acrobatics: handstand, various shoulder stands, free shoulder stand, backflips, somersaults, bell-swinging in groups of threes.
- Parallel bars: continuing Class 9 work with an emphasis on combining various movements.
- Horizontal bar: further improving on previous exercises, putting various elements together with an eye on harmony and flow, dropping from bar from a height with correct landing.
- Rings: straddle to front and back, simple somersaults on swinging and/or motionless rings.
- Jumps: increasing height, somersaults, jumps over box lengthwise.
- Mini-trampoline: somersaults forwards and backwards, exercises concentrating on twists and turns, also in combination with other apparatus, for example, vaulting box.
- Large trampoline: turns in roll and transverse axis, combining elements, jumping in pairs.
- Athletics: discus, 100 m and 200 m sprint, 400 m and middle-distance, relays, Cooper test (pupils run as far as possible in twelve minutes), high jump (straddle jump), long jump, triple jump and shot put.
- Games: basketball, handball, volleyball, ultimate frisbee, variations of Spaceball, baseball, fistball, tennis.
- Swimming: continuing the work done in Class 9.
- Dancing: interpretative dance, contact improvisation, modern dance.

Additional activities for Class 10

- Class trip with sporting emphasis.
- Hiking trips.
- Climbing.
- Skiing.
- Orienteering.
- Obstacle course.

The pupils also have the option of keeping a P.E. diary (see below), which will be used more in Class 12.

Information on sample lessons

Athletics: discus in the gym

After the exchange of greetings and a few words from the teacher giving a preview of the lesson to come, the pupils take part in a game of tag. This is designed to get them in the mood for working together in the coming lesson, while also blotting out any other issues which might be distracting them.

The times given for working on the discus-throwing technique are a rough guide only: practising the separate phases thoroughly is the most important thing. The aim is to produce a clean, flowing movement and a good throw.

Due to the weight of the discus, however, beginners sometimes develop a poor technique. It is therefore better to practise with rubber rings. As these are less dangerous, pupils can stand closer to one another and train more intensively. Once they have got the technique right, switching over to the real discus is straightforward.

Throwing the discus requires a lot more than just flair and intuition. The pupil must develop a feel for the discus and the movement, which takes place in the horizontal plane. For anyone feeling out of sorts, as little as fifteen minutes' discus training can restore harmony and well-being.

The Bothmer exercise The Discus has the same beneficial effects.

Game: frisbee

In this lesson, the students begin by taking an active part in the warm-up session. In learning the throwing technique, the frisbee immediately shows how successful and precise a throw is. When playing with changing partners, the pupils learn to adapt to new faces and distances as quickly as possible – an important skill in the game to come. Playing a simplified form of the game in small groups on a small pitch can be great motivation. Explaining how this game arose and discussing the spirit of the game should be part of the unit. This also goes for the other games and activities the students encounter.

Apparatus gymnastics: somersaults

In this lesson, the special form of the game Lying Tag means the players interact a great deal in quick succession. The variation, which involves boys and girls swapping places as runners, requires alertness and presence of mind – the perfect preparation for the challenging work on the gymnastics equipment to come.

The warm-up session with the ropes places the emphasis on concentration and rhythmical movement, where each pupil has a chance to improve on their performance.

The meditative Bothmer exercise Walking in the Horizontal invigorates the inner and outer movements of the pupils, alternating between the centre and the periphery. The teacher must observe the class carefully and gauge how far the students are willing to go with this exercise. Occasionally, individual students describe in their P.E. diaries how they come back to this exercise at home in an effort to improve.

It is important when it comes to working on the gymnastics equipment that the pupils feel confident in whoever is assisting them. There is also, occasionally, unintended intimate bodily contact. Teachers are advised to carefully consider groupings and pairings.

Somersaults

The aim here is not to go through all the somersault exercises as quickly as possible, but to allow the pupils to develop an inner feeling for the movement. Repeating this unit over a period of three weeks intensifies this experience. The more athletic pupils rapidly gain in confidence until they can perform a free somersault. For others, the added height of the somersault table helps them to concentrate on carrying out the correct movement.

As with the above exercise, consciously experiencing the back flip is more important than ticking off the various exercises one after another.

As they get to grips with the exercise, the pupils are asked to consider various questions. Where are they most awake when they carry out this movement? What goes through their mind just before they begin? How do they feel just after completing the exercise? Asking these questions will help the pupils to focus their minds on the activity and intensify their work.

There are several versions of the numbers game. Make sure to jot down which numbers and which games have already been done in order to avoid repetitions and increase the excitement. At the end of the lesson, it is sometimes good to turn attention to the atmosphere which prevailed in the games as well as the quality of the plays and moves. As usual, the lesson is concluded with everyone standing in a circle.

The P.E. diary

The idea of introducing this project arose while considering how to make young people more aware of the amount and quality of movement (or the lack of it) in their lives.

The project, which is undertaken on a voluntary basis, is introduced to the pupils at the start of Class 10. The pupils begin by noting down what sporting activity they do every day for a month. The important thing is that they try to write something each day without fail and that they be honest with themselves. As a rule, the work on the diary takes place between the autumn and Easter holidays. That gives the teacher enough time to read through them and, where appropriate, add any personal comments. Every few weeks, in the P.E. lesson, the teacher can remind the pupils about the diary. Some pupils do not wish to take part, which is fine, whereas others want to keep the diary for longer and hand it in at a later date, which is also fine.

Every pupil has their own ideas about how to keep the diary. Some use hardback bound notebooks and feature elaborate reports on jogging, cycling or some other activity they are engaged with. Others have loose sheets of paper fastened with paper clips, full of key words, abbreviations and charts. It is important to give pupils a free hand in the matter, while not forgetting to give them feedback on the content. It is also interesting to see all the things which count as sporting activity, ranging from 'dancing – 2 hours', 'walking the dog – 20 minutes', 'weight training with brother – 10 minutes' to 'vacuum cleaning at home – 15 minutes'. Pupils are often surprised about their general lack of movement, even those who see taking the dog for a walk as a sporting activity.

Sample Lesson: Athletics – discus in the gym. Duration: 80 mins			
Time	**Sequence of activities**	**Formation**	**Material used**
c. 3 mins.	The students form a circle and exchange greetings. The teacher gives the students a preview of the lesson and what to expect.	Standing in a circle.	None.
c. 10 mins.	Game: Animal Tag. 1. One student is chosen to be the hunter, who then attempts to tag as many of their classmates as they can. 2. Anyone being chased can save themselves not just by running away, but also by shouting out the name of an animal. The hunter must then choose another victim, or else they have the option of spinning round once on the spot before chasing the same classmate again. 3. No animal can be called twice. 4. Anyone tagged becomes the hunter.	Game of tag.	None.
c. 3 mins.	Discus technique – step 1. The students stand with their legs apart and their arms hanging down and slightly out to the side. They swing round, turning at the waist.	Standing in a line with plenty of space between students.	None.
c. 5 mins.	Discus technique – step 2. As well as learning how to hold the discus, the students practise releasing it in a single smooth motion. 1. Using a soft rubber ring as a discus, the teacher demonstrates the grip: fingers splayed, the ring/discus resting against the wrist and held in place by the tip of the middle finger. 2. From a standing position and with their arms still hanging down, the students let the ring roll forwards out of their hand. 3. The students then crouch low with their legs apart, and swinging their arm they let the ring roll away along the floor in as straight a line as possible. Rubber rings are safer to use to begin with and allow the students to train more intensively. Once they have mastered the correct technique, switching over to the proper discus is straightforward.	In a circle.	One rubber ring for each student.

Time	Sequence of activities	Formation	Material used
c. 15 mins.	Discus technique – step 3: 1. The pupils walk forward, holding their rubber ring with their arm out straight and palm turned upward. 2. They grasp the ring with their other hand and swing it downwards and back, then up again several times. This motion takes place in one plane. 3. The pupils repeat the exercise, but this time the impulse for swinging the arm is given by the motion of the pupil's hip: the right hip for right-handers, left hip for left-handers. 4. Now, on the upward swing, the pupil lets go of the ring, imparting a spinning motion with their hand. Final contact with the ring is with the little finger.	Standing in line, side by side.	As above.
c. 15 mins.	Practice session. Two groups face each other at opposite ends of the gym. They endeavour to throw the rings to one another, so that they fly upwards in an arc, rotating but not wobbling.	In teams, maximum of sixteen per side.	As above.
c. 10 mins.	Discus technique – step 4. Facing the direction of throw, the pupils now spin right round, taking three full steps before throwing. Pupils keep their knees bent and their centre of gravity low during the turn.	In groups of three, down the length of gym.	As above.
c. 15 mins.	Discus technique – step 5. The pupils practise throwing with one and a half turns, beginning by facing away from the direction of throw. The ring should rotate quickly in the air and at a slight slant without wobbling.	Three pupils standing next to each other.	As above.
c. 4 mins.	End of the lesson. The pupils take a few moments to reflect on the lesson and look forward to the next one. They exchange farewells.	Standing in a circle.	None.

Sample Lesson: Frisbee. Duration: 90 mins

Time	Sequence of activities	Formation	Material used
c. 5 mins.	The pupils walk together to the playing field.	–	None.
c. 4 mins.	The pupils form a circle and exchange greetings. The teacher gives the pupils a preview of the lesson and what to expect.	Standing in a circle.	None.
c. 6 mins.	Warm-up exercise. In groups of six the pupils run round the field, taking it in turns to lead off with a running exercise that the others follow. Change after a minute.	Small groups.	None.
c. 15 mins.	Throwing technique. In pairs, the students practise throwing and catching the frisbee, concentrating on their stance, their grip, their aim and the dynamics of the throw: a quick whip of the wrist at release as they focus on the target. The teacher discusses safety precautions relating to throwing and catching.	In pairs, spread out.	One frisbee per pair.
c. 5 mins.	Practising in motion. Still in pairs, the pupils practise throwing the frisbee while running to and fro. They need to keep the distance between them constant and aim for where the catcher will be rather than where they are.	As above.	As above.
c. 15 mins.	Short five-pass game. 1. The class is divided into teams of three players who occupy an area that is roughly 15 m x 15 m (50 ft x 50 ft). Each team tries to pass the frisbee five times, including any return passes to players. 2. The players throw from a standing position and pivot on their feet. 3. For a throw to be valid it must be at least one arm's length in distance. The aim is to practise rapid throwing and catching.	Game on field.	One frisbee per game; coloured team bands.
c. 25 mins.	Game: Cross Frisbee. 1. Four cones or skittles are set up in the shape of a cross, 35 m (115 ft) apart. 2. The class is divided into teams of seven. Passing to each other, each team tries to hit the skittles with the frisbee while players from the other teams attempt to intercept the frisbee. This game is good for practising quick, short moves, and learning to mark players and finding space, as well as gaining an overall picture of what is going on.	As above.	As above.
c. 10 mins.	End of the lesson. The students take a few moments to reflect on the lesson and look forward to the next one.	Standing in circle.	None.
c. 5 mins.	Return to school. The students exchange farewells.	–	None.

Sample Lesson: Apparatus gymnastics – somersaults. Duration: 90 mins			
Time	**Sequence of activities**	**Formation**	**Material used**
c. 2 mins.	The students form a circle and exchange greetings. The teacher gives the students a preview of the lesson and what to expect.	Standing in a circle.	None.
c. 5 mins.	Game: Lying Tag. 1. Two students are chosen to be the catcher and the runner. The rest of the students spread out across the gym and lie face down in pairs. 2. The catcher tries to catch the runner. 3. If the runner is caught, they swap roles and become the catcher. 4. At any time, the runner can lie down next to one of the pairs, making the one on the far side the next catcher. The present catcher then becomes the runner and the game continues. 5. In a different version of the game, mixed pairs are chosen at the beginning so that a boy and a girl lie face down, side by side. If the runner is a girl, she must lie down next to a girl so that the boy becomes the new catcher. The reverse happens if the runner is a boy.	Game of tag.	None.
c. 8 mins.	Warm-up. The students gather in a large circle, and each one is provided with a skipping rope. Exercises can include: ▸ skipping on the spot (100x); ▸ skipping on the spot backwards (100x); ▸ skipping forwards keeping legs together; ▸ skipping backwards keeping legs together; ▸ skipping one-legged, changing foot rhythmically; ▸ whipping the rope round twice in one jump; ▸ swinging rope on the left then right then over; ▸ the same swinging the rope backwards; ▸ crossing hands, skipping forwards and backwards; and ▸ free skipping in pairs.	Warm-up in a circle.	One rope per pupil.
c. 5 mins.	Bothmer exercise: Walking in the Horizontal. Recommended tips: keep a careful eye on the breadth of the movement and turning motions.	In lines, facing forward.	None.

Time	Sequence of activities	Formation	Material used
c. 20 mins.	Apparatus gymnastics: the somersault. Group A: Using the somersault belt, pupils practise backward somersaults, developing an awareness of the position of their body in space. Group B: A somersault table can be created using a section of a vaulting box covered with a large mat. Benches are placed on either side and a mini-trampoline at the front. Small mats are placed all around. The pupils then progress from simply jumping onto the somersault table to finally somersaulting onto it: 1. Jumping from the trampoline onto the somersault table. 2. Jumping onto the somersault table and into crouch before rolling forward on the large mat. 3. Jumping onto the somersault table into a roll. 4. Increasing the jumping height, until a somersault onto the table is possible. 5. Continue practising forward somersault. Getting a feel for the forward motion, coming out of the body curl in time and landing well are the main aims.	Two groups at work on gym apparatus.	Group A: small mats, somersault belts, ropes. Group B: two boxes, mini-trampoline, three benches, two large mats, small mats.
c. 20 mins.	Groups swap places.	As above.	As above.
c. 5 mins.	Changeover. Equipment is cleared away.	Clearing away.	None.
c. 20 mins.	Game: Numbers. 1. Students sit in two rows, facing each other along the centre line. If possible, opposing pairs should be of similar ability. 2. One row is given team bands; each pair gets a number. 3. The teams gather on opposing baselines behind benches that serve as boundaries. 4. The referee has lots of different balls. They call out the name of a game and a series of numbers, for example: 'Football. One, seven, twelve, fourteen, fifteen. Go!' 5. The players that have been called run onto the pitch and play against each other for two to three minutes or until a goal is scored, whichever comes first. 6. The players leave the field and a new game begins.	Running game.	Team bands, benches, goals (two small mats and six sticks for floorball), basketball baskets, handball, football, hockey ball, softball.
c. 3 mins.	Changeover. Equipment is cleared away.	Clearing away.	None.
c. 2 mins.	End of the lesson. Pupils stand in a circle. The teacher looks ahead to the next lesson. They exchange farewells.	Circle.	None.

HVXC

Class 11:
Taking Aim – the Javelin

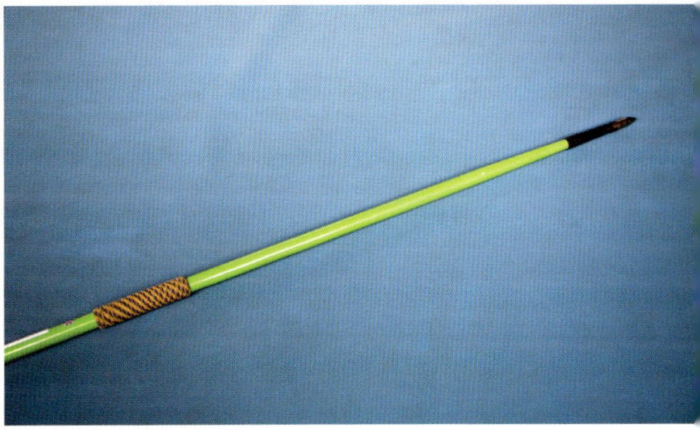

Class 11 pupils

Archery and javelin (which are both discussed later in the book) are the two disciplines that demonstrate more than any other what Class 11 is about: getting to the point. This is a challenging time for this age group. Each day confronts them with new challenges. The outside world with all its attractions exerts an enormous pull on them, distracting them from important matters closer to hand; new relationships give their lives new meaning but may also create new problems. Pupils in Class 11 want to know what life is all about. The capacity for logical thought that has been carefully nurtured in the first Upper School years continues to mature, allowing pupils to unravel complex structures and see the big picture. But at the same time, they are also preoccupied with that other, all-important question, 'Who am I?' Gradually, through their interests and passions, they begin to sense where this answer might lie and where it might lead them in the next few years. The target appears in the distance, in the future, and they take aim.

Approaches to teaching Class 11

In order to respond to the challenges confronting this age group, the lesson material must go hand in hand with an enormous amount of flexibility. The pupils need room to move and try their hand at different things, even at the cost of failure.

A highlight of this year is the opportunity of gaining more practical work experience, this time in the context of social work. Again, this has nothing to do with finding a future career; rather the value for students lies in the experience of being of service to others. Working with the elderly or those with disabilities, with children or with those in poor health, can be enormously beneficial and invigorating. During these few weeks outside the school, the students are presented with opportunities that can help them find their way within our modern, complex society, and they can learn a lot about the importance of tolerance and empathy.

For P.E. lessons, this stage of development means that movement is more consciously experienced and carried out. The educational value of throwing the javelin, where the athlete aims at a target which, ultimately, is out of reach, becomes clear. Alheidis von Bothmer says of this: 'The special thing about throwing the javelin is the fact that the target … is otherwise unattainable. It is, as it were, away up in the stars, in the region where ideals are at home.'[1] In formulating and striving towards their own goals, in making plans and arriving at decisions, the young person gains another little bit of independence; they become freer. Their capacity for thinking, feeling and willing has developed further and expresses itself in the quality of enthusiasm they bring to whatever they do.

Main aspects of the lessons

Purpose is now the watchword, as expressed through deliberate, focused movement. The power of thought, the ability to formulate an idea and then through the will to realise it in action, is also decisive. Lessons can be a lot more flexible at this stage, allowing room for pupils to make their own contributions. One of the sample lesson plans below gives pupils the opportunity to prepare and present an entire lesson themselves. This encourages young people to take on more responsibility and to formulate and achieve their own goals.

Suggested activities for Class 11

- Bothmer exercies: The Javelin, The Great Vertical, Movement Towards the Goal, Three Circles, and Lunge, which also forms part of the exercise, Movement Towards the Goal.
- Gymnastics: consolidating and improving on work with rope.
- Rhythmic sport gymnastics: choice of one piece of hand apparatus for developing choreography with various elements, this time with music.
- Floor gymnastics: creating, practising and performing a demanding combination of various elements.
- Apparatus gymnastics: developing a sequence of moves that link elegantly with each other for the purpose of performance.
- Acrobatics: exercises involving strength and dynamic movement are recommended.
- Artistry: consolidating exercises in one or two of the above areas, alone and with a partner.
- Athletics: javelin, discus, shot put, high jump, long jump, Cooper test (pupils run as far as possible in twelve minutes), 100 m and 200 m sprints, middle-distance (400 m and 800 m), hurdles, 4 x 100 m relay.
- Archery.
- Fencing.
- Games: handball, basketball, volleyball, baseball, ultimate frisbee, with the focus on emphasis technique and tactics as well as on teamwork.
- Swimming: practise swimming technique including turns, swimming underwater, diving (headfirst, forwards and backwards, from a height, Auerbach dive, from a headstand), water polo, life-saver certificate or underwater diving, synchronised swimming.
- Dancing: free dance, contact improvisation, maybe other modern forms of dance.

Additional activities for Class 11

- Class trip with sporting emphasis.
- Hiking trips.
- Climbing.
- Skiing.
- Circuit training.
- The pupils also have the option of keeping a P.E. diary (see below), which will be used more in Class 12.

Information on sample lessons

Athletics: javelin

The central motif for this unit, which is designed to continue over a period of weeks, is taking aim.

The lesson starts with Freeze, a game popular from Middle School now adapted for javelin throwing. Its purpose is to bring the class community back together as a working unit, after the lessons that usually precede the P.E. lesson.

During the initial steps, which introduce the throwing technique, the pupils focus on understanding cause and effect as well as on achieving accuracy. If they are willing to work hard and practise, then they will develop a firm basis for what comes next. Going through the throwing motion helps them to gain in confidence. The exercise featuring the matchsticks is also popular with pupils and certainly helps them make a good start with the five-step rhythm.

After all this preparatory work, throwing the actual javelin and seeing the progress they have made is a big moment for the young people.

The Bothmer exercise The Javelin is the perfect conclusion to the lesson. For a short moment, the pupils can, as it were, see themselves in the flight of the javelin.

Circuit training and ball skills

This unit is the first of a block of four. In order to evaluate circuit training properly, it is essential that the four units take place in consecutive weeks without interruption.

The lesson begins with another much-loved game from the Middle School, Pulling Turnips. The class is then divided into two groups, which should remain the same for all four weeks of the unit. For circuit training, each pupil keeps a record of their progress with each exercise. They work in pairs and each pupil starts at the same place on the circuit with their partner every week, something that is important for the final evaluation. If they wish, pupils can make extra notes concerning their health. They also record their heart rate at various intervals, namely before beginning on the circuit, then three and five minutes after training, as well as just before going to sleep in the evening. Of course, pupils may bring and use their own devices for taking their pulse.

After warming up and setting up the equipment, the pupils set off on the first circuit (thirty seconds' hard going, then thirty seconds' break for writing down results and moving to the next exercise unit).

Writing everything down motivates the pupils to improve as they can see clearly how they are progressing from week to week.

Typical of this age group is their desire to compare themselves with the others and work out their position in an imaginary league table. Although the emphasis should primarily be on individual progress, seeing where there is room for improvement based on external standards is also a good motivator. It is also relevant for achieving grades in state exams.

Keeping the circuit more or less unchanged over the three years of the Upper School and returning the notes the pupils have made at the end of their school time is heartily recommended.

The next part of the lesson deals with ball skills, where the focus is on the many different facets of basketball. The emphasis, however, is not simply on technique and tactics. We want to make the pupils aware of how the various parts of the body are involved in the action of the game: they need speed, stamina and agility in their limbs, they need to be alert to what is going on around them and quick to react, and no successful throw is possible without stability and balance. In the course of an exciting game, such observations are out of the question but should be elaborated on during training. Playing streetball is an option, if there is not enough room, but a proper game of basketball is of course a more appropriate test of skill.

After clearing away, it is good to get the whole class back together again for the Bothmer exercise The Scales. If the exercise is already well known, it is worth trying out different formations and inviting pupils to contribute their own thoughts and ideas. At times when the class has been occupied with projective geometry in the main lesson, pupils frequently offer imaginative ideas on how to carry out this exercise.

Finally, the pupils gather in a circle for a few moments of peace and quiet. They can reflect on their own personal highlights of the lesson, or just use the time to cool down.

Presenting a sporting discipline

Over the years pupils have grown used to taking over parts of the lesson, but special preparation is needed when they take over a whole double lesson in order to introduce a particular sporting discipline to their classmates. Beforehand, the pupil discusses with the teacher which particular activity would be appropriate and how the lesson might be planned and carried out. In addition, the student prepares a short, two-page summary of their chosen topic, which is given out to the rest of the class. This summary is later filed away and becomes part of a growing collection of documents on various activities and their supporting theory. The possibilities are endless. Alongside popular activities such as badminton, figure skating, riding, tennis, golf or football, other topics like fitness training can become fascinating and instructive lessons. In large classes, the lesson can be prepared and carried out with students working in pairs.

The way the lesson is carried out, as described in the sample lesson, is tried and tested. Often there is not enough time, especially with team games, but there is the option of reserving the following double lesson for a training session and game.

At the end, the pupils look back on the lesson together and their experiences of it. These lessons often provide opportunities for pupils to get to know a completely new activity that they otherwise might not have tried.

Offer constructive feedback to the pupils afterwards if they wish. This is meant as helpful advice for future presentations and does not appear in their reports. Many pupils are happy take up this offer.

The P.E. diary

In Class 11, work on the P.E. diary is taken up more consciously. At the beginning of the school year, there is a double lesson featuring three topics: stretching, strengthening and mobility. Muscles and sinews are put to the test and the question of bad posture is addressed. It can be gratifying for the teacher to see how the young people get to know their physical strengths and weaknesses as well as finding out which exercises do them good. It is helpful if they make a note of these exercises.

The teacher can help individual pupils compile a health and fitness plan. The pupils are asked to select five exercises, which they carry out on a daily basis while they are keeping their diaries. These exercises are either sketched or pasted into the front of their diaries. Otherwise, the same rules apply as in Class 10, namely short daily notes for at least one month about the various sporting activities they have done. The pupils can also choose to record other aspects relating to their health, such as coughs and colds, or menstruation pains.

In addition, every pupil is required to set themselves a special task, such as thirty minutes of non-stop jogging or a gymnastic exercise they have not yet mastered. They note down how successful they were in carrying out this challenge.

Below: the Bothmer exercise The Scales.

Sample Lesson: Athletics – javelin. Duration: 90 mins			
Time	**Sequence of activities**	**Formation**	**Material used**
c. 5 mins.	The students form a circle and exchange greetings. The teacher gives the students a preview of the lesson and what to expect.	Standing in a circle.	None.
c. 7 mins.	Tag game: Freeze. 1. The teacher demonstrates two positions in the course of a javelin throw: ▸ leaning back, left foot forward, and ▸ the moment when the javelin leaves hand. 2. Two players are chosen to chase the rest. 3. Anyone tagged freezes in one of the above positions. If another player taps them, they are freed.	Game of tag.	None.
c. 8 mins.	Javelin technique – step 1. The teacher gives out the javelins and shows the students three different ways of gripping the javelin: 1. The thumb-middle finger grip: the thumb and middle finger grip the javelin just behind the cord grip; the forefinger lies along the shaft. This is most common grip. 2. The thumb-forefinger grip: thumb and forefinger are wrapped around the shaft behind the grip; the other fingers are wrapped around the cord grip. This grip provides slightly less control when throwing the javelin. 3. The pinch grip: thumb, forefinger and middle finger hold the shaft behind the grip; the other two fingers are wrapped around the cord. There is less chance of straining the elbow with this grip.	In a line.	One javelin per pupil.
c. 5 mins.	Javelin technique – step 2. Holding the javelin with both hands, one over the other, and with the tip pointing down, the students place one foot forward and stretch up and back as far as possible. They throw the javelin so that it sticks in the ground about a metre in front of their feet. The end of the javelin should point straight back towards the thrower.	As above.	As above.
c. 5 mins.	Javelin technique – step 3. The same as above, except that now the tip of the javelin is pointing upward. The students throw their javelin up in a high arc to land point down in the ground.	As above.	As above.
c. 5 mins.	Javelin technique – step 4. The two previous exercises are carried out, this time with javelin held in one hand.	As above.	As above.

Time	Sequence of activities	Formation	Material used
c. 7 mins.	Javelin technique – step 5. The throwing motion. 1. The students work in pairs, with one standing behind the other. 2. The student in front adopts the sideways throwing position, and then, with their throwing hand, locks fingers with their partner behind them. 3. In a skipping movement (left-right-left or right-left-right depending on which is their throwing arm) the pupil draws their partner round to the front in a three-quarters rotation. The throwing hand should move above head height, or at least past the ear. 4. The roles are now reversed and the action is repeated. 5. The person behind should offer slight resistance to being brought forward. 6. This skipping motion can be repeated the length of the field.	In pairs, length of field.	As above.
c. 5 mins.	Javelin technique – step 6. Coordinating leg work and throwing the javelin. A top athlete offers the following tip: throw a matchstick instead of the javelin. That little bit of wood will soon be flying more than 15 m (50 ft). Repeat the standing throw until you have mastered the throwing technique.	Standing in a line.	As above.
c. 5 mins.	Javelin technique – step 7. The five-step rhythm. The pupils practise the first few steps of the five-step rhythm, up to drawing back the javelin just prior to the throw. 1. Standing sideways and starting with the left leg (right leg for left-handers) the pupil takes three steps: left (1) – right (2) – left (3). 2. On steps two and three, the pupil draws back their throwing arm.	As above.	As above.
c. 4 mins.	Javelin technique – step 8. The pupils carry out the full five steps. 1. Standing sideways and starting with the left leg, the pupil takes five steps: left (1) – right (2) – left (3) – right (4) – left (5). 2. On steps two and three, the pupil draws back their throwing arm. 3. Step four is a quick, gliding step with arm almost fully outstretched. 4. Step five has a braking effect and provides support for the throw.	As above.	As above.
c. 4 mins.	Javelin technique – step 9. The pupils put the five-step rhythm into practice.	As above.	As above.

Time	Sequence of activities	Formation	Material used
c. 7 mins.	Javelin technique – step 10. A short run-up is added to the five-step rhythm, accelerating to a mark where the five-step rhythm begins. When done with the javelin, the pupils hold the point slightly upwards at head height.	Together in a line, then individually.	As above.
c. 7 mins.	Javelin technique – step 11. The pupils practise the run-up, the five-step rhythm and the throw in separate stages.	Side by side, throwing one after another.	As above.
c. 4 mins.	Javelin technique – step 12. The pupils practise combining the different elements in a single flowing motion: the run-up, the five-step rhythm and the throw.	As above.	As above.
c. 7 mins.	Bothmer exercise: The Spear.	Two rows facing each other.	None.
c. 5 mins.	End of the lesson. The pupils take a few moments to reflect on the lesson and look forward to the next one. They exchange farewells.	Standing in a circle.	None.

Sample Lesson: Circuit training and ball skills. Duration: 80 mins			
Time	**Sequence of activities**	**Formation**	**Material used**
c. 3 mins.	The students form a circle and exchange greetings. The teacher gives the students a preview of the lesson and what to expect.	Standing in a circle.	None.
c. 12 mins.	Running game: Pulling Turnips. 1. The class is divided into two groups. The players in one group are the turnips and lie down on their stomachs on the baseline of the volleyball court, facing the centre line. The second group, starting at the centre line, tries to pull the turnips (by the pupils' hands) across the 'field'. 2. If they make it over the centre line, the turnips are free and can also free other turnips. 3. However, two students are chosen to be foxes who try to prevent the players from pulling turnips. 4. If the foxes succeed, the players also become turnips and lie behind the baseline. 5. If a turnip is drawn by a player who is tagged by a fox, the turnip can remain where they are instead of going back behind the baselines with the other player. 6. The aim of the game is to free all turnips. 7. The groups change over when the game ends; two new foxes are chosen.	Running game.	Team bands of different colours.
c. 3 mins.	The class is divided into two groups. Group A begins with circuit training while Group B practises basketball skills.	Standing in a circle.	None.
c. 25 mins.	Group A: The pupils set up a variety of equipment in a circuit. Each pupil is given a sheet of paper to record their progress with each exercise. One of the pupils leads the rest in a warm-up, working through the various exercises in turn. When they finish, they measure their pulse at intervals of three and five minutes. It is worth the pupils paying special attention to the question: 'What helps me to calm down after an exercise?' Group B: Short warm-up focusing on footwork and ball skills. This is followed by free practice either alone, with a partner or in small groups. The pupils practise: ▸ repeated layups; ▸ simple attacks in threes; and ▸ one-on-one game.	Working with a partner through the various exercises.	Group A: various equipment for circuit training. Group B: one basketball per student, team bands if necessary.

<table>
<tr><th>Time</th><th>Sequence of activities</th><th>Formation</th><th>Material used</th></tr>
<tr><td>c. 2 mins.</td><td>The students form a circle and exchange greetings. The teacher gives the students a preview of the lesson and what to expect.</td><td>Standing in a circle.</td><td>None.</td></tr>
<tr><td>c. 5 mins.</td><td>Game: Lying Tag.
1. Two students are chosen to be the catcher and the runner. The rest of the students spread out across the gym and lie face down in pairs.
2. The catcher tries to catch the runner.
3. If the runner is caught, they swap roles and become the catcher.
4. At any time, the runner can lie down next to one of the pairs, making the one on the far side the next catcher. The present catcher then becomes the runner and the game continues.
5. In a different version of the game, mixed pairs are chosen at the beginning so that a boy and a girl lie face down, side by side. If the runner is a girl, she must lie down next to a girl so that the boy becomes the new catcher. The reverse happens if the runner is a boy.</td><td>Game of tag.</td><td>None.</td></tr>
<tr><td>c. 8 mins.</td><td>Warm-up. The pupils gather in a large circle, and each one is provided with a skipping rope. Exercises can include:
▸ skipping on the spot (100x);
▸ skipping on the spot backwards (100x);
▸ skipping forwards keeping legs together;
▸ skipping backwards keeping legs together;
▸ skipping one-legged, changing foot rhythmically;
▸ whipping the rope round twice in one jump;
▸ swinging rope on the left then right then over;
▸ the same swinging the rope backwards;
▸ crossing hands, skipping forwards and backwards; and
▸ free skipping in pairs.</td><td>Warm-up in a circle.</td><td>One rope per pupil.</td></tr>
<tr><td>c. 5 mins.</td><td>Bothmer exercise: Walking in the Horizontal. Recommended tips: keep a careful eye on the breadth of the movement and turning motions.</td><td>In lines, facing forward.</td><td>None.</td></tr>
</table>

Sample Lesson: Presenting a sporting discipline: 90 mins			
Time	Sequence of activities	Formation	Material used
c. 3 mins.	The students form a circle and exchange greetings. The teacher hands over to the student who is taking the lesson.	Standing in a circle.	None.
c. 15 mins.	Introduction. The student introduces their chosen activity. This part of the presentation can include a brief history of the sport, the rules of the game, equipment used, forms of competition, well-known athletes within the discipline, preconditions for playing and the health aspects of the game. The student can also include a critical assessment of the activity as well as their own feelings about the game and the appeal it has to them. It is good to leave time at the end to answer any questions from classmates.	Sitting in a circle.	Display materials/ equipment: whiteboard, pictures, video screen if required.
c. 70 mins	Practical exercises. Warm-up, followed by time spent learning any necessary skills and techniques. A short game or competition to finish if possible.	Activity dependent.	Activity dependent.
c. 2 mins.	End of the lesson. The students take a few moments to reflect on the lesson and provide feedback on it. They look ahead to the coming lesson. They exchange farewells.	Standing in a circle.	None.

Class 12:
Freedom in Movement and Action – Awareness and Responsibility

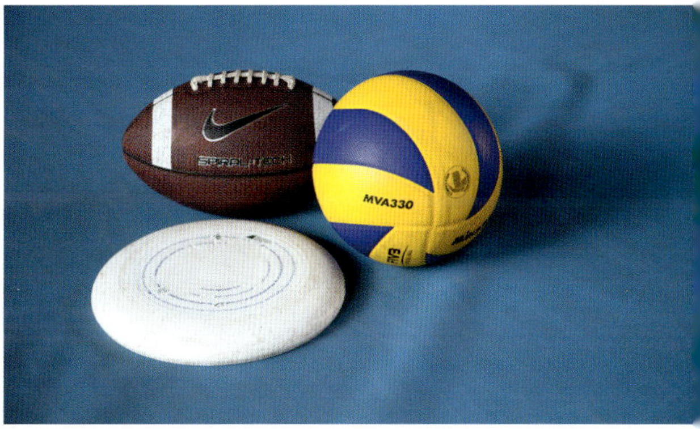

Class 12 pupils

In the final year of the Upper School the pupils work on various artistic projects as well as presenting a larger project on a self-chosen topic that they have worked on over the entire year. In both cases, they are given an opportunity not only to showcase their work, but also to demonstrate that they have a broad understanding of their chosen topic. This fits with the two main themes of the year, which are concerned with personal responsibility and learning to take a broad view of things or seeing the overall picture. Many topics are discussed with this approach in mind, so that the pupils can see how they fit into a larger context. The pupils are able to work independently on all topics and need very little help from others. A further highlight of Class 12 is the class play, in which the entire class community takes part, each person contributing their own particular skills and talents to make the project a success.

Approaches to teaching Class 12

The themes of personal responsibility and gaining an overview carry over into the work the pupils undertake in P.E. Working alone or in small teams, they get the opportunity to plan and carry out their own lessons. This freedom to choose lesson content encourages them not only to repeat well-known exercises in their ongoing efforts to perfect them, but also to try out new things.

At the same time they learn to assess difficulties and problems as they arise.

The Bothmer exercises that the pupils have been performing since Class 3 enable them to recognise qualities in themselves that go far beyond simple physical growth: they present a picture of the human as a spiritual being, ready and willing to act responsibly for the good of their community.

Suggested activities for Class 12

- Bothmer exercises: The Dome, The Long Closing, Turning on the Inclined Plane, as well as working through past exercises; choreographic work on separate exercises in groups, combinations of exercises.
- Gymnastics: continuing working with rod and rope; choreographing elements.

- Rhythmic gymnastics: individual training as well as choreographic work in groups, free programme with one piece of hand apparatus.
- Floor and apparatus gymnastics: exacting combination of exercises, each pupil contributing according to their ability, with an assessment that can appear, when necessary, in the final grade.
- Acrobatics and artistry: demanding combinations of exercises, choreographed elements developed for individual and group performance, perhaps for an audience.
- Athletics: 4 x 100 m relay, 5,000 m, where possible pole vault, Cooper test (pupils run as far as possible in twelve minutes), continued practice of disciplines already learned.
- Games: technical skills and rules of sports, fair play, taking on the role of referee.
- Swimming: medley relay, improving swimming technique, Cooper test, water polo, diving, continued practice of rescue technique.
- Dancing: further work in the various styles, where possible with specialist tuition.

Additional activities for Class 12

- Class trip with sporting emphasis.
- Hiking trips.
- Climbing.
- Skiing.
- Orienteering.
- Keeping a P.E. diary.

Information on sample lessons

Apparatus gymnastics, free programme

During this lesson, pupils take responsibility for the different activities the class will do together. To start, one pupil chooses a game. Depending on how much time is available it might be best to choose a game the pupils know well. It is often the case that the teacher must decide whether to take part in the game or not. Although the pupils enjoy having their teacher in the game with them, the teacher also has the opportunity to stand back and observe the class in general and individual pupils in particular. The warm-up session that follows the game is also the task of one of the pupils.

Working on the gymnastics apparatus shows just how much the students have learned in the twelve years of P.E. lessons. After a short planning session, the pupils set up the equipment. They are quite used to working on their own and giving each other advice and support. In lessons like these, the teacher is on hand to keep a watchful eye on the various groups, making sure the pupils are safe and supported, and to offer encouragement to those individuals who need it.

Pupils should be given enough freedom and scope to concentrate on their favourite apparatus. Enthusiasm for one particular piece of equipment, together with hours of intensive training, may well lead to the performance of a brilliant free programme. This is especially important given that the free programme, which Class 12 pupils have to work on as a form of self-assessment, contributes to their final grades.

Once the work on the apparatus is over and the equipment has been cleared away, the pupils perform a combination of two Bothmer exercises of their choice. The Dome and The Long Closing, for example, when performed at the same time and in the right formation, allow the pupils to experience their surroundings in a very special way. And if the main lesson happens to be focused on the architecture project, then these exercises can have a complementary effect on the how pupils think about and experience space.

Athletics: pole vault

This discipline is particularly suitable for Class 12 pupils as it represents a culmination of all the work done in athletics lessons over the previous years, bringing together many of the key elements. If it is not possible to do this in school, it is still worthwhile looking for an alternative location, or at least improvising in some way, so that the pupils get some idea of how glorious this discipline can be.

The relay race at the beginning sets the mood and gets the pupils used to handling the pole. Following this there is a step-by-step description of the pole-vaulting technique. The most important thing is to allow sufficient time for the pupils to try out the moves and enjoy a phase of serious training.

A good camera and video analysis are recommended to enable the pupils to see what they are doing from a different perspective.

Instead of describing a third sample lesson, there follows a wide-ranging collection of ideas for P.E. lessons in Class 12. Every Waldorf school has its own characteristic features in Class 12, in addition to the general recommendations such as the class play, the individual self-chosen project, and artistic performance. Many schools also offer the pupils a choice of specialist subjects that demand intensive study. Here are some suggestions that have their roots in the area of movement, games and physical education.

Some schools include Bothmer exercises in the artistic work alongside art, eurythmy and music. In this case, the pupils work hard perfecting a variety of exercises and creating appropriate choreography over several months, before performing on stage for the whole school community.

In producing the class play, the pupils can use the P.E. lessons to develop and rehearse the various movements and dance elements. By the same token, any project work with a sporting dimension can become a practical part of other lessons.

Those pupils who have been pursuing a particular activity for several years often stage impressive demonstrations for classmates. What is more, some pupils in Class 12 are already experienced trainers in sports clubs they belong to. It is also worthwhile getting a professional athlete to come and give the young people a trial lesson in some activity they might otherwise never get to know.

Some Waldorf schools hold a circus every year, and the pupils of the Upper School are responsible for putting on a variety of shows. The amazing artistic and acrobatic performances on display all result from the hard work done in the P.E. lessons. Some classes also take the opportunity to put on performances for the school community featuring dance, acrobatics and other disciplines, in order to finance a class trip. Every time the pupils of Class 12 appear on stage in public at any one of the school festivals, they serve as role models, showing the younger pupils what they have achieved in their P.E. lessons. These are special moments in the school year.

All of these various ideas need time to develop before being brought to fruition, time that is well spent in P.E. lessons. Other classes and other teachers will have their own ideas, many of which will arise out of the particular situation of the school and the pupils, but there are no limits to what can be achieved.

The P.E. Diary

Although students have had the option to keep a P.E. diary in classes 10 and 11, in Class 12 it can play a more central role in their experience of physical education. If the teacher has not already done so in previous years, they can give the students clear, written instructions on how to keep their diary. Now they work completely on their own through to the Easter break, when they hand the diary to the teacher. These instructions (some carried over from Class 11) include making brief notes on their sporting activities over the course of four weeks, choosing five daily exercises to complete, as well as selecting a particular individual task to work on. In addition, each pupil is asked to set aside four or five minutes each day during which they are still and silent, and to make a note in their diary on how this went. Finally, they should include a few words of self-reflection in which they assess how well they feel they have done with the project. Pupils often express appreciation for being allowed to work so independently. They also appreciate feedback from the teacher in the form of a short comment at the back of the diary.

Sample Lesson: Apparatus gymnastics – free programme. Duration: 90 mins			
Time	Sequence of activities	Formation	Material used
c. 3 mins.	The students form a circle and exchange greetings. The teacher gives the students a preview of the lesson and what to expect. They discuss who is doing what and who is taking responsibility for each activity.	Standing in a circle.	None.
c. 12 mins.	One of the students chooses a game for the class to play, for example a ball game or a game of tag.	Game.	Activity dependent.
c. 15 mins.	Warm-up session for the gymnastics, organised and led by a student.	Warm-up.	Activity dependent.
c. 45 mins.	Apparatus gymnastics. Each student has developed a free programme based on two different pieces of equipment. The students set up the equipment and discuss how they want to proceed. Those students working on the same piece of equipment practise in groups. The teacher meanwhile goes around the groups, making sure they are safe and offering advice and support where necessary.	Work on apparatus.	Mats and various equipment.
c. 5 mins.	Changeover. The equipment is dismantled and cleared away.	Clearing away equipment.	None.
c. 7 mins.	Bothmer exercises: The Dome and The Long Closing. The class perform the exercises together. Suggested variation: every second pupil performs The Dome while the others perform The Long Closing. Change after three runs through. Finally, the class performs The Long Closing together.	Standing in a circle.	None.
c. 3 mins.	End of the lesson. The students take a few moments to reflect on the lesson and look forward to the next one. They exchange farewells.	Standing in a circle.	None.

Sample Lesson: Athletics – pole vault. Duration: 90 mins			
Time	**Sequence of activities**	**Formation**	**Material used**
c. 5 mins.	The students form a circle and exchange greetings. The teacher gives the students a preview of the lesson and what to expect.	Standing in a circle.	None.
c. 10 mins.	Pole vault – step 1: standing jumps. 1. The students practise standing jumps from the vaulting box while holding the pole. One hand grips the pole high up, the other at head height. 2. This is followed by a jump with a short run-up onto a big mat. The student aims to land in a straddle position or with the pole between their legs. 3. The students take it in turns with the teacher, helping to direct the pole. Time should be allowed for each student to receive feedback from the teacher.	In a row, one after another.	Box, pole, large mats or sandpit.
c. 10 mins.	Pole vault – step 2: getting accustomed to flight. 1. The students continue to practise jumps from the box, this time without help from the teacher, although the teacher remains on hand to supervise. 2. It is important that the student grips the pole to the end of the jump, keeping their upper arm straight. The free leg remains bent. 3. The students can work in pairs if they wish.	As above.	As above.
c. 10 mins.	Pole vault – step 3: jumping over the canyon. 1. Two boxes are placed lengthwise to form the run-up opposite a pile of large mats. 2. The student stands at the opposite end of the run-up, holding the pole high in their hand, meaning towards the top end of the pole. The other end of the pole is placed on a small mat tucked just under the pile of large mats. 3. The student takes the run-up and vaults across the gap, or 'canyon', to land on the three large mats. As they jump, they keep the pole on the opposite side of their body to their top hand (on their left side if the pole is held in their right hand and vice versa). 4. The pupils take it in turns, with the teacher offering feedback and support.	As above.	Poles, large mats, small mat, 2 boxes
c. 5 mins.	Pole vault – step 4: holding the pole. 1. The student rests the pole on their right shoulder and grips it with their right hand from below. With their left hand they grip the pole from above just in front of their chest. Both thumbs are on the outer edge of the pole. 2. The student lowers the pole to their side. The hand at the rear puts pressure on the pole so that the tip rises above head height. 3. As many students can practise as poles are available.	Group work.	One pole per student.

Time	Sequence of activities	Formation	Material used
c. 10 mins.	Pole vault – step 5: the run-up and placing the pole. 1. Practising the run-up and placing the pole initially takes the form of a jousting game. Three medicine balls are placed on a box at the far end of the gym. The students, pretending to be knights, run across the hall and attempt to push one of the balls off the box with the end of the pole. 2. Alternatively, they can try to hit a small rubber ring lying on the floor. 3. If there is enough equipment, two to three students can practise simultaneously. 4. Time should be allowed for the teacher to provide feedback on each attempt.	Three rows.	Three medicine balls, box, poles, three rubber rings.
c. 15 mins.	Pole vault – step 6: first vaulting attempts. 1. The students take it in turns jumping up onto a mound of soft mats, tucking the end of the pole under the mats as in step 3.	Standing in a line.	Poles, large and small mats.
–	It is always possible to have another group of students working on gymnastics apparatus at the same time, performing related movements, for example, on the horizontal bar, swinging up with a half-twist.	Group work.	Bar, mats.
c. 15 mins.	Pole vault – step 7: the final stage. 1. The students practise vaulting with a longer run-up onto a mound of mats, performing a half-turn in the air, and keeping hold of pole until landing, their upper arm straight. 2. Next, they practise vaulting over an elastic rope (ideally a Zacharias crossbar), slowly increasing the height.	Standing in a line.	As above, plus elastic rope (a Zacharias high-jump crossbar if possible), high-jump stands.
c. 5 mins.	A review of the lesson. This might take the form of asking two of the more capable students to perform the pole vault. The rest of the class then comment on the technique as a summary of what they've learned in the lesson. The pole vaulters describe how they experienced their 'flight'. The pupils clear the equipment away.	Semi-circle.	As above.
c. 5 mins.	End of the lesson. The students take a few moments to reflect on the lesson and look forward to the next one. They exchange farewells.	Standing in a circle.	None.

Below: the Bothmer exercise The Long Closing.

Part Three
Exploring a Range of Games and Activities

What We Do in P.E. Lessons and Why

Gerlinde Idler

Any attempt to portray the full range of physical education in Waldorf schools in one book is bound to fail. But we can at least take a look at the more well-known games and activities that are taught in European schools, where the authors of this book are based. Limiting ourselves to the more established activities, such as the Bothmer exercises, apparatus gymnastics, games, and activities like swimming and athletics, allows us to discuss the special quality of the each discipline. Thus, the selection here is exemplary yet could easily be extended, especially in parts of the world that have different games and sporting traditions. Since the pedagogical value of each and every sporting discipline deserves attention, we hope that this book encourages a stimulating discussion on other such activities too.

The Bothmer exercises are fundamental to P.E. in Waldorf schools. The meticulous observations made by Fritz Graf von Bothmer, whose aim was to take physical education in a new direction, led to the development of a sequence of exercises that form the basis of all P.E. lessons in Waldorf schools. These exercises help teachers assess how their students are progressing, they take account of the special qualities that different activities have, and they address how certain sequences of movement can support and encourage development. Partly due to the complexity of the topic, there are two essays on the subject in this section of the book.

The aim of P.E. in Waldorf schools is to help students establish firm foundations in their relationships with each other and their surroundings. As a result they learn to move more freely and with greater confidence through the world. This applies to the entire Waldorf school curriculum of course, but in P.E. it does not mean practising sequences of movement or fixed drills in order to attain perfection in a particular discipline. Instead, it means focusing on experiencing the quality of movement, something that is hard to express in words. P.E. in Waldorf schools is not about developing physical sporting skills, with their technique and sequence of movements, but much more the way the young people experience what they are doing and how they are moving.

To demonstrate what this means, here are two examples: swimming in Class 5 and archery in Class 11. In the case of swimming, which begins as a school subject in Class 5, the students return to the horizontal plane from their upright position, and find themselves in an element with little gravitational pull. In order to stay above water (and more so when they want to move forwards) the young child must learn a completely new way of moving that involves balance, rhythm and breathing technique. This is exactly what the human body goes through when puberty sets in and the young person must find their inner bearings. Developing self-confidence, learning to move safely in the medium of water, and plucking up courage to dive in from a height are, metaphorically speaking, the same attributes that young people need to get themselves through the next phase of their lives.

By the time they get to Class 11, things are a little different. In archery, the archer stands with both feet planted firmly on the ground, calm and collected. They set their mind on the distant target and take aim, waiting to feel the right moment to finally release the arrow. The way the archer thinks and then acts has a special quality, which is important and typical for the young person in Class 11. Shooting a bow and arrow satisfies a particular need, and gives them developmental support.

Experiences such as these help young people meet all sorts of challenges.

Another aim of P.E. in Waldorf schools is to cultivate a high degree of flexibility or versatility, not purely for its own sake but as a counterbalance to the level of specialisation and automatic movement that occurs when learning complex sequences, such as for high diving or football. From a pedagogical point of view, the way children and adolescents develop is best served by offering them the widest range of activities. This is part of our attempt to address body, soul and spirit – admittedly not an easy task, but utterly worthwhile. We find that with this approach, children and adolescents will respond with the greatest enthusiasm to their P.E. lessons.

In the following essays, the authors, all experts in their respective fields, have taken great care to outline the various qualities of movement developed by their particular activity and the significance for specific age groups. Each essay is as unique as the activity it describes, inviting us to immerse ourselves in the wonderful world of movement, in the hope and expectation that our imaginations will be fired and we will discover something new.

Qualities of Movement

Gerlinde Idler

Before we can talk about the quality of a movement, it is of course necessary to experience it. The aim of twelve years of physical education in Waldorf schools is to give students the widest possible range of such experiences. In this sense, P.E. lessons, including the first two years of games and roundelays, form an integral part of the whole Waldorf curriculum. The aim is not to produce specialists but to engage children and adolescents in as many different activities as possible. The confidence and self-belief this develops helps young people become fully fledged, active members of society. Viewed in this light, the teaching of P.E. in Waldorf schools is not simply a physical education, but a vital part of a truly human education.

All physical movement is a reflection of a person's inner life, an external image of what is going on in their soul. P.E. can therefore be understood as offering an education for the soul, something the P.E. teacher must keep constantly in mind. As with other subjects, it is important to consider the essence of P.E. This means learning to recognise the intrinsic quality of a particular movement or activity and observing the effect it has on children's development.

It is generally agreed that we each have so-called 'movement memory', which we add to continually over the course of our lives. The movements that are most vividly and most deeply ingrained in this memory come from our early years: there is our first tumble on the ground as we learn to walk, or, a little later, our first solo bike ride. It is not possible to recall many of these 'first' movements, but if we manage to do so we may recollect the special feeling we had at the time – the differences in the movements can be clearly felt. Each movement has an effect on children's thinking, feeling and willing. Rudolf Steiner often describes how interwoven these three faculties are. They are so interconnected that any movement in one area automatically leads to an adjustment in the other two. For this reason, a movement must be seen as an impulse that exerts an influence on the whole structure. Looking at the quality of any particular movement therefore goes hand in hand with recognising the quality of the impulse.

Similarly, different aspects of movement which must be taken up and learned can be assigned to different parts of the body: arms and legs are responsible for free movement and for carrying out actions, the torso is the seat of rhythm, and the head is the calming element, providing a clear overview. All three areas are dependent on each other, and bringing them together in a harmonious balance represents a big challenge. There is a tendency in many sports to focus only on one particular area, thus failing to take into account the threefold nature of the human being. In Waldorf schools, the approach to teaching P.E. aims to counteract this one-sided approach, without being dogmatic or hostile towards any particular sports or games. Rudolf Kischnick writes: 'What we are aiming for is a culture of movement which develops in an artistic direction and which truly deserves the name "art of movement".'[1] This makes it clear that P.E. is part of the art of education.

Movement – that is, a completed action in a defined space – gives structure to time and can be examined in a number of ways. For example, where does the movement begin? How does it progress? Where and, more importantly, how does it stop? Does the person performing the movement gain strength from it, or does it just fizzle out? If we compare how children move during a game of tag with how adults undergoing physiotherapy utilise a particular piece of equipment, each step exactly prescribed, then we can see immediately that the answers to the above questions will be very different. The difference in quality between the two types of movement is obvious. Both movements have a special meaning; both fulfil a special purpose.

A further aspect to consider when choosing what activities to offer children and young people is their age. Every sporting activity has a special affinity to a particular age group and should not be

offered to children when they are too young for it. Games that have strict, technical rules and require specialist technique are unsuitable for the Lower School classes. On the other hand, creeping through a magic forest together and engaging in imaginative play is much more appropriate for children of that age (see Class 2 sample lesson). Games that involve throwing a ball to hit a classmate and remove them from the game are not suitable for students in Class 4 – not because their throwing is poor, but because this gesture has no place in their emotional make-up. Generally speaking, the games played before the onset of puberty have a completely different quality to those which come in the Upper School. The head – where rationality, strategy and a more detached overview originate – is not yet free and the demands that come with more complicated activities should not be made of it too early.

Concentration is a spiritual quality that appears with the birth of the astral body. Only after puberty does it become possible to perform meaningful exercises and sporting activities such as fencing. The fencer must be light and fluid in their movements: from where their feet touch the floor to the tips of their fingers on the handle through to the point of the rapier, everything must flow in a single movement. Even the space in front of them, which the fencer penetrates, becomes part of the movement. Inner calm, foresight (anticipating what their opponent will do) and poise, the balance between limbs, torso and head, must all be brought together in perfect interplay. This is really only possible in the Upper School, ideally in Class 11. Any earlier and the sophisticated moves inherent in fencing are too difficult.

The basis of P.E. in many Waldorf schools is the Bothmer exercises, developed by Fritz Graf von Bothmer after many years of closely observing his students. When performed properly, these exercises enable students to experience a variety of movements and their different qualities. For teachers and students, they are a helpful way to cultivate a feeling for balance and proportion in movement.

In order to get the most from these exercises, it is necessary to practise the art of keen observation. Often, we only register single movements, which, without inner activity, are little more than photographs. But if we attain an inner experience of the *dynamics* of movement, we can make endless observations. No one movement is exactly like another, and with a highly trained eye, the quality of a particular movement is more easily identified.

The aim of P.E. in Waldorf schools is to lead young people to inner freedom, giving them the confidence to act in a given space, rather than simply reacting to what is already going on. As human beings we are in a position to consciously carry out our own movements and set our own targets, and this requires a high level of reflection the older we get. How movement can serve as a mediator between our inner life and the outside world, between what we want to achieve and how we can achieve it, are important questions. If teachers manage to raise these questions in the minds of their students during lessons, then it will lead them to a better understanding of the gesture or individual characteristics of the particular game or activity. And it is through this movement and gesture that the creative power of the soul is experienced and expressed.

The Bothmer Exercises: A New Form of Physical Education

Adrian Constantinescu, Eric van Wijnen

Each person defines the space around themselves.
Fritz Graf von Bothmer

When Rudolf Steiner founded the first Waldorf school in Stuttgart in 1919, physical education was not included in the curriculum. There was a good reason for this. Steiner was convinced that 'gymnastics, moreover, has become void of all sense or meaning' and that it had become 'an activity that follows the body entirely'.[1] However, in the same lecture, he also stated (as he had done in previous lectures) that gymnastic exercise was nevertheless important for healthy development. But in which form?

Three years later, Steiner asked Fritz Graf von Bothmer, an inexperienced teacher at the time, to develop a completely new form of physical education. Thus, it came about that von Bothmer, by closely observing how movement skills emerge in children and young people, produced a series of gymnastic exercises designed to promote healthy development. Although quite archaic in character, they correspond to principles of movement that underpin specific age groups, and they follow children and adolescents through clearly defined stages of spatial development. This means that in every exercise there is a developmental stage that expresses itself through the movement.

The Bothmer exercises are a way of getting to know one's own body better and to take control of it. The exercises allow paticipants to experience the different qualities of spatial dimensions as well as their own individuality. This helps them develop their own standpoint and a healthy interest in the world around them. At the same time, the exercises offer P.E. teachers a key to understanding how movement skills develop and, as such, are the basis for all P.E. lessons. Ideally, in combination with all the various games and activities, such as gymnastics, athletics and swimming, the Bothmer exercises form an important part of children's healthy development.

Bothmer's approach was revolutionary and it has lost none of its relevance for teaching P.E. today. The aim remains to help children and young people develop into the space around them, and the common observation that children are now less active than in the past makes this practice more necessary than ever. In an interview, Katrin Hörnlein describes the development of children as 'lacking in activity', which has a direct effect on their social skills.[2] Children need limits and boundaries, and they need to experience them physically, even painfully sometimes. This is impossible without activity and it is just as difficult when parents are over-protective, in the manner of hovering so-called 'helicopter' parents.

If we look at how children develop, we see a process of tremendous growth that begins at the head and gradually makes its way down to the feet. The head grows, then the upper body, then the arms and legs, and finally the hands and feet. But if we observe how children take hold of their bodies, how they become accustomed to them and become more aware of them, we recognise a tendency in the opposite direction, namely from the extremities – feet and hands first, then arms, legs, torso and finally head.

Children develop their own special form of awareness and spatial consciousness, which initially is very different from that of adults. Children live in their own highly imaginative world. They are completely absorbed in what they are doing, and the joy they experience through their light-hearted play is obvious to all. As the years go by, they enter into a more structured, more concentrated relationship with their surroundings. While they are treading this path, their awareness of movement changes. A teacher who is attentive to this is in a good position to support them every step of the way.

In his lectures, Rudolf Steiner often points out how important it is to 'awaken' growing children and adolescents. This should not be done by addressing them intellectually, but rather by strengthening the will:

> With the limbs it is different again. Here, from the first moment of life, spirit, soul and body are intimately connected; they all flow into one another. Moreover it is here that the child is first fully awake, as those who have to bring up these lively, kicking little creatures in their babyhood very well know. Everything is awake, but absolutely unformed. This is the great secret of human beings: when we are born our head spirit is already very highly developed, but asleep. Our head soul, when we are born, is very highly developed, but it only dreams. The spirit and soul have yet gradually to awaken. The limb human being is indeed fully awake at birth, but unformed, undeveloped.
>
> All we have really to do is to develop the limb human being and part of the chest human being. For after that it is the task of the limb human being and chest human being to awaken the head human being. Here we come to the true function of teaching and education. You have to develop the limb human being and part of the chest human being, and then let this … awaken the other part of the chest human being and the head human being.
>
> From this we can see that the child brings something of great consequence to meet us. They meet us with a perfected spirit and relatively perfected soul, which they have brought through birth. All we have to do is to develop that part of their spirit which is not yet perfect, and that part of their soul which is as yet still less perfect.[3]

Such is the teacher's task: first to activate the limbs and then, when the time comes and taking into consideration the age and development of their students, to use the activity of the limbs to address the intellect.

The Bothmer exercises provide P.E. teachers with an invaluable resource for mastering this exacting educational task. They can be employed as the first step

in a journey of discovery into the world of movement, or they can be used as the culmination of a particular lesson, one that takes up and reflects the activities that have gone before in a powerful movement.

Thorough training in the Bothmer exercises helps teachers become more aware of the strength and significance of the different exercises. As a result, they are better able to assess the quality of other kinds of movement. This serves as a useful tool when it comes to observing their students more closely and forming a clearer picture of the nature and quality of their own movements.

Each of the Bothmer exercises can be approached in a variety of ways in order to experience a new relationship to our surroundings. New spatial relationships arise through changing conditions, through a shift in balance or through inversion, and these changing conditions help develop a more alert understanding of the world and our own self.

The period that spans children's time at the school can be divided into roughly four stage of development, including puberty. Each stage has a different focal point and requires a different approach to teaching. These are outlined below.

The Lower School: the power of images

Emotionally, younger children live in imaginative pictures. Therefore, instead of offering them adult games which have been adapted for children, they should be given traditional children's games, such as obstacle courses and roundelays, in which archetypal stories and images, of the kind usually found in fairy tales, are brought to life.

The Middle School: the mechanics of movement

Gymnastic exercises are appropriate at the point when children begin to wake up to a greater self-consciousness, leaving behind the dreamlike world of pictures. They allow a rhythmical struggle with the forces of gravity. The exercises become more complex in structure and geometric clarity. In running and jumping, the interplay of lightness and heaviness is directly experienced. The dynamics of inner life and the outside world find expression when children's bodies shift between contraction and expansion, between tension and release.

Puberty: depth and gravity

For young people going through puberty and having to come to terms with the changes taking place in their bodies, gravity is a constant challenge. It continually makes itself felt in their bearing and their movement. The corresponding Bothmer exercises teach them to work with gravity rather than trying to resist it, to include it in what they do. In this way, amid all the changes taking place, they achieve a new inner balance, and they finally arrive at their own standpoint.

The Upper School: extending the range of movement with body, soul and spirit

The next stage consists in overcoming the pull of gravity, which is accomplished by teens opening up to the space around them.

In the Euclidean concept of space, there is no qualitative difference between above and below, front and back, right and left. Nevertheless, if we look at how small children come to terms with their bodies through movement or how we ourselves, as adults, relate to the dimensions of space around us, then we can see that there are in fact considerable differences in quality. The six directions (above-below, left-right, front-back) and the three planes (horizontal, symmetrical, frontal) have specific characteristics. The horizontal plane relates to our emotional life, the symmetrical plane to consciousness and decisiveness, and the frontal plane to the present and to truth, ethics and the will. By practising selected movements and activities, young people are able to grasp these qualities.

***

The following example illustrates why the challenge of a particular Bothmer exercise – The Fall into Space – is particularly appropriate for students going through puberty.

With the changes of puberty, the natural harmony that governed children's bodies has dwindled away, and they no longer feel in tune with either themselves or their surroundings. Their minds are vibrant and powerful, but there is a marked dissonance to their will, which often refuses to do what these newly adolescent students intended – something that can lead to emotional troubles. In short, adolescents seek friction; they are often at war with themselves and the world.

In this exercise, students encounter both surrounding space and the lightness and heaviness of their bodies.[4]

- Standing straight and with feet together, the students raise their arms up and stretch their bodies.
- They then allow themselves to fall forward before arresting their fall and recovering their balance at the last moment by putting out their leg.
- At the same time, they cross their arms and swing them up again without touching the ground.
- Pausing for a split second in this position, the students realise the precarious position they are in.
- The students swing their arms up again, returning to an upright position, while turning through 180°.
- There then follows another fall, with the other leg coming forward to prevent a tumble, but this time there is no arm movement.

- The students slowly drop their arms so their hands touch the floor. They can now feel their bodies stretching from their fingertips to their toes.
- The students swing their hands upwards, straightening up and returning to the starting position. The exercise is finished.

There will have been a number of falling exercises in lessons prior to this one – for example, falling forwards and backwards onto a mat, or falling from a vaulting box into the outstretched arms of classmates. This particular exercise is about courage. The experience of falling is an intense one: there is the feeling of heaviness, the challenge of prolonging the fall to the last moment, the students' experience of their own body weight, and the strength required to stop the fall in time.

In carrying out this exercise, students experience the qualities of space, height, depth and width and ask themselves a number of questions: 'Dare I let myself fall? Can I stop myself in time? Can I keep my balance? Have I got a good sense of orientation when turning?' By performing the exercise, students are able to find the answers to these questions, and the direct encounter with their inner selves, as well as the confrontation with forces of resistance, make a valuable contribution to their development.

The exercises von Bothmer devised are unique in their clarity and precision. They give the teacher an excellent way of observing how children and adolescents are developing. What is more, they help children develop and step into the world around them in a healthy, confident manner. They are a significant contribution to holistic, age-appropriate education, something which seems now more important than ever.

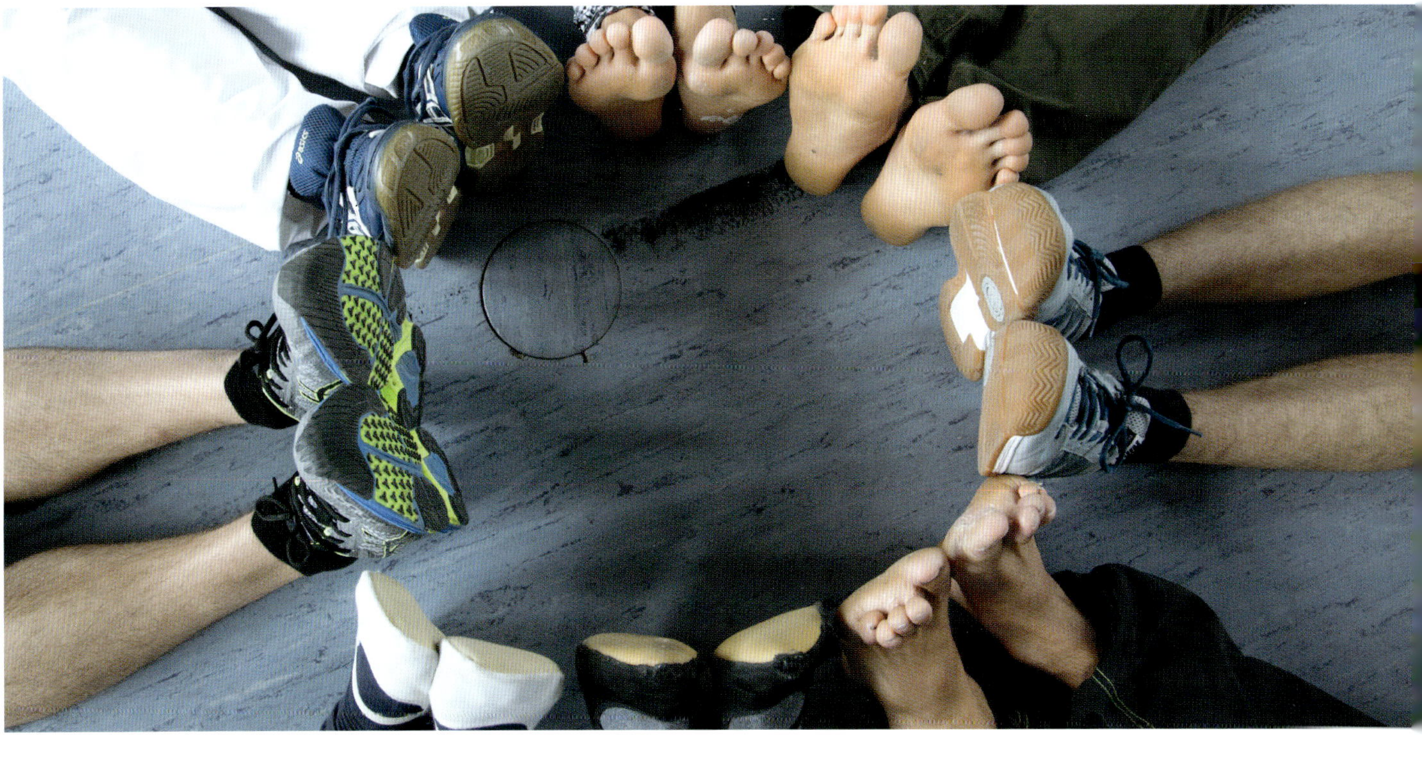

The Bothmer Exercises in Practice: A Personal Experience

Benz Schaffner

I will never forget the time I found myself in the Himalayas at the age of twenty-one. I was standing on Shivapuri Peak, a site sacred among Hindus. It was sunrise and, looking over the mountain range towards Mount Everest, I performed the so-called Walking Exercises, found in the Bothmer exercises. Beforehand, I was simply overwhelmed by the panoramic view: the light, the dense foliage of the jungle covering the mountainside, the enormous, barren mountains all around with their luminescent snowfields. I sat there, then stood up and walked up and down, utterly fascinated. Overjoyed at being part of the moment, I began to go through the Walking Exercises and the whole situation took on an extra dimension. The endless space around me seemed to penetrate my being but, at the same time, it passed right through me. The periphery and the centre drew closer and closer until I saw both as one entity, creating for me a moment of the utmost fulfilment.

From that moment up to the present day, the Bothmer exercises have played an important part in my lessons. I have grown to appreciate the exercises more and more. I have seen the way the children and young students progress with them through their time at school, and how the exercises have given them a sure foothold in the world in both a physical and a metaphorical sense.

A few years ago, I met an ex-student of mine who had left Waldorf education and was now preparing for his final exams at a state school. In the course of our conversation he asked me, 'How come I remember gymnastics at the Waldorf school as being quite different from what we do at my present school?'

I asked him what he meant by 'different'.

'At the state school, gymnastics is basically a warm-up exercise for what follows: it gets the blood circulating and there are one or two exercises for stretching and improving bodily strength. It was like that at the Waldorf school, except that the Bothmer exercises enhanced it all. They weren't just warm-up exercises, there was much more to them than that. I felt what it was like to stand upright quite differently, I felt myself as an individual, occupying my own space, fully conscious of my body. In Class 12, when we did the Cross Exercise, I experienced my own body very differently to when we had done press-ups and other fitness exercises. The exercises had a much deeper meaning than those of conventional gymnastics. You don't acquire good posture by simply tensing muscles and lifting weights, you get it by becoming a physical presence in your surroundings.'

Impressively, my ex-student had answered his own question.

The twenty-eight exercises devised by Fritz Graf von Bothmer in Stuttgart between 1922 and 1938 allow teachers of physical education to work with students on three levels: on the physical level through the students' heightened awareness of their own bodies, on the soul level through the development of their spatial awareness, and on the level of the spirit in the way they structure and objectify the surrounding space through their movements (essentially, projecting themselves into it).[1] The Bothmer exercises also enable P.E. teachers to work hand in hand with other subjects by incorporating the content of other lessons.

What follows is not an essay about preparing and carrying out the exercises, but much more an attempt to describe how rewarding it can be to work on these Bothmer exercises together with the children and experience the progress they make.

The Bothmer exercises in P.E. lessons

Although the importance of the Bothmer exercises is made clear to all young Waldorf P.E. teachers during their teacher training, experienced colleagues are quick to say how difficult it is to make the exercises an essential part of each lesson. A certain amount of courage is needed to engage with them, to appreciate

and communicate their worth. Working with the students on these exercises is always an intensive part of every lesson and is something that requires the teacher's undivided attention. The conflicts that can sometimes arise between teacher and students over the exercises, as well as the inner conflicts that teachers and students go through, can be formidable, and this is exactly where the inner flame of passion for teaching has to burn most intensely.

Children today want to be fully involved in the lessons. They want to know how each unit of the lesson relates to them and their personal situation. The teacher therefore should find the right way to address each age group and put the particular exercise into the context of their everyday lives. If I want to introduce the Light Beat/Heavy Beat exercise to Class 5 students, then I have to find some connection to their own experience, to the world they live in. For example, at our school there is a regular circus performance at the Christmas fair in which the students of Class 5 are enthusiastic participants. What, from a Waldorf point of view, are the important educational aspects of performing in the circus arena?

Including content from other lessons – examples from Classes 5, 6 and 7

As Rudolf Steiner describes in his image of the human being, children of this age group are physically well-proportioned. The length of their bones in relation to each other will never be as harmonious as they are now. In this wonderful bodily harmony there is an interplay of 'light' and 'heavy' extremes, and I can integrate these qualities into the various exercises in order to help students achieve inner balance. For example, the more 'lightness', the more the element of weight will be experienced in an exercise: the higher the jump, the greater the sense of heaviness when coming down. Children swing to and fro between incarnation and excarnation, something they take great pleasure in at this age, and during this intensive activity significant developmental steps are taking place. Freeing ourselves up (for example, when we jump) and regaining control (coming down to earth) are primal experiences, which will be acted out time and again in many other contexts later on in life. The world of the circus is swift to adopt many exercises which embody this approach.

Another facet of the circus is the importance of teamwork. Between the various acts, we have to dismantle the equipment and prepare for the next act, quickly but without rushing. A lot of the acts involve synchronised movement: for example, seven children perform forward rolls together, ending in a standing position all at the same time – not easy, especially when other children are performing cartwheels alongside them. The whole performance culminates in an enormous pyramid. The aim of the circus project is for every child in the class to feel proud of the part they play in the whole. This experience can be called to mind, when the Bothmer exercise Light Beat/Heavy Beat is introduced.

This has shown me that the best way to get the children to experience the element of lightness is when they work together. During the exercises, we try, as a class, to jump together and really feel what it is like to be in the air. The children can decide for themselves whether it has worked or not. Interestingly, the students are quick and perceptive with self-criticism. The momentum of the Bothmer exercise has something in common with the circus. And we can take pleasure in this, inasmuch as this Light Beat/Heavy Beat exercise is a legitimate part of the process. If the exercise can be built into the beginning of the performance, the moment when all the performers take to the ring, this breathes real life into it.

In Class 6, the children get their first taste of geometry in the main lesson. In P.E., we introduce The Triangle as the corresponding Bothmer exercise. Keeping their legs straight and their feet apart, the children try to touch their toes with their fingertips. Through this simple but clearly defined movement, the students experience their bodies in a new light – most evidently through the physical tension which it creates as they reach down. The triangle is then reversed as they straighten up, opening their arms to the sky and bringing their feet together. During the changeover, when the students open up in both directions, the tips of two triangles meet in the middle of their bodies like an hourglass.

As in all the other subjects, the element of achievement plays its part here. When the children make a real effort and practise hard they are able to make progress towards their aim and this increases their enjoyment. By the end of the sixth school year, almost all the students are able to stretch down to their toes, which has an incredibly motivating effect.

The Triangle has a tremendous amount to offer. There is the moment where the apex points to the heavens and the legs are wide apart and firmly on the ground, and vice versa, when the arms open to the sky and feet are together at the bottom. One aspect of the triangle that we encounter often in life is that of the trinity. In Class 6, we work with this trinity on an age-appropriate level, namely in the physical plane. This is a healthy introduction to a phenomenon which can then develop further in the years to come.

If we now turn to puberty we are faced with new challenges. For some students, any form of movement is too strenuous, whereas others have energy to spare. Many youngsters need to test how far they can go and are completely goal-oriented. What then is the role of the Bothmer exercises during this phase of development?

Class 7 is when I introduce long-distance running. I start with 800 metres, a middle distance. It is enough to begin with and it is important that no student should feel that they cannot cope. To begin with, we concentrate on rhythm and breathing technique. On the first runs, I lead the field and set a pace which ensures that everyone can keep up. Towards the end, students may choose their own pace.

I touch upon the issue of breathing technique with caution. At the start, I always pose the following question: 'When I breathe in, does my stomach contract or expand?' The right answer almost always comes as a surprise. Roughly 80 per cent of the young people answer that the stomach contracts. And why? They are so used to breathing higher up, within the ribcage, that it pulls the stomach inwards. After a long run, however, it is easy to practise the right breathing technique in which the stomach actually expands when breathing in. The students immediately feel an improvement. They experience this for themselves simply by placing a hand on the stomach. This is the right time to integrate the Bothmer exercises.

I begin with simple arm-swinging exercises which strengthen the breathing before proceeding to the exercise known as The Rhythm.[2] This exercise can reduce the breathing and pulse rate following strenuous activity, something I was able to test for myself with a pulsometer when I was a member of the national pentathlon team. I have yet to find a better exercise for slowing down the pulse. The young people see for themselves how quickly they recover.

I would like to elaborate on a further aspect of this exercise, in which two circles are described, a large and a smaller one, which cross at one point, the only real impulse in the exercise, which otherwise consists of rhythmical, flowing motion. This reflects how the circulatory system in the body functions. The heart is situated at the centre of the two circulatory systems, one operating through the lungs, the other on the periphery. The dynamics of the exercise reflect in the surrounding space exactly what is taking place in the body. Although I would only discuss the causality of this phenomenon with Upper School students, the students of Class 7 can at least feel the pleasant, calming effect.

Adolescents in the throes of puberty often have trouble coming to terms with the Bothmer exercises, as they require that we open up and reveal something of our inner life – something children this age are reluctant to do. They are much happier keeping themselves to themselves and disclosing as few of their shortcomings as possible. A dynamic exercise with lots of movement can be a great help here. The exercise Jump to Middle Point can often fit the bill. The expression 'flying high one minute, down in the depths the next', a perfect description of young people at this age, is reflected in this exercise, in which we draw together, preparing for the jump, before explosively outstretching arms and legs. In order to increase this explosive effect, we might, after the jump into the centre, leave out a small jump in between.[3] This variation appeals to Class 9 in particular.

In my lessons, the exercise Fall to the Point has developed in a special direction. Not long ago, I noticed that students were engaging in a half-hearted manner with this exercise. Every time we were on the point of moving from the crouching position to the stretching position, they would begin giggling. This happened with every Class 8. After a few years, I realised that the students of classes 8 and 9 were unable to cope with this inner preparation – something about it induced a kind of nervousness or self-consciousness in them that made them giggle. From that moment on, I incorporated a dynamic, swinging movement into this thrust upwards, and since then students have taken part in this exercise much more willingly and with greater seriousness. This has led to a further inner development in Class 10. By then, students are at an age when they can understand the reason for *removing* the swinging motion. This metamorphoses into inner activity, which in turn enables the young people to understand and better get to grips with the Bothmer exercises.

Finally, I would like to say a few words about how best to introduce the Bothmer exercises into lessons. Meaningful movement is an important foundation stone for education and students have a right to expect their teacher to perform these exercises well and with the utmost conviction before they join in themselves. At the beginning of this essay, I spoke of the changes that can be observed when children perform the Bothmer exercises, and teachers can experience similar changes in themselves when preparing this special form of movement for their lessons. They can learn a lot about themselves while wrestling with these exercises. Accepting this self-educational aspect enables teachers to see similar progress in their students as, slowly but surely, they disclose their inner selves. The precondition for this perceptive ability is that teachers are completely at home with the Bothmer exercises.

As I have described above, teachers should be willing to adapt the exercises if the circumstances of their lessons and the needs of their students demand it, changing the dynamics of a particular exercise for the benefit of the group as a whole as well for each individual student. Students will appreciate this flexibility and are likely to engage more enthusiastically with the exercises as a result. When teachers demonstrate their commitment to their students' progress and well-being, when teachers appear authentic and genuine, this helps to strengthen the educative relationship. This sense of trust is a thrilling aspect of any student–teacher relationship.

Above: The Opening Exercise.

P.E. Lessons in Classes 1 and 2: Age-appropriate Movement and the Significance of Images

Christiane Weide

For classes 1 and 2, Waldorf schools offer a special form of physical education that places a particular emphasis on play. The central idea is to provide the children with forms of movement that are appropriate to their age and, as the name 'gymnastic games' suggests, that incorporate the element of play.

This 'games' lesson should be given at least once a week by the P.E. teacher with the assistance of the children's class teacher. The advantage of this pairing is that the P.E. teacher gets to know the children with the class teacher's help, while the class teacher gets to see how their students behave in a different environment from the classroom. The P.E. teacher's expertise and the class teacher's familiarity with the children complement each other well. Both teachers are able to recognise children who experience difficulties in movement, and the school doctor or therapist can be invited to the lessons to make their own assessments – assuming the children's parents consent to this beforehand.

The various games help the children develop their social skills, teaching them to be considerate towards their classmates, to wait patiently for their turn, and to take care not to be too rough, among other things. This develops confidence within the class community.

If the school has a gym or sports hall, the lessons should of course take place there, but if there is no gym, then the classroom must suffice or else a large hall, foyer or the playground. These alternatives mean that teachers must be inventive and ready to improvise. It may be necessary to split up the class, although this should be seen as a drastic measure as it limits the feeling of togetherness and inhibits social learning in the class community.

At this age, children love to be in motion, but teachers shouldn't expect every child to have acquired full control over the various types of movement. These include running without bumping into others, hopping on one leg, bounding on two, walking on all fours, climbing and swinging from rung to rung across monkey bars, and skipping, as well as throwing and catching a ball. During lessons, P.E. teachers can begin to remedy any deficits by providing a wide range of movement in all areas, as well as relying on many of the tried-and-tested games for children.

The world of games is rich and diverse, and it is worth planning the school year around projects that last for several weeks, just as the class teacher does. One project might feature just games, while another might be a combination of games and practising with skipping ropes, hoops and balls; still another might be a short obstacle course with gymnastics equipment set up as a 'magic forest'.

For Class 1, games in a circle accompanied by singing and chanting, as well as tag games that feature capture and release, are ideal. They give small children a sense of security within the class community, and from this safe platform they learn to venture out on their own.

Teachers use their imagination to introduce the games, and the children slip into the various roles that feature in the stories they hear. The children's imaginative powers are stimulated and they become emotionally involved in the activity. Achieving some particular physiological training effect is not the aim here; we want to spur the children into action on the strength of the pictures they produce with their own imaginations.

Class 1 games

The good cook walks into the vegetable garden and the vegetable children run to escape. The cook touches any vegetable children they catch with their dishcloth. The chosen vegetables sit in the pot (the centre circle of the gym), which slowly gets filled. 'Take care, little vegetable children, not to bump against the sides of the pot, or you might tumble in!' Finally, when all the vegetable children are in the pot, the teacher walks round, asking the individual children which vegetable they are.

The story provides the rules and the run of play, as well as the boundaries to the playing area, and the children are part of the story. Compare this story approach with a matter-of-fact account of the rules of the game: somebody is the catcher, who tries to tag the others. Anyone tagged is 'out' and sits down in the centre circle. Anyone who accidentally steps into the circle is also 'out'. The lack of a story in this description means that the children go hungry. They simply follow instructions with no emotional involvement, something which ought to be avoided in this age group.

Firing children's imaginations within the framework of stories is the basic principle of lessons at this age. It begins even before the children arrive in the hall or whatever space has been set aside for the P.E. lesson. The children are greeted in the classroom with a special verse before being escorted to the lesson; likewise they are brought back to the classroom with a recurring rhyme or song. This provides the children with a sense of security before they enter the wide spaces of the sports hall, where they might otherwise soon feel lost. This framework to the lessons, which remains constant, keeps children from becoming wild and uncontrolled. The verse the teacher chants when leading the class to the lesson has something eminently reassuring about it.

The following verse, 'The Giant Snake', has proven popular in games lessons. It calls for a variety of forms and movements, which give the children a better sense of orientation when entering the gym.[1]

The Giant Snake

(Entering the gym) The giant snake is on the way
From where it hides the live-long day.
The head comes first and without fail
Miles of snake until the tail.

Its pace is slow, the line is straight
Onwards to the garden gate.
Keep to this line, go straight ahead,
And be careful where you tread.

Now it moves from side to side,
In a zig-zag! See it glide,
Wriggling from left to right,
Slithering with all its might,

Into a circle, round and wide
Where it starts to curl inside,
On and on, so closely pressed,
Until it makes a cosy nest.

Now its path is just the same,
Circling back the way it came,
Out of the dark, back into the sun,
The snake is home, the journey done. *(Arms raised)*

A variety of verses and images, as well as a set of signals that have been agreed on, are also useful for bridging the gap between games. In this way, the general mood engendered by the images and stories can be maintained. It is all one long game for the children.

One example of such a verse might be:

> Let's go wandering,
> let's wander through the land,
> and at the journey's end,
> in a circle we stand.

The teacher walks around as they recite this, gathering the children as they go. The children come together in the 'sun circle' or meet in the middle for the 'tea party', with the teacher sitting down with them.

If the children in the circle are still restless and fidgety, another short verse can help: 'Tip to tip and stump to stump'. While standing, the children tap the toes of their left foot with the toes of their right, as the teacher says, 'Tip to tip.' Then they do it the other way around. Next, the children tap their left knee with their right heel and vice versa as the teacher says, 'Stump to stump.'[2] The teacher varies the speed, emphasis, and pitch of voice – even whispering at times to really hold the children's attention – while speaking the verse. The children join in the mood of the exercise and calm down. Then, the teacher can begin relating a story to introduce the next game.

Ideally, the end of the lesson is also structured. For example, the children might be led out of the gym to the words:

> Hand in hand, and off we go,
> not too fast and not too slow,
> all together hand in hand,
> away we march, a merry band.

I advise against repeating a game in the same lesson, however much the children clamour for it. In this way, the children are more attentive to the course of the game and identify more strongly with the story. Every game has its own occasion, and this helps maintain the joy and excitement they have for it over several weeks. If a game is not a success, the teacher might give the corresponding story some thought, making changes where they feel necessary. They certainly shouldn't explain it intellectually, as this would put an immediate stop to any emotional involvement the children have with it. There is also nothing wrong with leaving a game on the shelf for a while, before reintroducing it at a later, more suitable, time. There need to be alternating phases of activity and calm, the children should not become breathless or over-excited with too many hectic games. On a normal school day, there will be other lessons that need attentiveness after P.E.

The game 'Fire, Water, Storm' is one that can be played in endless variations, with imaginative suggestions coming from the children themselves. In this game, the whole class runs around the gym. One person shouts, 'Storm!', at which point the children get into a protective position to shelter themselves from the storm. Whoever is the last to finish the gesture is the next to call out another word. In Class 1, no child is ever made to leave the game for being last; the emphasis is always on movement in many variations. What children in Class 1 need most is to feel safe within the group: skipping, running and climbing completely carefree, side by side with a classmate. Being tagged and having to leave the game can be introduced in Class 2.

Class 2 games

In Class 2, the children begin to enjoy the recurring ideas connected with the images and stories, and perform the corresponding actions not only quickly but also gracefully. They enjoy the feeling of 'I can do this. I've done it!' The daredevils in the class are reminded to hold back a little, while the dreamers are encouraged to try their luck. The children who,

for example, fail to reach a certain stage in a game, may go to the teacher who allows them to name the next stage. They should also get used to running in a clockwise direction, because they learn to tell the time in Class 2. Through running they experience the hands of the clock more directly.

In the project lessons, which only have games at the beginning and end, try to choose games that practise coordination and dexterity, as well as introducing exercises that need a certain amount of courage.

For skipping, every child gets a rope and can go all over the gym practising on their own, or together, running through and jumping over a long rope. A song and verse can help here too, for example:

> Come on, come on, run through the gate,
> Then turn once more before you're late.

Hearing this, the children are encouraged to try their luck and go for it.

After the skipping, the children might be asked to balance on a 'tree trunk' (one of the benches) moving forward and back, sidestepping then crossing their legs. Further adventures might involve leaping over a stone (a small box) or climbing a ladder or a tree (a climbing wall or a pole).

Learning to handle a ball is also something which can take place in the form of free practice. In the gym, despite the apparent chaos, everyone has to keep an eye out for their classmates as they throw the balls up in the air or to each other. At the agreed signal (maybe a tambourine – anything but a shrill whistle), all the children gather in the middle, in the 'sun circle' or at the 'tea party', rolling or throwing their balls back to the teacher.

With rhythmical running and jumping, to the beat of a tambourine or handclap, the teacher gets the students moving in an orderly fashion. This is a useful strategy when the children appear restive, turbulent or simply tired.

In warmer months, activities can be held outside, barefoot on grass if possible. Mini relay races, which also call for agility and dexterity, allow the children to run at full speed. Naturally, some of them will ask who won – the competitive spirit can appear as early as Class 1 – but here, too, a story can help change the mood. The teacher casts the children as dwarves who must run, skip, jump and sneak to a castle – the different stages of the relay – in order to discover a secret treasure and bring it back to the others. The teacher tells each child which group or stage (running, skipping, jumping or sneaking) they belong to. This shifts the focus away from the competitive element that would likely dominate in a flat-out race, and infuses the activity with a more playful, imaginative quality.

In Class 2 the world of fables provides good material for stories. Children adopt the characters of various animals: they are as strong as an ox, as cunning as a fox, as brave as a lion, as quiet as a mouse, and

so on. Their ability to identify with the true nature of the various animals is impressive. The dialogues that occur in the fables enable the children to act at the right moment. For any rhythmical running – or jumping, skipping, walking, creeping or weaving – the children can continue to imitate the different animals. Some story examples are: 'Wolf in Sheep's Clothing', 'Cat and Mouse' and 'The Hawk and the Hen'.

To begin the lesson, one of the children leads the class into the gym, with the teacher following them in. Silently, the leader paces out the well-known paths of the giant snake, familiar to them from Class 1. In the course of the year, each child gets a chance to do this. Similarly, at the end of the lesson, one child leads the class out of the gym. Using one of the side lines for orientation creates an orderly exit as well as having a calming effect on the children.

For all the changeovers during a lesson, standing in a circle, clapping, stamping or whispering is the recommended method. Perhaps a mouse, which the teacher pretends to hold cupped in their hands, is set free to scuttle around the circle between the children's legs. The children have to jump, one after another, at the moment the mouse rushes past.

There is further practice with the skipping rope and ball. The children learn to cross the rope in front of them, to skip backwards and to skip with and without a small hop between. Standing in a circle, they practise rolling, throwing and bouncing a ball all the way round. A song or verse is the perfect accompaniment for this:

Roll, little ball, and off you go,
Not too fast and not too slow,
Round the circle, on your way,
And back to me another day.

Then change the words to 'Bounce, little ball' and then 'Fly, little ball'. For the first verse, the children sit in a circle and roll the ball from one to another round the circle. Then they all stand up and bounce the ball from one to another. Finally, they throw the ball.

In the forest (made of gymnastics equipment), equally exciting adventures take place. The children have to climb onto a boulder (a vaulting box covered by a mat), jump down into a small lake, perform a forward roll from a stepping stone (a small box) onto a mat, then balance over a bridge (a bench resting on two boxes). The P.E. teacher and the class teacher accompany the children around the course, giving support and encouragement where necessary.

Sometimes the P.E. teacher encounters children who take no interest in these games or who find it difficult to fit into group play. Such children must be met with patience and a gentle but nevertheless firm insistence. A short break can help here, allowing children who feel this way to sit and watch for a while before the teacher gently encourages them to have a go. Another strategy is keeping the reluctant child close to you throughout the lesson.

I would like to wish my fellow P.E. teachers great enjoyment in teaching this wonderful subject, and hope they continue to find an endless source of ideas to enrich their lessons and stimulate the healthy development of children through movement. It is my hope that with these few lines I have been able to contribute to that goal.

P.E. Lessons in Classes 3 and 4: 'What are we playing today?'

Christiane Weide

> By means of gymnastics and sport, human beings fit themselves into external space, adapt themselves to the world, experiment to see whether they fit in with the world in this way or in that. That is not language, that is not a revelation of the human being, but rather a demand the world makes upon human beings that they should be fit for the world and be able to find their way into it.[1]
>
> *Rudolf Steiner*

The playful approach to physical education ends after Class 2. From now on Waldorf teachers talk more of 'P.E.' than 'games' lessons. Games are still played, embedded as always in age-appropriate images, but now the emphasis is more on being a member of a team. Today, this approach is more important than ever. Even at this young age there are children who detach themselves from the group and demand too much attention as individuals.

As an antidote to this, children can play lots of games together that stimulate their imagination.

Images and stories enable children to immerse themselves in the worlds the games create. The fantasy element is still appropriate for children at this stage, but the games are not played simply for fun and to be active. The children learn stamina, coordination and dexterity, and to play by the rules, but above all they learn social competence. This means being considerate and respectful to one another as well as being brave and taking the initiative. The games form one part of the lesson and give the teacher a chance not only to introduce valuable movement skills but also to be pedagogically effective in a variety of areas.

Example games for Class 3

In tag games, where children find themselves 'enchanted' and then 'released', the challenge for the children is not just to avoid being caught or 'enchanted' themselves, but to risk being caught in order to save others. There is also an element of patience: children must wait until they are rescued. The games are also designed to overcome any personal animosities within the class community or between groups of children, for example, between the boys and the girls. In the heat of the moment, everyone is prepared to help a classmate.

One example of such a game is Bear Tag (also known as Chain Tag). The teacher tells the story of bears returning from the forest, where they have been enjoying a feast of honey. They play tag, and the first bear to be tagged gets stuck to their fellow bear's sticky paws and must run along with them. When four or more bears are running in a chain, they divide into two groups. This continues until all the bears have been caught. Similar games worthy of mention include Octopus; Fly, Little Bird; and Parcels (see instructions below).

At this age, it is best not to play too many games in a single lesson, otherwise the lesson takes on a breathless, hectic character, with the children clamouring for yet another turn. Sometimes, doing less achieves more. The children should be given plenty of time to play each game and there should also be time to go into any questions they have. When games are repeated in the coming lessons, the children will feel more at home with them.

Example games and relays for Class 4

At this age, children run and jump around the gym, full of energy and enthusiasm. A certain egotism also makes itself felt. The challenge facing the teacher is to find imaginative ways of channelling all this positive energy and to get children to work together as a team. Relay games provide a great opportunity to do just this, and there are countless ways of dressing them up in exciting stories. Competing and winning are not the important aspects here, but rather courage, dexterity, agility, team spirit, individual performance and the quality of movement.

Examples of suitable stories for relay races could include some of the following. The farmers are on the way to market carrying sacks of potatoes (medicine balls), or they are driving their geese (various balls) to the meadow and have to overcome a variety of obstacles (benches, segments of vaulting boxes, cones). Strength and agility are what count here. When speed is called for, the image of the postman is particularly apt. They may have an express delivery, which they carry over, under and around various obstacles. Fragile goods also have to be transported (for example, the children have to move backwards, becoming more aware of their surroundings and the way they move). The farmers can be rewarded with a good harvest, the postmen with a big stamp collection. The main thing is that it be a genuine part of the story.

Children are sticklers for fair play. During the relay races the various tasks must be performed according to the rules and the teacher must ensure they are observed.

Every age group has its own special games. The children will be proud to have reached a higher stage. In Class 4, the games become more complex. In the tag games, more sophisticated movement sequences are required. In the case of Parcels (see below), which may be introduced towards the end of Class 3, and tag games where children free a classmate by leapfrogging over them, strong, controlled jumping is called for.

Class 4 tag games require chains of children to work in unison, which encourages functioning as a team. There is also Guards and Robbers (see Class 4 sample lesson, p. 71), where the guardians have to be brave and skilful just as the robbers have to be quick and vigilant.

Another suitable team game, which is also a lot of fun, is Tambourine Ball (see below).

Parcels

Three or four postmen are doing their rounds. Any children they tag become 'parcels', curling up into a ball on the floor. This parcel can only be released with the help of two classmates working as a team. One crouches down beside the parcel and the other leaps over both of them, keeping their feet together. The game is over when all the children are on the ground as parcels.

Fly, Little Bird

The children spread out around the gym. One child throws a rubber ring into the air and calls out, 'Fly, little bird, and come back soon!' and then sits down. The other children try to catch the bird (ring). Whoever catches it throws it up again, repeating the call and sitting down. This goes on until only two children are left standing. The one holding the ring is now the bird catcher. All the other children jump up and run off. Any birds (children) who are caught sit at the side. When all the children have been caught, the game is over.

Octopus

The children pretend they are fish swimming from one side of the sea (the gym) to the other. In the middle, one of the children pretends to be a big octopus, holding an 'ink ball' (a softball), waiting to catch them. The children chant, 'One, two, three, you can't catch me!' and try to 'swim' past the octopus. The child playing the octopus catches the fish by touching them with the ball (in a later version of the game, they can throw the ball at the fish). Any fish that are touched by the ball become octopuses themselves. They remain in one place and attempt to touch the fish with their tentacles as they swim past. The game is over when all the fish have been caught and are sitting on the seabed as little octopuses.

Tambourine Ball

The class is divided into two teams. Members of Team A sit on benches near a vaulting box with a tambourine on it, while Team B spreads out around the gym. The first player on Team A takes a ball and throws it as far as they can, then they run round and round the box, tapping the tambourine each time they complete a lap. The team counts the laps out loud.

Meanwhile, Team B must place the ball on the vaulting box as quickly as possible. However, there is a particular sequence of actions they must perform before they can do this. The player who catches the ball stays where they are and the rest of the team form a line behind them, standing with their feet apart. The player who caught the ball then sends it rolling through the tunnel. If the ball rolls out of the tunnel, they have to start again. The player who receives the ball at the end of the tunnel takes it up and runs to place it on the vaulting box. Now it is the turn of the next player on Team A to throw the ball. When every member of Team A has had a turn, the teams swap over.

An Anthroposophical Approach to Play: Cultivating Confidence and Empowerment

Eric van Wijnen

> We don't stop playing
> because we grow old;
> we grow old
> because we stop playing.
>
> *George Bernard Shaw*

As a young schoolboy, I remember playing practically every free minute – indoors as well as outdoors. My playground was the neighbourhood. There were certain boundaries that had to be respected and which were pushed back year by year. At the edge of the town, I could climb trees, play ball and hide-and-seek, jump over ditches and run behind the wheelbarrow with my brothers. Often, the older boys were my role models. I would go out into the country with them and climb giant trees to enjoy the view. Climbing back down was a new, rather frightening experience, as it was more difficult. There was no television, and I was away with my friends until it was time for bed. Each season had its own special games, which reappeared as if by magic when the time came round again. Every child joined in. From the rich soil of all these experiences grew my interest in sport. These times had an enormous effect on my later life. Years later, as a P.E. teacher, I tried to recall them and have encouraged my students to do likewise.

This is why I now give my Class 12 students the task of writing their own 'movement autobiography', with parental help if possible. 'How did I learn to walk? What was typical about the way I moved? What activities did I particularly enjoy, which ones did I dislike? How did I play with other children?' The young people are also asked to reflect on the various stages of their journey through school, asking themselves, for example, which sporting activities they preferred and which ones they disliked.

It is interesting to see how each child discovers their own motivation and preference for a particular activity, and how much it means to them to be 'good' at something. Every sporting activity has its own emotional ethos to which a person may be attracted and in which the experiences they have are their very own.

'What do you learn when you are at play?' This is a question I often ask my older students, just after a game has finished. In any game, children are constantly interacting with each other and with the world around them. The pedagogical benefits of play can therefore be found in the activity itself. For example, in a ball game some children need to learn to hold back rather than hog the ball all the time, whereas other children need to learn to shake off their timidity and take a more active role in the game. When children are at play, they are actively involved in the outside world.

There are various anthroposophical approaches to assessing the value of play. In this regard, it can be helpful to cast an eye on the polarities that form part of our human make-up, and how these polarities relate to each other and find equilibrium in the centre. Muscles are situated between skin and bone, and the basic tension in them determines our relationship between our inner world and the world around us. It is also the basis for our ability not just to feel and perceive – in both directions, outwards and inwards – but also to concentrate. Tightening and relaxing our muscles is not something we are always conscious of, but as with throwing and catching a ball, both components must be present: a conscious alertness as well as an easing of tension in the moment of catching.

In puberty, the distance between the centre and the periphery changes as the limbs lengthen rapidly. Adolescents have to learn to cope with all the accompanying awkwardness and to arrive at a new relationship between the physical body and their surroundings. In the diagrams set out below, Bernard Lievegoed provides a picture of the interaction between children and their surroundings.[1]

First phase: pre-school children (0–7 years)

At this age, the most important connection to the outside world runs in one direction: from the outside inwards. The experiences that children have are not yet registered in the seat of their ego.

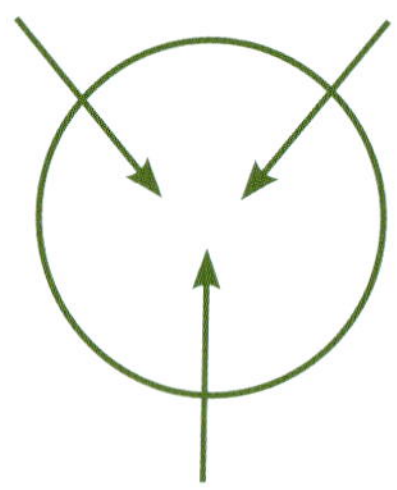

On the topic of play, Lievegoed says, 'At play, the child can practise ways to become what their innermost impulses dictate, ignoring all exterior considerations.'[2]

Second phase: children in the Lower School (7–14 years)

With their ego forces, children create a safe, clearly defined world around themselves, as indicated by the arrows radiating out from the centre.

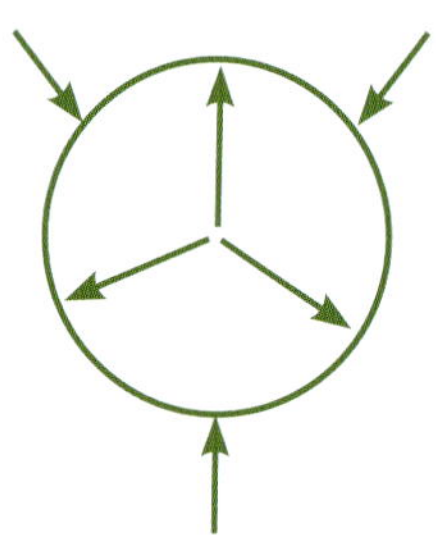

Third phase: puberty and the adolescence (14–18 years)

During this phase, young people break out to conquer the world. This is the so-called 'Sturm und Drang' period, the 'storm and stress' of the adolescent years. It is characterised by a strong outward impulse that creates a new relationship to the world and leads to a corresponding strengthening of the ego. The aims and desires that young people have now encounter the restrictions of the outside world and must be adjusted or reconsidered.

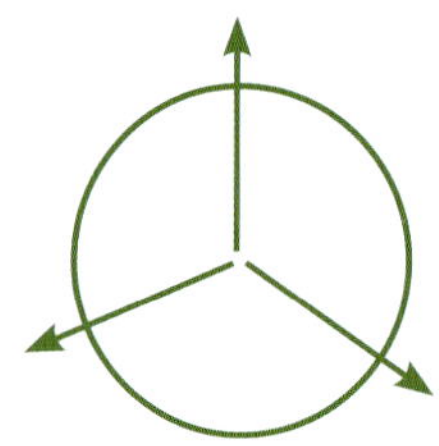

On reaching adulthood, we finally establish equilibrium between both worlds, with a balanced correlation between activity (outwards) and experience (inwards).

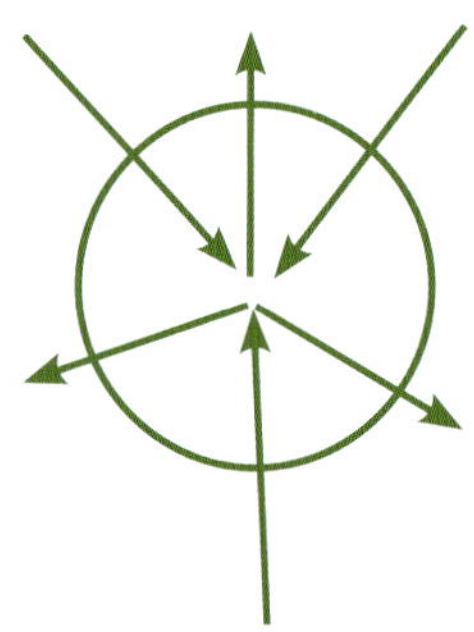

The importance of play in childhood development

Play is such an essential component of children's development that it has been set down as a basic right in the Convention on the Rights of the Child (article 31, paragraph 1). A position paper written for the Association for Childhood Education International 2002, says:

> Children are growing up in a rapidly changing world characterised by dramatic shifts in what all children are expected to know and be able to do. Higher and tougher standards of learning for all populations of students are focusing on a narrow view of learning. Consequently, students have less time and opportunity to play than did children of previous generations. Few would disagree that the primary goal of education is student learning and that all educators, families and policymakers bear the responsibility of making learning accessible to all children. Decades of research has documented that play has a crucial role in the optimal growth, learning and development of children from infancy through adolescence. Yet, this need is being challenged, and so children's right to play must be defended by adults, especially educators and parents.[3]

Lievegoed singles out the imagination as the driving force that enables small children to develop inner lives of their own. Children need play in order to channel their experiences and transform them into something useful. It allows them to observe with a certain objectivity what they have experienced and store it in their memories, ready for recall at a later time. This helps them cope with new situations. This approach is not a reflective or cognitive process but rather an intuitive one: it takes place on an emotional rather than a rational level. During play, children react to the continually changing situations of the game and this gives them opportunities to practise different ways of exploring and expressing their innermost impulses. Where should they run? To whom should they throw the ball and when? How do they time the perfect throw? Do they feel confident to speak up during the game, or do they prefer to keep a low profile? As Lievegoed says, 'The powers of the imagination confront the outside world and transform it according to their inner needs.'[4]

These examples show the numerous possibilities available to children at play. They are required to become active and find their own relationship to the game being played, and while this is a matter of will, children must also understand what needs to be done – in other words, how to play the game. This mostly takes place in the emotional centre, which acts as an agent between the intellect and the will. Imaginative activity is also needed to acquire a grasp of the rules and tactics. This knowledge flows into the action and may eventually lead to decision-making and responsibility. Throughout, children strive to find a balance between being so immersed in the game that they forget what is going on around them, and so intent on maintaining control that they miss out on all of the fun.

Sometimes, when faced with an obstacle, children are thrown back on themselves in order to find a solution, but then there are moments when everything flows together, effortlessly and without obstruction, and children can lose themselves in play. In these moments they are able to build a bridge between themselves and the outside world and the result is pure joy.

The main aim of Waldorf education is to lead the students to freedom. This means that the young person is able to realise their true potential and set themselves aims for the future. 'Who am I? What am I capable of? What do I want in life?' An educational system that recognises how children change over the course of their time at school, and reflects this in the method and content of teaching, is invaluable in helping young people overcome all inner and outer obstacles on their way to self-realisation. This of course is an ideal that can only be achieved gradually.

In the light of this educational challenge, we might wonder what contribution physical education can make. How important are games? A well-known line from Friedrich Schiller's *On the Aesthetic Education of Man* reads, 'Human beings are only at play when we are in the fullest sense of the word, "human", and we are never so authentically human than when we are at play.'[5] Schiller's picture of the human being compares with the definition of freedom described above, to which, in our most elevated moments, we can aspire. The creative power we possess as human beings has its seat in our desire to play, which, according to Schiller, makes its first appearance in small children. Play is the first primitive expression of the creative instinct by which something new arises out of what already exists. This is why, for children, play is the training ground for their emerging creative will.

Games in the Upper School

Although many of the games played in Waldorf schools are just as common in state schools, such as volleyball, basketball and handball, when deciding which ones to include the Waldorf method gives closer consideration to the children's stage of development.

For example, competitive games are best suited to older children who have learned to assert themselves more and are able to command the space around them. These are typical characteristics of competitive games. Pushing themselves and seeing how far they can go is also part of this. The games that the younger children play in the early years up to the end of Class 6 gradually prepare them for the competitive games of the Upper School.

Fifteen year olds have reached that phase in which they need friction, and they deliberately seek out conflict in order to learn more about themselves and the world. Yet this new consciousness is fragile and full of contradictions. They are constantly dealing with questions such as: 'Should I stand my ground or back down?' They need challenges and genuine confrontations, and these can sometimes be of an extreme nature. It is often all or nothing with young people; everything is black or white and grey areas seldom occur. It can take a while for them to open themselves up to the world and to appreciate it in all its contrasts and contradictions.

Rugby, for both boys and girls, and sometimes with mixed teams, has proved to be an excellent choice of game for this phase. The intense physicality of the game means that students soon overcome any reservations they may have about physical contact, given that tackling is an intrinsic part of the game, and a strong sense of fair play helps to balance out its roughness. Volleyball, handball and basketball also invoke the competitive spirit.

At sixteen, emotions are running riot, the personality is defining itself more and more, and the power of judgement is becoming more sophisticated. Spatially, young people develop an affinity with the horizontal plane: this is the plane in which face-to-face encounters with others take place. It is the same with games. The players have to become alert to interaction, to all the facets of teamwork. When the team players are well attuned to one another, they can enjoy a free-flowing game.

The special quality of the horizontal plane comes into its own and is perfectly demonstrated in Ultimate, formerly known as Ultimate Frisbee. Players from one team throw the frisbee to one another while members of the other team try to intercept it. The aim of the game is to catch the frisbee in the designated end zone. Running with the disc is not allowed. It takes a strong team to score the point. Ultimate is great for training and improving the power of judgement: each player has to be aware of the situation, make split-second decisions and spring into action. Because there is no referee, the players follow the game closely and decide on infringements together. The spirit of the game engenders respect for the opponent.

In Class 11, students becomes more concerned with their future. The power of thought and that of judgment are now highly developed. At this age, the burning questions are: 'What talents do I have? What do I want? What am I capable of?'

The spatial dimension of making decisions, of judging and taking aim at a target, is in the sagittal or longitudinal plane. In anatomy this refers to the imaginary line down the middle of the body that divides it into left and right parts. Precision, focus and concentration are qualities that help young people to prepare for their future. Baseball or softball improve these skills through pitching and striking. During the game, it becomes clear whether a player can anticipate the run of play or not. At best, they forget themselves and go with the flow, reacting automatically. They grasp the overall picture, are creative and adapt quickly to new situations, and their aim is true. A combination of presence of mind and talent helps better players dictate the run of play.

Sometimes, when learning how to play a game, certain movement sequences are trained intensively in drills, but these are more or less detached from the game in question. Real learning only takes place during the game itself, and this is where to start, practising in small groups or in pairs. This is where the pleasures of a technically difficult game like volleyball can be discovered.

The students in Class 12, in the context of their movement biographies, are now in a position to look back and recall the games they played in earlier years. They are able to draw on their shared experiences and use it to plan lessons of their own. In the games too, the strengths they have developed in thinking, feeling and willing become more apparent, and the teacher can observe qualities such as determination, restraint, flexibility, stamina and empathy.

An essay on games should not leave the topic of coeducation unmentioned. Whereas it sometimes makes sense to separate boys and girls (for example, when exercising on certain gymnastic equipment), games offer a great opportunity for all to play together, and provide a framework for learning to get on with each other. Especially during puberty, young people must learn where certain lines have to be drawn, but they can also learn how natural reticence and fear of contact may be carefully overcome. In any particular situation during a game, every player is free to decide for themselves the extent to which they seek physical contact with their opponents. In dodgeball, when boys are only allowed to throw at other boys, the girls can take on the role of a protective shield. Even mixed rugby is possible, as long as the rules are adhered to and the players treat each other with respect. This opens up enormous potential for development.

In summary, it should be said that playing is of inestimable value for the healthy development of children and adolescents. In the Waldorf curriculum, the element of play is a key part of a comprehensive educational approach, providing an age-appropriate stage upon which children and adolescents can learn and progress. Where possible, adults should make sure that the children in their care get ample opportunities to engage in free forms of play above and beyond P.E. lessons at school. In this respect, even the design of the school playground has relevance. Where there is a warm, inviting and safe environment, children find it easier to join in games and cultivate their love for play.

Apparatus and Floor Gymnastics: Between Tension and Dynamics

Alexander Koekebakker,
Claudio Czak-Lindemann

> When a person performs gymnastics, activating their muscles without needing to think about what they are doing, developing their skills directly and intuitively, then they truly engage in self-educative play.[1]
>
> *Rudolf Steiner*

Working on gymnastics apparatus is an effective means of encouraging self-educative skills in students and furthering their development. On the gymnastics apparatus, students are in the grip of physical forces – they feel the strain the exercises place on them and the strength they demand from them. If the P.E. teacher manages to introduce the exercises so that students fully experience them, it can lead to a healthy form of practising while playing. The physical and pedagogical effects, the qualities of the various movements and how they may be experienced, are described in the table overleaf.

The basic movements and their qualities

In apparatus gymnastics, we can postulate the following basic movements: rolling, arm support, swinging, tension, turning and jumping. Close observation of these movements brings to light greatly varying qualities.

Basic movement	Physical level	Emotional level	Direction of movement
Rolling.	Contract, tighten.	Hold – let go; Loss – recovery; Within – without.	
Support.	Strength, tension, balance.	Rest and motion.	
Tension.	Hold shape.	Connecting and shaping.	
Swinging.	Sweeping, turning rhythm; heaviness (downswing), lightness (upswing).	Rhythm of the breath; incarnating (breathing in), excarnating (breathing out).	
Turning on a horizontal axis.	Tension in the middle.	Turning in the horizontal plane around a point.	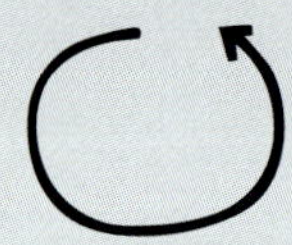
Turning on a vertical axis.	Tension in the middle.	Turning in the vertical plane around a point.	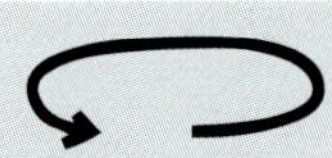
Jumping.	Concentration, focus.	Letting go, taking hold, overcoming.	
Stretching.	Form.	Light, purposeful.	

Above: the basic movements in apparatus gymnastics.

P.E. teachers who take the various aspects of the chart opposite into account are in a position to observe their students in action and give them specific advice on how to progress further. The important thing is to observe and to, at least initially, refrain from assessing and judging. The terms listed in this chart are guides for seeing movement in a new light. They make it possible to read how a child really moves and help them to develop.

The qualities mentioned above can be demonstrated and elaborated upon in the example of a flying roll.

Confidence, direction and rhythm are part of each and every movement. Confidence is a prerequisite for performing any given movement, direction gives structure and clarity to the movement, and rhythm helps us to immerse ourselves in a flowing movement.

If we take the average thirteen year old, we see a stage of emotional development that exists in tension between a certain degree of insecurity on the one hand and a desire to find out what is going on in the world on the other. Caught in this flux, they are looking for structure and orientation.

	In the preparatory phase, the body tenses up and the young gymnast plucks up courage. As soon as they overcome any qualms they may have, they gather their strength and jump.
	A short moment of letting go leads to the contraction of the muscles before the phase of flying through the air.
	In landing and rolling, there is a short phase of loss of self during a soft landing on the mat.
	In emerging from the forward roll, the child comes back to their senses and regains orientation.

Above: the stages of a flying roll.

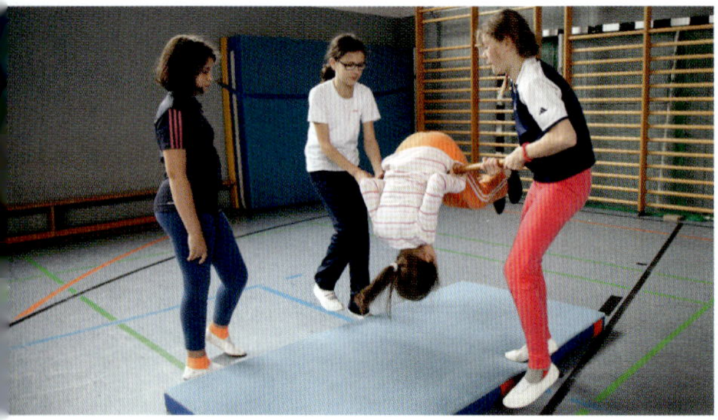

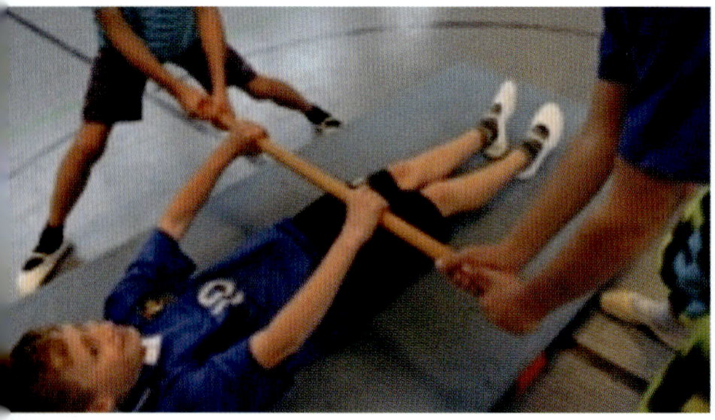

The best way to reach this age group through the medium of movement combines elements of rhythm, courage and lightness – exactly what the flying roll demands of the thirteen year old. Finding the courage to take the plunge boosts their self-confidence, while the tension and structure involved have a regulative effect. The ability to let go and then come back to themselves gives students a feeling of security, which helps them to regulate their emotions.

Apparatus gymnastics from classes 3 to 5

During this time children get to know the various pieces of equipment and become confident in using them. This is important preparation for the gymnastics lessons they will have in their later school years.

Classes 3 and 4

Working on the gymnastics equipment takes on a central role in classes 3 and 4. Although it will still be a while before the children perform specific exercises on one piece of apparatus, in the meantime they enjoy navigating the obstacle courses and imaginary landscapes that are set up for them. Each child chooses the approach that suits them best, experimenting and discovering new things through play. The equipment becomes the framework that the children adapt to their individual requirements. Through contact with the apparatus, they gain confidence and learn to take pleasure in the activity. By placing the action in an imaginary context, through a story or by describing a vivid image, the children can immerse themselves in what is going on.

In Class 3, the emphasis is more on togetherness, whereas in Class 4, the exercises are more individual: each child works more on their own when facing the various challenges.

Class 5

The obstacle courses now take on the form of apparatus circuits, with the emphasis on heavy and light qualities. Little tests of courage have a wake-up effect, giving each student a clear indication of where they stand and what they can do. The aim is not to perfect any particular exercise but to develop flowing gymnastic movements.

Three steps for performing a hip circle in Class 6

This approach is a creative way of introducing exercises on the horizontal bar, taking the individual ability of each child into consideration.

- **Step 1:** two children kneel either side of a small mat, holding a rod in both hands. A third child lies face up under the rod and grasps it with both hands shoulder-width apart.
- **Step 2:** the child lying on their back brings their feet over the rod and their own head and, at just the right moment, the two children either side pull the rod upwards. The student in the middle spins around the rod and finishes in a kneeling position, still holding on to the rod.
- **Step 3:** this involves the children either side coming to a standing position at the same time as the third student rolls up and backwards, keeping their arms straight. The student likewise finishes in a standing position. (A warning for the teacher: the two helpers must be strong enough to take the weight of their classmate!)
- **Step 4:** the two children holding the rod stand next to the wall bars, each resting one elbow on a bar at collarbone height. Caution: the correct grip on the rod is important. Both thumbs must be pointing upwards before the fingers close around the rod.
- **Step 5:** finally, the students can try the same exercise but without the help of the wall bars.

The way the gymnast and their two supporting classmates experience the exercise are closely connected. The momentum to swing up is initiated by the gymnast and reinforced by the other two students. In this way, the physical laws at work this movement can be clearly felt by both parties. This method of practising is a good, intermediate stage on the way to working on the static horizontal and asymmetrical bars.

How an exercise develops: from handstand to front handspring

From Class 6 onwards, the handstand can be integrated into all lessons as one of the basic movements. The handstand requires a high level of control over the body, a completely new orientation in relation to above and below, as well as confidence in one's own strength to support oneself. All of this provides a whole range of possibilities for lessons.

Class 6

At this age, young students are experiencing their own bodies in a more conscious manner. There is a growing interest in lengths, measurements and relationships. Since strength in the arms is not yet well developed, the handstand should only be practised for short periods and not in the form of serious training. Further options include:

- a handstand workshop with exercises laid down by the teacher;
- students create their own exercises; and
- practising the handstand as homework.

In this work, each student takes the time to find their own style of practising. Working in small groups is good for creating mutual trust, while making progress with the technique and giving each other the necessary support.

Class 7

The students continue working on the handstand, with the emphasis on momentum and body tension. Arm strength can be improved by the students holding themselves on the palms of their hands in a crouching position after rolling out of the handstand.

Class 8

Now that the students are becoming stronger, the handstand can be practised as an exercise in strength and stamina. With support from other students, the handstand can be practised starting from a press-up position or lying face down at the wall. Work on a front handspring from the box onto a soft mat can also begin and then be continued using a knee-high bar, a mini-trampoline and a soft mat.

Class 9

As the students' strength increases, and control over their bodies becomes more sophisticated, more exact work on the front handspring is possible. It is a perfect time to combine gymnastics and acrobatics. In the case of the acrobatic shoulder stand, strong support and stability are demanded of the person on the ground, while their partner trains body tension.

For the handspring, two students stand either side of the student and hold them securely, carrying them through the flip-over. This involves one hand supporting at the shoulder while the other hand grips the opposite hip, the forearms of the two students crossing in the middle of the student's back. In this way they are able to turn the student around their centre of gravity, letting go only when they are in a standing position.

In a further exercise, a mini-trampoline and a vaulting box can be used to practise the element of arm support as well as the flying phase.

Class 10

The young students are now able to work on the handstand and the front handspring using momentum rather than strength. Arm strength, momentum and body tension become one harmonious unit. Working from a higher level and landing on a soft mat are recommended. Students can begin with a slow front handspring, starting from a handstand and with students giving support as described above, and then continue building momentum until they can do it with a short run-up and a jump. In this way, the students are able to practise on their own and fairly quickly manage a front handspring without support.

Class 11

Once the students have grown accustomed to the front handspring, they can begin practising it on level ground and in combination with other moves. It can also be done over the vaulting box using a springboard, and even lengthwise over the box. Giving the chance to create and work on a sequence of moves works wonders for this age group.

Class 12

During the final school year, the task is to integrate the handstand (and rolling out of it) and the front handspring in a freestyle programme and perform all the exercises in one harmonious, flowing sequence. From now on, the front handspring and its many variations can be improved upon, depending on the ability of the individual gymnast.

Developing confidence

Depending on the demands a gymnastic exercise makes, students can struggle to complete certain exercises. This initial failure engenders a feeling of humility. But when, with the right guidance, they are able to overcome the obstacle and go on, they grow more confident and develop greater faith in their abilities. In this way, students learn to face up to difficult situations and take further steps in their development.

At this stage, the importance of the student–teacher relationship is worth mentioning. This can be fairly close or remain more distant, but in either case it gives gymnastics an active social component. Trust in the care and the competence of the teacher enables students to surpass themselves and continue making progress. Pleasure and creativity come to the fore and exercises set by the teacher can take a back seat. The activity becomes the responsibility of the students so that the focus is not only on well-performed exercises.

In our experience, there is a lot of potential for development in apparatus gymnastics. Confidence and courage are fundamental human qualities that are of supreme importance in everyday life. The ideas we have set out above aim to encourage teachers to take an honest look at the well-known stock gymnastics exercises and breathe new life into them.

Athletics: A Wealth of Challenges

Jürg Bigler

Athletics offers ideal support in helping young people develop physically and emotionally. Here, we practise the most basic human actions of running, jumping and throwing alongside other rhythms and patterns of movement. As will be shown below, a sequence of disciplines, each one suitable for a particular age group, can easily be slotted into the school curriculum.

In Class 5, the children learn about Greek culture and the origin of the Olympic Games in their history lessons. At this age, like the statues of classical Greece, their bodily proportions are in perfect harmony and they become Olympic athletes with their heart and soul. In Switzerland, in the course of a long summer's day, a number of schools meet to recreate their own Olympic Games in mixed teams. Class 5 teams from various schools all over the country, even from neighbouring countries, gather around the Olympic flame and then compete in all the ancient Greek athletics disciplines, including chariot races and wrestling. Although for this age group the emphasis is deliberately placed on the team performance, an outstanding individual performance may be honoured with a laurel wreath.

Classical athletics really begins in Class 6 and coincides with the changing anatomy of the young people as adolescence approaches. The harmonious proportions of the eleven year old disappear. The muscles grow longer, the longest being in the legs. For this reason, we find all sorts of running games on the curriculum, as well as sprints, crouch starts, cross-country runs and orienteering. The aim is for children to develop stamina, the staying power to work at some particular skill. They run relays, practising passing the baton and sprinting off to perfection. Eventually, every student is able to run through and pass the baton with the hand in exactly the right position. Along with a variety of relay races, there are also obstacle courses and cross-country team competitions as well run-up practice for javelin. As we shall see below, a definite sequence suggests itself: running, jumping, shot put, discus, javelin, and even pole vault. This range of activity encompasses the whole of our physical being, starting at the bottom and ending at the top. It also corresponds to stages of human development, from walking, skipping, then spinning around and throwing objects with true aim.

In Class 7, the ligaments and tendons grow stronger. From an anthroposophical point of view, this is the time for all sorts of jumping activities, such as the long jump and the high jump. Because the Fosbury Flop has dominated the scene for so long, other techniques such as the straddle jump and scissor jump have been neglected. Nevertheless, the adolescents should be given the chance to try out a wide variety of jumping techniques, including any they invent themselves. The only rule for the high jump is that the take-off be one-footed! One idea is to hold high-jump competitions where the heights of three different jumping styles are added up to give the final result. Competitions are fair when, rather than aiming to jump higher than anyone else, the aim is to achieve the smallest possible distance between a person's own height and the height of their jump. If the various jumping styles are introduced as they appeared chronologically in the past, the young people also get a chance to understand the historical development of this sporting discipline. If outdoor practice is rain-affected, long-jump training can be continued in the gym, using equipment such as the vaulting box, springboards and the soft mats. With these artificial aids, the actual time in the air can be increased, enabling the separate phases of the jump to be experienced more consciously and more intensively. At the same time, work continues on practising sprints, sprint starts and relays.

When we come to Class 8, the students have a feel for their own bodies and are ready to be challenged. In learning the shot put, for example, they experience the flowing transition of many different movements and experience resistance from the shot that must be overcome. This is also a good time for a first attempt at pole vaulting. After the run-up and take-off, there follows a swift sequence of movements on the pole that culminate in a handstand. Ancient pictures show how horsemen used to swing themselves up into the saddle using a long pole. In this way, children also spring over ditches and streams. Swiss Athletics, the governing body for athletics in Switzerland, has endeavoured to breathe new life into this traditional sport by designing projects and offering training courses. For example, a teacher might take their Middle School class out into the woods, equipped with poles, and practise leaping over tree trunks or hopping over various sectors drawn on the forest floor with sticks. Finally, they might try their luck over ditches and streams. They could also practise pole-vault technique, using a rope hanging from a branch, Tarzan-style. Practising long jumps with the pole is also worthwhile, for which the normal long-jump pit is quite suitable. It is also a good time for slingball, which involves throwing a leather ball attached to a strap. This can be practised individually or in the form of team games.

In Class 9, purposeful, controlled movement is required as students continue to practise the different styles of shot put – the spin style, the O'Brien Glide – and tackle the sophisticated technique of hurdling. A central motif for this age group is 'contraction and release'. In the shot put there is contraction as the students gather their strength before the throw and then release with the throw itself; in the hurdles and the high jump, the students experience contraction during the run-up and then release as they soar through the air. The high jump, with its famous Fosbury Flop, is a wonderful example of this motif. With other high-jump techniques, such as the scissor jump and the straddle jump, the athlete lands on their feet. In the case of the Fosbury Flop (which significantly is not called a jump), the athlete lands on their neck, something only made possible with the advent of thick foam mats. As this technique demands a certain amount of confidence to take a leap backwards into the unknown as it were, it is a valuable exercise in contraction and release and learning to let go that characterises the period following puberty.

In Class 10, our work is focused on feeling and developing momentum. Training is not just a question of marshalling the will but also about cultivating a particular feeling sense for the activity. When the students throw the discus their aim must be good so that it lands in the designated area, and as it sails through the air the discus must rotate evenly without wobbling. The students must have a really good feel for this. In addition, with its emphasis on balance and graceful movement, this activity has a harmonising, therapeutic effect. In the case of the triple jump, another technically challenging discipline, the necessary momentum has to be carefully distributed over the three jumps. Working on the different stages of the triple-jump rhythm provides an interesting challenge, and by varying their speed and energy, students can experience the hop, step and jump sequence in all sorts of different ways. If necessary, practice can take place indoors, with a run-up of mats and a large foam mat to land on, which is softer on the joints and an exciting challenge for the students. Another splendid way to enhance students' feeling for movement is when flying round the curve in the first half of the 200 m sprint.

An exemplary discipline for Class 11 is the javelin. Along with the horizontal dimension of the run-up, we have the added dimension of height. The act of aiming comprises both controlled emotion and intention, or purposeful thought. The latter in particular has a liberating effect on students, enabling them to focus their strength on a single point. Throwing the javelin therefore has a close affinity with the process of thinking itself: the thrower despatches their javelin – a symbolic bolt of lightning that represents their intention – in the hope that it arrives at its target. Interestingly, the flight of the javelin corresponds to the symmetry of the human countenance. When lost in thought, a person often follows this line unconsciously with their forefinger, touching the middle of their forehead, the root of their nose, their lips and chin.

During Class 12 all the different disciplines are practised and improved upon. Ideally, the students should get to know the 4 x 100 m relay race – the team race par excellence! This is an event with an eminently social component and requires perfect cooperation. Only when the individual performance is combined with a good baton-passing technique together with a teammate is success assured.

The decathlon is a great project for Class 12 as a way of bringing together the various athletic disciplines. The pole vault is likewise a wonderful way of rounding off twelve years of P.E. lessons. In one single vault there are elements of all the classical athletic disciplines, one after another: the sprint, the long jump, shot put and javelin are particularly conspicuous. By means of photography, it can clearly be shown that features of all four recur identically in performing the pole vault. It is as if, in each of the various disciplines, the students discover a piece of the jigsaw necessary to perform the pole vault. In the final strides the pole vaulter takes towards the box, just before they plant the pole, you have the same picture as the 100 m sprinter ten strides before the finishing line. Immediately after take-off, the vaulter mirrors the long jumper as they rise up into the air, and as they work the pole, their arms bent just before they push up into a handstand, they resemble the shot putter. The action of pushing the pole away as they cross the bar is comparable to the release of the javelin, just as the javelin thrower coming to a stop at the moment of throwing, is like the vaulter hanging onto the pole after planting it in the box.

Athletics is a wonderful means of giving an additional boost to physical and emotional development. How effective these activities are can be seen in the fact that many renowned acting schools have athletics on their curriculum. Since acting plays such a large part in Waldorf education, certain athletic disciplines can be called upon as part of preparation for theatre productions. Rudolf Steiner elaborated on the effect that walking, running, throwing discus and javelin, and even wrestling has on articulation, the stream of speech, hand and arm movements, facial expression and much more.[1] Running technique is the basis for further jumping and throwing disciplines. A solid grounding in footwork and the ABCs of running are the key to mastering the twisting and turning of the shot put, discus throwing, sling ball and the hammer.

In many ways the classical disciplines of athletics are more relevant in today's world, where people often feel isolated from one another, than the latest fitness craze. In contrast to fitness training, which can be a solitary pursuit, athletics can only be enjoyed in a club setting. This means that the participants must be able to rely on and be committed to each other. Annual local and regional club competitions create a tremendous sense of belonging and team spirit, and there is also the promise of going on to qualify for an international meeting.

Athletics has long enjoyed a wonderful alliance with culture and science, which is perhaps not so apparent today. But once, between the years of 476 and 372 BC, the town of Crotone in Southern Italy produced 200 Olympic champions.[2] This was where Pythagoras and his student Milon lived. They were also great friends and endeavoured to unite the two opposites of elite sport and science. Pythagoras is best known today for his theorem concerning right-angled triangles. Nevertheless, he too was an Olympic champion. And Milon, the proverbial super athlete, was responsible for a book on the natural sciences entitled *Physica*.

Athletics opens the door to a whole world of interdisciplinary work. It obviously provides material for history lessons, being an important aspect of the study of ancient cultures. The five classical disciplines underwent many changes in the long, colourful history of the Olympic Games. In P.E. lessons, it is possible to study, and try out, ancient long-jump techniques as well as different styles of running and throwing. Athletics also lends itself to art history projects, studying representations of human beings in motion. There are lots of bronze and stone sculptures as well as painted vases that provide wonderfully instructive examples of this. In physics as well, the ideal trajectories of balls and javelins or the best angle for a long-jump take-off can be calculated. In social studies, the constant striving of athletes to break records and win medals can be studied in connection with questions of discipline and ethics and the pressure applied on athletes to achieve the very highest standards. How can they best train their minds as well as their bodies to provide them with the focus they need, and in the absence of that what are the consequences of taking performance-enhancing drugs? Neither are English teachers left without inspiration for interdisciplinary units. One possible text for study is *The Loneliness of the Long-Distance Runner*, by Alan Sillitoe, dealing with an outsider in society.

Considering the broad spectrum of alternatives on offer today, the field of athletics is holding its own remarkably well. It offers a wealth of different training possibilities and there is no hurry to specialise in one particular discipline. Ideally, athletics requires training twice a week, fixed times that help many adolescents through the rough waters of puberty while enabling them to grow strong and develop their skill. Many leading athletes, having completed their competitive careers, return to their clubs and take on the job of long-term trainers, passing on their expertise to following generations.

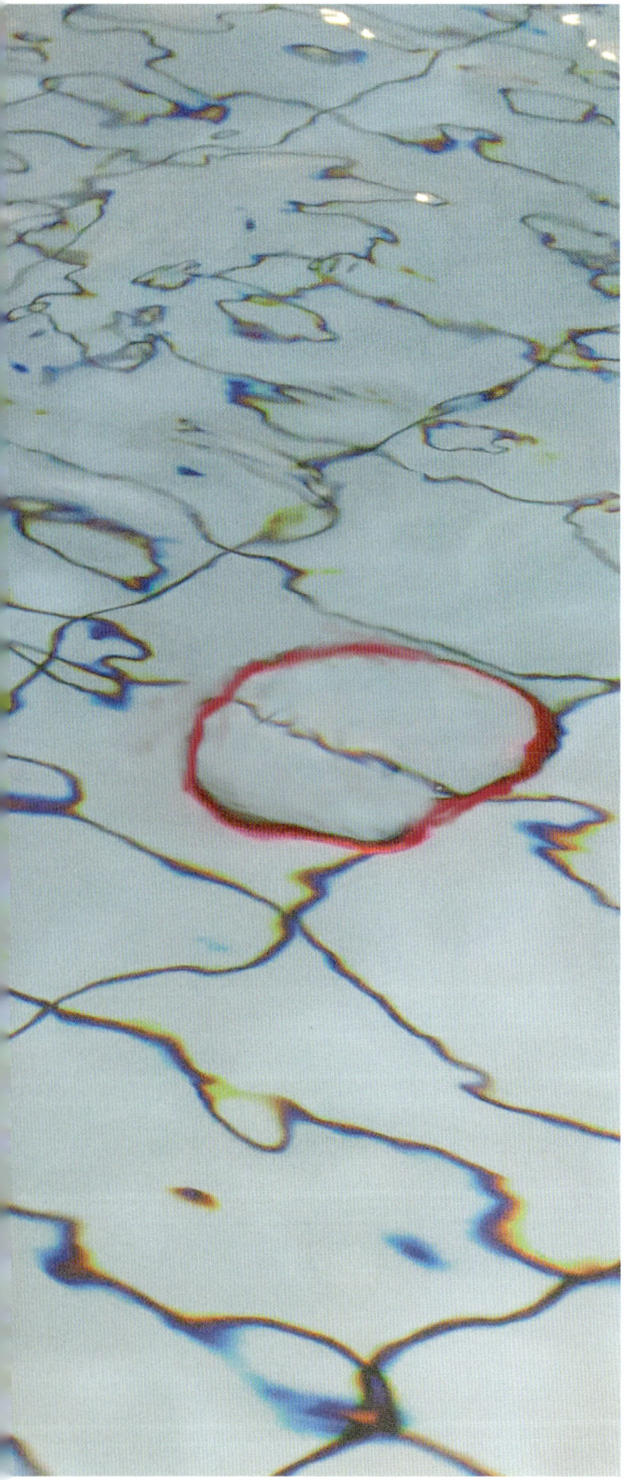

Swimming: The Pool as a Classroom

Gerlinde Idler

Swimming is acknowledged as an obligatory skill, and in many countries it has a fixed place on the school curriculum. In Waldorf schools, it represents a healthy supplement to the other areas of P.E. lessons, namely games, the Bothmer exercises and apparatus gymnastics. Most children and young people take great pleasure in being in the water and enjoy the freedom of movement and the apparent weightlessness they experience there. When they go swimming, they relinquish their hold on something they have invested a lot of time and energy in achieving: the ability to stand and walk upright. Being able to take this backward step, as it were, requires emotional stability and good coordination. This is why swimming offers so many age-appropriate opportunities to help and encourage children and adolescents in their physical and emotional development.

Swimming in the Lower, Middle and Upper Schools

Swimming lessons in Waldorf schools place particular focus on finding the right time and method for introducing and teaching the chosen exercises. They take into account Rudolf Steiner's picture of the human being and his proposals for setting down a curriculum. The main aim is not to master the perfect front-crawl technique, for example, but rather to give students, in the way they tackle the tasks at hand and experience the implicit qualities of movement, the opportunities to progress and develop further. It is important that the teacher, when planning their lessons, keep an eye on the developmental stage of the students and the composition of the group.

Another of Rudolf Steiner's proposals was to consider individual students in relation to the four classical temperaments.[1] This is meant only as a rough guideline and does not seek to judge or pigeonhole students in any way, but the idea can be helpful in preparing lessons. In the case of swimming lessons, taking the temperaments into consideration might lead the teacher to make the following observations: the more sanguine children are attracted to diving in, whereas the more phlegmatic children prefer being underwater; children who tend towards the more melancholic temperament are suited to long-distance swimming and show great stamina, while the more choleric children love all games in the water that are exciting and competitive. It can be helpful therefore, and as long as circumstances allow, if there is something for every child in each lesson.

For students in the Lower School, the best way to get them accustomed to the water is with a playful approach, capturing their imagination with stories. It is a gradual process, using various gliding exercises to teach them good coordination and good body posture – even when some of them have already learned to swim and feel quite at home in the water.

Many of the games and exercises from P.E. lessons can be carried out in the teaching pool or the shallow end of a larger pool, with the aim of improving the children's sense of orientation. Similarly, among other things, the groundwork for the right breathing technique can be laid. We are not yet occupied with perfecting the different swimming styles but simply enjoying being in the water, so that the basics of diving and swimming can be learned confidently and without fear. Two games, Mind the Witch and Carry the Cup, exemplify this approach. In the former, anyone tagged by the three children wearing bathing caps (the witches) stand with their legs apart in the shallow end. They can be freed if a classmate dives down and swims between their legs. Carry the Cup is a relay race between two or more groups, in which the children transport plastic cups filled with water on the ends of their floats.

According to Rudolf Kischnik, swimming should not become a part of P.E. lessons in Waldorf schools before the fifth school year:

> The best time to learn swimming is between the ages of ten and twelve. This is the time when children are most attracted to the element of water … and take to swimming most easily. The reason for this is that they are still bathed in etheric forces, but at the same time they are beginning to raise their heads in a much more independent way. Certain parallels can be observed here. The picture of the swimmer, gliding along with their head above the water, corresponds to gradually being able to think independently and logically. Every physical exercise has an affinity with a particular age group and swimming is especially for ten and eleven year olds.[2]

Today, we would say that this is the time for practising (and later mastering) the various swimming styles; learning to swim at an earlier age is of course preferable.

According to Günther Frank, ages ten to twelve are best for improving coordination and developing swimming skills.[3] From an anthroposophical point of view, a rhythmical approach to work and exercise is the most effective for this age group. A rhythmical approach makes hard work easier. The first two swimming styles of breaststroke and backstroke can now be tried out, albeit with no claim to perfection. As ever, the emphasis is on an imaginative approach, with exercises presented in story form (see sample lesson for Class 5, pp. 84-6). In the same playful way, all the various pieces of swimming equipment, goggles, floats, flippers, paddles, hoops, bricks and diving rings, can be introduced if they are to hand.

We will now look at how the various activities of diving and swimming are developed through the years from an anthroposophical point of view.

Class 5

In the game Burying the Treasure the student enters the water from the side of the pool, diving in, if possible, and places a diving ring (the treasure) on the bottom of the pool. On the next attempt, they try to place it further away. The emphasis is on immersing themselves in the spirit of the story and completing the task elegantly and to the best of their abilities. The actual distance travelled underwater is not measured.

Class 6

This is when students really begin to practise their swimming technique, building on the basic rhythmical movements they learned in the previous year. The main focus is on breaststroke, with its breathing technique, and backstroke. Students are asked to swim geometrical forms as well as other, clearly described, abstract shapes. There are the first, short competitive races too. Students are proud to attain one of the standard swimming badges. Distances swum underwater can be measured objectively, so that each child's achievement is clearly seen and felt by them.

Class 7

The young people now want to test how far they can go. In response to this, long-distance swimming appears on the agenda alongside other challenging tasks. For example, students are asked to swim underwater as far away from the side of the pool as they think they can get and still be able to turn around and get back without coming up for air. In this way, they learn what their limits are and how to conserve their energy. They also learn to practise on their own. Another task might be to have students estimate how many lengths they can swim in eight minutes doing breaststroke. Classmates and/or the teacher then compare the actual results with the individual guesses.

Now is also the time to start diving from a height as a test of courage. Jumps hitherto performed forwards can now be attempted backwards. Some of the main exercises in gymnastics, such as somersaults and cartwheels, can be brought in.

As far as swimming technique is concerned, the focus remains on breaststroke and backstroke. The more demanding front crawl also makes an appearance.[5]

Class 8

If it can be organised, a swimming project lasting six to eight weeks is recommended for this age group. This can be an activity that focuses on rhythm, harmony and creative movement, like synchronised swimming, or one that requires strength and stamina, like long-distance swimming, relay races, water polo, or carrying objects underwater. Practising the different swimming styles the students have already learned continues, and a new one, the butterfly stroke, is introduced, with its powerful, rhythmical stroke. Turning techniques and rescue skills are also developed further.

At this point, it is worth mentioning the interdisciplinary nature of the Waldorf curriculum and the way subjects can overlap and reinforce each other. In classes 7 and 8, for example, students learn about levers and the laws that operate in concert with them. In physics, the logic of these laws is meant to bring truculent adolescents to at least a certain amount of insight and understanding: brute force alone cannot guarantee success and, with a portion of cunning (and knowledge of how levers work), a weaker person may still win the day. Of course, these same laws come into effect when lifting weights or moving bulky objects in water. It is therefore worthwhile giving movement techniques serious consideration.

Similarly, in biology, lessons that deal with health and fitness share a common ground with swimming lessons. Exercising in water is easier on the joints, and movement in general is smoother and gentler. Physical limitations can be cushioned and, after an accident, mobility restored more quickly.

Class 9

In his comments on the Waldorf curriculum, E. A. Karl Stockmeyer remarks on how the content of most subjects in the Middle School recurs in the Upper School in reverse order.[5] For swimming lessons in the Upper School, this would mean taking up the butterfly stroke again in Class 9, having first been introduced in Class 8, improving front-crawl technique in Class 10, intensifying work on the backstroke in Class 11 and, finally, perfecting the technically more demanding breaststroke in Class 12.

Class 10

In the Upper School, there are further opportunities to vary the experience of students. In swimming lessons, the students might be given the chance to work more intensively on a project they have chosen themselves, or to take a course in high diving, or lifesaving, always depending on what resources are available and what can be reasonably organised. Often specialist instructors are required for this. If, however, the P.E. teacher has the necessary proven skills and all legal considerations are clarified beforehand, they can lead the course themselves.

Improving swimming technique in the course of a project lasting several weeks is also in tune with young people's stage of development. Making further progress with swimming turns (contracting, rolling, stretching) is a natural continuation of other work undertaken in the P.E. lessons of Class 9.

Class 11

The focus now, from an anthroposophical point of view, is increasingly on individualisation, with students encouraged to take on greater responsibility. Students might prepare talks on various water sports, taking sports theory into account. Alternatively, they could also give lectures with an interdisciplinary angle, examining aspects of swimming in the light of phenomena dealt with in biology and chemistry lessons. Endurance tests and long-distance swimming – open water is also an option – are age-appropriate challenges for the students of classes 11 and 12.

Class 12

Medley swimming is an activity that combines everything the students have learned over the years: the technique of four different swimming styles, the personal rhythm each student finds for themselves, the flying start, endurance, and the art of self-assessment. When it comes to a medley relay race, the individual contributes their own special skill to the success of the team.

In conclusion, swimming offers children and adolescents the chance to continue enjoying healthy activity, not only during but also well beyond their time at school. The aim of swimming lessons in Waldorf schools is to enable children to feel at ease in water and confident in what they can achieve there.

Folk Dancing: Expressing Soul and Character

Astrid Jochens

> As long as people live and breathe, they will convert melodies and rhythms into movement. This is what we call 'dance'.[1]
>
> *Manfred Stingel*

In all ages, in all cultures, people have danced. The earliest evidence for this fundamental form of expression can be found in the cave paintings of the Pyrenees, which are 30,000 years old. Dance originally served as a form of worship that connected human beings with the gods and the cosmos.[2] In the Old Testament, King David danced before the ark of the covenant, accompanied by people with lutes and harps and bells. Pictures from ancient Egypt and Greece offer further evidence of the ritual importance of dance. In classical Greece dance was also considered a necessary part of a good upbringing. The ancient Greeks had a saying, 'Dance is the firstborn of the arts. They who do not dance, know nothing about life.' Furthermore, there was a war dance, which prepared warriors for combat, a sporting way of toughening them up. The victory celebrations that followed the Olympic and the Delphic games were further opportunities for great numbers of people to dance together.[3] Dance was also of great significance in the Roman Empire.[4] Tacitus (c. AD 58–120) was particularly impressed by the Germanic sword dances, which were aimed at bringing success in hunting and war.

In all cultures, we find dances performed for different seasons, for fertility, and at weddings and burials. It was believed that ritual dances could ward off illness, plague and natural catastrophes. The indigenous peoples of America, Africa and Australia have always had knowledge of ritual dances that have healing powers.

But alongside these ritual forms, dance has also existed simply as a way of enhancing and expressing a joy for life. In Europe, in the Middle Ages, the Church tried to forbid these heathen customs, calling them the work of the Devil. The spirit of that age was against any form of individual action, and dancing was seen as a way of giving reign to personal forms of expression, of doing your own thing. But the Church was not able to enforce this completely and the ordinary people constantly found opportunities for covert celebrations and dancing. The upshot was that many heathen elements, including the various dances, were taken over by and neatly adapted to Christian festivals. In the twentieth century, folk dancing became less and less popular, pushed back into smaller, regional and social niches as more modern forms of dance took its place. The urgent drive towards individualisation, characteristic of our modern age, is seemingly incompatible with the group experience of dancing together to the sound of antiquated music.

In many European countries, folk dancing still takes place in a convivial atmosphere at traditional festivals, weddings and other celebrations. In Greece, Hungary and Scotland it can even be found on the school curriculum. In Germany, the attraction of traditional dance can be seen in the number of Israeli

dance groups, African dance workshops and other dancing groups that celebrate international folklore.

Folk dances can be distinguished according to ethnic and geographical considerations. Japanese dance is very different from that of indigenous Africans or Americans. We can even see different styles within the borders of Europe: the people of south-east Europe dance differently from the English; Russian dance is easily distinguishable from that of Spain. The down-to-earth dances of the Bretons have a different character to the dreamlike, floating dances of the Irish, which have a special place among the regional dance styles. The tempo and ever-changing rhythms of Balkan dances demand vitality and controlled power. The feet move elegantly and lightly, while the upper body remains upright. The Irish dances, accompanied by harp, bells and dreamlike melodies, give us a glimpse of the country's past, imbued with myths and stories of supernatural beings. The steps are light and airy, with sprightly pirouettes. Everywhere we look, we see dance evolving in a singular fashion. It expresses something particular in the soul and character of a people, in the way they see the world and the surroundings they inhabit. In this way, each country reveals something of its charm and of its secrets through its dances.

But there are certain features that all folk dances have in common, no matter where in the world they originate. Every dance defines a particular space through an ordered sequence of movement, performed to a rhythm provided by instruments or song. If we abandon ourselves to this rhythm, we can find ourselves floating across the room, moving lightly and spiritedly and with a spring in our step as the music takes hold of us. We are carried by the rhythm and feel almost weightless. What is more, we do not get tired, we can dance effortlessly for hours on end.

Where does this feeling of lightness come from?

Rudolf Steiner said that not only do we have a physical body, perceptible to our physical senses, but we also have an etheric or life body. The etheric forces are what endow the physical body with life and cause it to grow. In contrast to the physical body, they are not subject to the laws of the material world. While the physical body has to obey the law of gravity, and without energy would simply lie like a stone on the ground, the etheric body, as Steiner puts it, 'always wants to move around the earth'.[5] That is to say, while the physical body tends towards being static and heavy, with the etheric body, it is just the opposite: moving and rotating, it gives itself over to lightness.

> The etheric body wants to make circular movements … and so the person dances. Dancing is usually a matter of someone not wanting to follow their physical body but their etheric body. The desire to dance actually exists so that a person may forget their physical body and can feel themselves to be a spirit that belongs to the cosmos.[6]

It is easy to see from these remarks how the inherent lightness in every dancing movement can help overcome the fatigue of daily routine. It is also important for the development of children. Children are continually growing, and the forces responsible for their growth are those of the etheric body, which, as we have seen, is keen to perform dancing movements. Every time we dance with children, therefore, we are stimulating the forces that promote healthy growth within them.

In what follows, I would like to outline how certain dances might be taught at school. These ideas come from my years of experience; they are presented as suggestions.

Kindergarten

During their first seven years, children learn mostly through imitation, which makes dances and rhythmical games perfect teaching methods. [7] These can be chosen according to some seasonal activity. For example, the kindergarten teacher demonstrates how the farmer goes about harvesting and the children imitate the movements. Then the group performs a harvest dance, in which the kindergarten teacher leads the children round, running and hopping, although they do not necessarily keep in step!

The Lower School

Classes 1 and 2

For children of this age, a fun dance for them to take part in is 'Hey, nimble dwarves!', in which they skip hand in hand in a circle. There is no change of direction, as this would disturb the harmony of the movement for children. In the middle of the circle, the children who have been chosen to be dwarves also skip to the music. When the first part of the dance is over, everyone stands still. Each dwarf stands in front of a child in the circle and they hop from one foot to the other, stretching out their free foot with each hop. At the end of this section, the children selected by the dwarves join them in the middle and the dance begins again. During this dance, the children are enchanted by the fairy-tale mood, something which the circle, with its warm, encompassing character, enforces.

Class 3

Around the ages of nine and ten, children reach a decisive stage in their development. They become aware of the distinction between themselves and the outside world, between subject and object. Rudolf Steiner calls this stage 'crossing the Rubicon'. On the curriculum, learning about traditional crafts and professions, for example blacksmith, stonemason, farmer and carpenter, is designed to help them adapt to this new situation. Corresponding dances that feature the working person take up this motif. In one dance children might the emulate the typical movements of the cobbler, followed by a fast-moving gallop, after which the children imitate the action of repairing a shoe. Finally, after 'work' is over, each child takes a partner and, holding hands, they dance round and round in celebration.

Class 4

A typical circle dance for Class 4 is the Seven Jump, a dance from the sixteenth century that was widespread in Central Europe. It begins with eight steps to the right and then eight to the left, followed by four steps forwards and four steps back again. Now we have the first jump – left foot, heel and toe. Then the dance begins again. Six further jumps follow after the standard beginning, getting more and more complicated. The dancers need more and more strength and concentration to get through to the end, where, kneeling down, nose to the ground, they prepare to spring back to the starting position. This ancient dance draws something from the world of poetry, namely from the stave rhyme or alliterative verse, which is traditionally part of the Class 4 curriculum. This is designed to strengthen the will, the power of determination. In stave rhymes, this is achieved by alliteration; in the dance, it is the rapid jump back.

Class 5

One of the main topics covered in history lessons in Class 5 is ancient Greece. Although the great philosophers do not play a prominent part in the actual lessons, they are significant in that they pave the way for a greater, rational comprehension of the world. Many of the Greek folk dances symbolise this step forward: the closed circle dances of the earlier classes now open up into a semi-circle. These dances also make a perfect conclusion to the Olympic Games, which take place in this school year. Aphroditis, Tsamikos, Zorbas and Syrtos are all forms of Greek folk dances and are recommended.

Class 6

With the onset of puberty, children begin to feel a growing sense of independence. They are searching for their place in the world, their own standpoint, and they are quick to defend it. Anyone who has ever taught this age group knows how vehemently twelve year olds will give their opinions. The Madeleine dance helps them meet this need to find a standpoint. Each dancer has their own starting point, which they have to return to after sixteen hops and skips. Since there are seven other dancers who have exactly the same aim, it is important they do not lose sight of their starting point (their standpoint) and not be put off by comings and goings of others.

Classes 7 and 8

This is the age when the force of gravity is most strongly felt – as typified in the popular imagination by the lethargic teenager with heavy limbs. A number of dances are suited for this stage of development. Square dances, with their stately pace, are good for more reserved children or those less sure of themselves, whereas those with more experience in dancing are likely to find the more vigorous Balkan dances a fair challenge. Moreover, the many different steps mostly carried out on the balls of the feet are a good antidote to the heaviness and lethargy typical of this age. With the right music, the young people will soon overcome their sluggishness and get into the swing of things.

The Upper School

Despite full timetables, if there is a chance to do folk dancing with students, it should be seized with both hands. This form of dance contrasts sharply with the way young people usually dance today, but it still gives them the opportunity to experience something of their innermost selves, to explore how they feel within a group and what effect they have on it. This can be a significant experience on the way to finding one's individuality.

We can see the benefits of folk dancing in three ways. Firstly, there is the physical aspect. Dancing improves physical agility and suppleness. The dancer has to find the rhythm and perform the prescribed steps in exactly the right moment. This is good training for coordination, strength, stamina and concentration. Furthermore, the physical body learns to carry out meaningful movements, meaningful in the sense that they have significance for the soul and allow it to express itself through the dance.

This brings us to the next aspect, which relates to the soul. Folk dancing is an eminently social activity that fosters a communal feeling. Through our encounters with the other dancers we are lifted out of our everyday routine and feel lighter and happier. As Kurt Neff writes:

> The adult who puts his arm round his partner in the ballroom, and the child who skips along in the street, both forget themselves, overcoming the pull of gravity and rising above daily routine.[8]

The third level relates to how traditional folk dancing reflects and allows people to engage with the cosmos. First and foremost, we have the circle as the archetypal cosmic form. This serves to bring individuals together, each of whom may be dancing in smaller circles, revolving around themselves just as they are revolving round the centre or the sun. The lemniscate formation, the figure of eight lying on its side, represents a constant interaction of within and without. It allows us to open up to the world as sensory beings, but also to repose within ourselves as thinking beings. Finally, the spiral formation shows how the circle can be condensed into a final point. Crossing the threshold, a new opening leads back to a new beginning. On the basis of these examples, a microcosmic copy of the macrocosmic order can be reproduced. As Neff also writes:

> For what is this dance of the stars and this interlocking of the planets and the stars and the common measure and wonderful harmony of their movements but rehearsals of the primeval cosmic dance?[9]

Modern Dance: Questioning Traditional Forms

Bernard Thiry

Dance is a form of interacting playfully with the space around us. It activates the dancer and encourages them to experiment with the limits and laws of their own body. When dancing, we learn to keep to a rhythm and tempo and to internalise a sequence of steps. Dancing addresses the powers of the will in particular, helping young people to find orientation and to increase their interest in the world around them. It can take us on journeys through different countries, cultures, traditions and landscapes. Last but not least, dance brings people together.

For children and adolescents, a dance workshop or an intensive block of dancing lessons can make a marvellous contribution towards harmonious and balanced development. For this reason, it is important to always be on the lookout for dances with educational value while, at the same time, constantly questioning the traditional forms and methods. In these rapidly changing times, it is hard to predict which dance will be in vogue tomorrow, and being fashionable is not sufficient criteria for introducing a dance into lessons. But neither is it appropriate to dismiss out of hand everything that emerges from modern culture, such as hip hop, jazz dance, modern dance, and rhythm and blues (R&B).

In any given lesson, what is possible will depend on the teacher and their students. The older the children, the more they will be involved in choosing the content of the lesson. In the role of counsellor, the teacher can help the young people develop criteria for assessing particular dances, even ones that do not yet exist. Some questions you may consider are: what is the best way of getting students to appreciate all the various qualities of movement? What are your pedagogical intentions in introducing a particular dance to the students? How can you reach young people in their particular stage of development?

It helps to connect with the content of other subjects that combine to make one big picture, in particular subjects that focus on movement, including the inner movement we perhaps find most clearly in art and modelling lessons. In principle, each lesson contributes to developing the students' capacity for judgement. During their time at school, the students get to know the different qualities of movement better and better, without ever judging or condemning them. Questions can be considered and discussed with the students concerning the attitude of the dancer, the sequence of the steps, the relationship to the music as well as the intention of the dance. In coming to an appreciative opinion of modern, contemporary forms of dance, the students become more self-reliant and independent.

One possible form of movement that could help students find a basic understanding of other forms of free dance is contact improvisation. This is an improvised dance technique in which the dancers support and use each other's weight while in motion. Although younger children are usually fine with bodily contact, with the onset of puberty there are very definite inhibitions. In such circumstances, contact improvisation can be carried out using various objects, such as a ball, a chair, a wall or a tree, before gradually leading to working with a partner when the young people feel more comfortable. No person is an island. We are all connected, and we need each other in order to develop and find out who we are.

Working in contact with a person or an object and using this technique to learn more about gravity, pressure and the surrounding space can lead to experiencing the world in new ways and finding new relationships to the people and things around us. If during the dance we are supporting our partner, we must stand firm and be alert to the shift in weight; if we are being supported, we must keep our balance and stretch and spread out our limbs to distribute our weight more evenly. In both instances we are completely in the moment.

A journey through the various forms of dance is one special way of experiencing different cultures. Almost every modern dance has its origins in some particular culture and region and carries these roots within it. For example, there are dances from southern African cultures that are notable for their energy, rhythm and constant contact with the ground. The waves of movement come from the earth and are transmitted into the entire body; the repetitive quality is the rule and is learned by imitation. Students may be inspired by dance traditions from many places. Consider southern Europe, eastern Europe, the Indian subcontinent, China or American First Nations cultures. It will always be important to see from a historical and sociopolitical viewpoint exactly where the roots of a particular dance lie. Certain dances, like modern jazz dance, give the students a chance to develop skills by joining together elements from other forms of dance, such as ballroom dancing, contemporary dance and Bollywood dance.

In order to create a balanced relationship to the various forms of dance, it is essential to vary the dances and to select those that are suitable for the particular age group. We should never shrink from trying out completely new dances. A teacher who combines a sensitivity for movement and space with a strong grasp of gesture and modern music will surely have a healthy knack of choosing the right dances. They will be able to inspire their students and encourage them to become enthusiastic dancers.

Rhythmic Gymnastics and the Bothmer Exercises

Silvia Tampe

In rhythmic gymnastics we find three elements combined in one sporting discipline: rhythm, sport and gymnastics, elements we will discuss further in the following essay. We will also consider whether rhythmic gymnastics and the Bothmer exercises, two very different disciplines, actually have anything in common. Is rhythmic gymnastics compatible with the anthroposophical picture of the human being and with the Waldorf curriculum?

Before taking a closer look at rhythmic gymnastics and the rhythm of the Bothmer exercises, let us consider the term 'rhythm' itself. Every living thing has been created by means of rhythm and is sustained by it. We live our entire lives in rhythmical processes. Some of these rhythms we experience consciously, such as the alternation between day and night, and waking and sleeping, others we experience less consciously, such inhaling and exhaling, and then there are some that we are completely unaware of, like the rhythms that govern our internal organs. Any imbalance can lead to illness, and a rhythm that supports our physiological processes creates health and strength.

On this subject, Thomas Hardtmuth writes:

> Rhythm is an elementary principle of all vital processes … The ratio of a single rhythm to any other is a whole-number one and thus we see how the various rhythms are to a certain extent synchronised. For example, the ratio of the pulse to the rate of breathing is 4:1, the basic oscillation of the arteries in relation to the pulse is 2:1, and that of breathing to the rhythmical blood fluctuations is 1:3 … All the rhythmical structures as well as our bodily proportions are a compendium of primal cosmic rhythms.[1]

Hardtmuth goes on to describe how the rhythmical nature of our bodily functions and our external physical proportions represent music in an organic form. This throws an interesting light on the relationship between gymnastics and music.

Rhythm takes a central position in both the Bothmer exercises and rhythmic gymnastics, but there are essential differences. Inwardly and outwardly, the focus is on completely different aspects. This essay attempts to clarify this distinction so that both forms of exercise can be employed in an educationally effective way, helping children and adolescents in their healthy development.

Rhythmic gymnastics is defined as a form of artistic gymnastics, a type of physical education and a competitive sports discipline. It developed out of competitive gymnastics and combines elements taken from dance and acrobatics. Gymnasts must be incredibly strong and supple and possess a high level of concentration and bodily control to meet the demands placed on them. Gymnasts work with five pieces of hand apparatus – rope, ball, hoop, ribbon and club – and movements are generally accompanied by instrumental music. The first competition was held in 1948 in what is now St Petersburg but was then called Leningrad. Although there are competitions for male gymnasts in the USA and Japan, by and large rhythmic gymnastics is a sport dominated by women.

The Bothmer exercises on the other hand have neither artistic background nor artistic claim, and their purpose is neither fitness nor expression but the healthy development of children and adolescents. This is not gymnastics in the traditional sense. The exercises were devised by Fritz Graf von Bothmer at the suggestion of Rudolf Steiner (see pp. 196f). Bothmer combined close observation of the children and their various age groups at the first Waldorf school in Stuttgart with his knowledge of ancient Greek sculpture and architecture to create his exercises. The disciplines that make up the pentathlon – running, jumping, wrestling, discus and javelin – are the proverbial pillars on which this form of movement rests, and the laws of projective geometry are the lynchpin of all the movements. Each exercise, in its entirety, is a picture of the corresponding age group from an anthroposophical point of view. The various movements not only support the children and adolescents in their physical development but also take into account the emotional and spiritual situation of the age group. For this reason, the Bothmer exercises are a pedagogical tool: they complement P.E. lessons and are also able to enrich other school subjects.

The Bothmer exercises are also recognised as an effective form of movement therapy. They have a special affinity with physical and spatial laws, and they can perhaps help bring emotional and physiological rhythms into balance – especially the exercise called The Rhythm.

How then, within the framework of gymnastic schooling, can we put these rhythms to good use in the various stages of a child's development?

It might be mentioned at this point that rhythm ought to be an important element of every lesson. Clearly, it has enormous significance in all the disciplines of P.E., for example, the rhythm of running in athletics, or the run-ups in jumping or gymnastics. Whether swimming or taking part in winter sports, motion is defined by rhythm, and it is our task to use the element of rhythm in the most appropriate way for each age group. Take skipping. In classes 1 and 2, the spoken word defines the rhythm of the skipping. The children love the chants and rhymes that go with skipping and hopping. The pleasure they feel lasts well into classes 3 and 4. When the teacher and a helper swing the heavy rope, this represents a huge challenge to the students. With the corresponding words chanted in time to the turning rope, the run-up and jump alternate in a lively and harmonious fashion. The rope, as a gateway, opens and closes non-stop.

Skipping chants

The great gate is open,
Run up then run through,
And start straight away!

Or:

Teddy bear, Teddy bear, turn around,
Teddy bear, Teddy bear, bend right down,
Teddy bear, Teddy bear, hop on one leg,
Teddy bear, Teddy bear, go down a peg,
Teddy bear, Teddy bear, build a house
(*Children put both hands above their head to form a roof.*)
Teddy bear, Teddy bear, run outside!

Or:

Baby Jane,
Golden chain,
Golden shoe,
How old are you?
(*The children skip their age before jumping out of the moving rope.)*

The rhythms of speech, as pleasurable as they are, support the children's movements. At the level of language there is word play and every child increases their own store of images, something that is nourishing for their souls. All sorts of skills are practised too, such as twists and turns, one-legged hops, skipping in a crouching position or even with eyes shut. We can make things more difficult, for example by having the children skip with their own rope in and out of the heavy rope, or even into and out of a double heavy rope. In the latter, two heavy ropes are swung in opposing directions, so that when one of them is on the rise the other is falling. In Class 7, the art of skipping reaches a certain climax, although it can still be practised and improved on in the Upper School classes – the older students may even devise their own choreographies.

In rhythmic gymnastics, the basic approach to working with the rope as a piece of hand apparatus is completely different. Music plays a significant part. It is stimulating and uplifting, and its rhythm also helps to determine and structure the gymnast's routine. A gymnastic dance is greatly influenced by the personality of the gymnast and the way they experience the music on the one hand, while on the other hand obeying clearly defined rules and laws.

With the introduction of the five pieces of hand apparatus mentioned above, a wealth of new movements can be experienced. Each piece of equipment has its own special characteristics, and students must learn to adapt their own dynamic style to each one. A high degree of skill and coordination is required. As an example, let us consider a gymnast working with the ribbon. On this subject, Alina Wallmann writes:

> The students feel the flow of the ribbon, which they are themselves controlling … When the gymnast's movements harmonise with the ribbon, it leads to a feeling of lightness: the ribbon floats, flies, swoops and swirls, quite soundlessly in the air. If there is a cracking or slapping sound, then the student is not sufficiently at one with the ribbon, the movements are being carried out too powerfully. The movements must be flowing and dynamic, so that you can see and feel the bond between the gymnast and the ribbon. … The rhythm helps the changeovers to go smoothly.[3]

There are two different techniques for setting the ribbon in motion, one using the shoulder, the other the wrist. The former produces larger, sweeping movements, the latter smaller, swifter ones. If the movements are carried out half-heartedly or with insufficient care, then according to Wallmann, a sort of 'feather duster' effect appears, which is of course neither correct nor desirable.

Depending on which piece of hand apparatus is being used, various skills such as rolling, throwing, catching, bouncing, swinging and circling can be practised. When the hand apparatus is in the air for a longer time, the gymnast has their hands free to perform other floor exercises. These consist of five basic types: the springing step in preparation for a jump, walking, running, jumping and pivoting. There are also seven so-called groups of elements: steps, jumps, balances, rotations, flexibilities, waves and floor elements.

In order to reach an adequate level of proficiency in rhythmic gymnastics in all its complexity, you need special training from a qualified trainer beginning in early childhood. As P.E. teachers and teachers of movement at Waldorf schools, however, we have other aims. Versatility is key to fostering the holistic development of the whole person, and when rhythmic gymnastics becomes a part of P.E. lessons in the Upper School, the context is always an anthroposophical one. On the way to finding their own rhythm, the young students have worked on the laws governing the surrounding space and gained a greater awareness of them. As students of Class 10, they have now progressed beyond the burdensome time of puberty and are in a sovereign position to adapt their powers of movement to music. They have greater physical and inner strength. They are more emotionally settled and are able to 'face the music' and convert it into movement without getting carried away. Students are more self-determined in dealing with important aspects of rhythmic gymnastics such as expression and self-confidence. This explains why students must be at least sixteen before they can meet the demands of the discipline without losing themselves entirely in the rhythm. From now on, it is possible to work with elements of rhythmic gymnastics, maybe even reaching a level good enough for school-leaving exams. Before this age, short choreographed exercises with hand apparatus, unaccompanied by music, are possible.

One Bothmer exercise that plays a central role in Class 10 is Discus. The students stand at the centre and, at the same time, reach out into the space around them towards the periphery. The young adolescents need to keep their balance between zenith and nadir. The horizontal arm movements are performed with such rhythmic intensity that it is as though the horizon is pushed back, something that forms an intrinsic part of development for this age group. From within themselves and unaided by music, the students increase the dynamic activity towards the target. There is no hand apparatus, as in rhythmic gymnastics, and certainly there is no discus. A real discus is thrown in the athletics block that accompanies the gymnastic exercises, whereas in the corresponding Bothmer exercise we deliberately do without it.

It is worth attempting Discus using a piece of hand apparatus, namely the ribbon, which allows students to relate to and experience the surrounding space quite differently. The ribbon draws paths, making them visible in the air, but the sense of different planes is suspended. In a way, the ribbon transforms students into artistic draughtsmen, where otherwise they would be architect and discus thrower.

In similar fashion, students can experience the Bothmer exercise known as the The Vortex (see illustration on facing page). Performing this exercise with a ribbon in each hand affects the arm movements and can even become an acoustic experience. With

the turning points being so significant, the way the surrounding space is experienced gains a completely new quality.

In the Bothmer exercise Slinging Circles, large, circling movements are performed with both arms, accompanied by steps from side to side. If these large, circling movements, which move forward in loops (typical for Bothmer exercises), are performed with a club in each hand, then the circles seem to be smaller, but this allows the students to practise with rhythmical accents: when the clubs are swung up to the highest point, they are tapped against each other. Swinging the arms parallel to each other becomes somehow more tangible and to a certain extent more spirited. In this way, the clubs lend the exercise a new dimension.

If we consider each piece of hand apparatus separately, we discover an enormous range of possibilities. The shape and the composition of ball, rope, hoop, ribbon and club vary immensely, each piece of equipment obeying its own specific physical laws. While they are simply used for games in the first four classes, in the Middle and Upper Schools they are serious pieces of sports equipment. Balls and ropes are employed so universally through all the different age groups that floor and apparatus gymnastics, athletics and the many team games are hard to imagine without them. In kindergarten, children love it when a ball is introduced into their games and budding schoolchildren can even fashion their own skipping ropes. With endless patience, they form and sandpaper the wooden handles until they attain a smooth finish. How proud they are when they finally manage to skip through a full circle, or even more. All rhythmical work with this versatile piece of equipment has great educational value. With sufficient practice, skipping can improve dexterity and coordination.

The hoop can be used not just as hand apparatus but also for the many tasks involving running and jumping, such as when children manage to slip through a moving hoop. In the first years of school, a hoop can be almost anything: a mossy patch in the forest, a puddle on the path, and can even serve as a take-off mark for leapfrog.

The Bothmer exercise called The Vortex.[4]

Classes 3 and 4

In the roundelays and the playful, rhythmically chanted verses of classes 3 and 4, we see the interplay of heavy and light. With the help of vivid images found in the first Bothmer roundelay, connected with the building of a house ('Windows as high as the sky and as wide as a river, the steadfast pillars'), the children are able to connect their inner world with the world around them. The images are not simply pictures transferred from the outer world, but rather stem from inner spiritual experience. A wonderful example of this is the bell tower in the second roundelay for Class 4. The extremely spirited 'Toll the bells ... in the storm' becomes tranquil and still. From the breadth and the height and the depth of the space surrounding them, the children come to a standstill. They have come down to earth.

Classes 5 and 6

The Bothmer exercises known as Light Beat/Heavy Beat require very concentrated movements that draw the students' attention to the pauses between the rhythmical motion. These pauses, quite still and without music, have the power to harmonise an entire class. The coordination of arms and legs during the exercises is not automatic, but is brought about by the rhythm itself, something which becomes particularly clear when the exercises are performed in staggered fashion, where groups of students carry out the various sections as in a musical round. Some variations on the exercises – for example, where throwing and bouncing a ball are added to the rhythm – are taken up eagerly as tests of skill. Any set tasks and games that thrive on rhythm are a form of salutogenesis (relating to the sustaining of physical and mental health and well-being) for young people going through puberty. This is a difficult time, when the proportions of their bodies and their extremities are changing. Through the laws of geometry and the dynamic movements that underpin the Bothmer exercises, the children are able to work on their physical bodies. One exercise worth mentioning briefly here that helps with this and that children encounter in Class 6 is The Triangle.

Class 8

The exercise Jump to Middle Point contains a rhythmical element that the children must strive to create themselves. They experience how they do not

get very far without momentum and realise the need to find their own centre and the motivation that can come from it. Meeting this challenge opens up a completely new area for practice for young people.

Class 9

The students find a new way to tackle the element of rhythm in the Class 9 exercise Fall to the Point, which derives its energy from the power of the four elements, earth, water, air and fire, and the resistance they put up. The stepping exercise The Frontal Walk (also known as the Rhythm of Two Interlacing Circles), also helps to create much needed calm after the tumultuous time of puberty.

Class 11

Finally, let us take a quick glance at the Class 11 exercise The Scales (see photo illustrations below).[5] This involves getting to grips with a point of balance that is in constant motion while at the same time aiming at a moving target, all in one flowing movement. Here, projective geometry does not simply lend support but actually points the way. This is a genuine physical challenge for the students, who are now seventeen and eighteen years old. Again, they must find the balance in themselves, this time in relationship to their surroundings.

Long ago, Aristotle described the expressive character of the hands, when he compared the hand with the soul.[6] In the Bothmer exercises the open palm plays a large part in defining the quality of the space – it reaches out or is open to receive, it does not simply mark it out. In rhythmic gymnastics the hand has a different purpose. It is generally used to manipulate a piece of hand apparatus and carry out various acrobatic challenges.

Alheidis von Bothmer, daughter-in-law of Fritz Graf von Bothmer, characterised the hands as follows:

> The hands are very fine sense organs for the invisible forces in the space surrounding us. In gymnastic exercises, it is the hands which make contact with these forces … That is only possible, if the hands are alert … After some practice, the work the hands perform can be felt in the area of the heart.[7]

For pedagogical reasons this contact is broken in those exercises where the students form their hands into fists. As Alheidis von Bothmer goes on to write:

> In gymnastic terms, a serviceable fist is one in which the fingers are carefully folded into the palm and the thumb rests protectively over them. This fist is enclosing something but not crushing it, and it is warm. Once it is opened, the life force streams out of it.[8]

My renewed studies on rhythm have led me once more to ascertaining that we constantly encounter rhythm in all its diversity. In Waldorf education, it is particularly exemplary in the subject of dance, eurythmy and every sort of handicraft.

In this essay, I have endeavoured to link external movements with a deeper meaning. This process reminds me to a certain extent of Grimms' fairy tale 'The Three Feathers', in which important things are sought after and found deep down under the surface.

These remarks lay no claim to being complete. My aim has been to pose some questions and give them some thought. We can look in a new light at Rudolf Steiner's instructions to the teachers of the first Waldorf School to ensure that children attain physical health. The aim of developing children's emotional and spiritual powers on the same basis remains an ongoing task, but it can be best achieved by moving together.

The School Circus: Combining Strength and Agility

Alfred Schachl

The circus has always been a melting pot of different people who each possess some special skill or ability. The costumes, the music the atmosphere of the Big Top all combine to place everyone under their spell.

During puberty, adolescents have to learn to cope with their often turbulent emotions and the rapid changes their bodies are going through as well as anxieties that arise, including anxiety over their future. Their search for kicks, for that rush of adrenalin, can lead to a range of dangerous activities, from substance abuse to extreme sports. Circus activities give young people opportunities that go beyond what normal P.E. lessons can offer. Physical activities such as acrobatics and balancing exercises strengthen the sense of self as well as the sense of balance, and help young people cope with their fears and uncertainties. Practising juggling or performing magic tricks improves dexterity and hand–eye coordination, and trains stamina and perseverance. Working with a partner or in a group has enormous social value for young people. It teaches them tolerance and how to deal with conflict, and they learn to rely on others and to step back or accept a subordinate role in order to allow someone else their moment to shine. They learn to see each other as role models. A spectator watching two young people performing a routine on the trapeze can hardly imagine how much hard work has gone into producing such a level of elegance and aesthetic beauty. Furthermore, by working together, by overcoming stage fright and other personal dramas together, young people gain a very special inner strength.

In Germany, there are over a hundred circus groups of all shapes and sizes at Waldorf schools: permanent working groups, circus clubs, circuses within the class community and project initiatives that encompass more than one class or school.

At these schools, two types of performance have emerged: the traditional show in the circus ring, and the stage show. Both forms go through a classic list of different acts, but increasingly they have begun to adopt a common theme or overarching story into which the various acts fit. Embedding the work in images and stories is particularly good for integrating less able children and those with additional learning needs. Indeed, the circus atmosphere described above, and the many ways of clothing the acts in wondrous stories, make the circus a valuable addition to all schools with children with additional learning needs.

Whilst the classical circus ring, with everyone sitting round in a circle, is more suitable for young spectators, the stage show is a better way for the older students to showcase their skills. This can also include project work, including the major project undertaken in Class 12. Working in cooperation with other circus groups and schools, with clubs and professional artists who then take part in the show together with the students, opens many new horizons. It is a marvellous experience for participants and underpins the creative, collaborative qualities the circus has always stood for.

The acts in circus performances fall into four main categories: acrobatics, juggling, clowning and magic. Acrobatics includes leaps and jumps as well as partner acrobatics (human pyramids), aerial acrobatics (the trapeze), and equilibrium or balancing (the tight rope, the unicycle). During the various jumps, the acrobat briefly loses their orientation and must regain it in a split-second. In practice, qualities such as strength, bodily control, suppleness, presence of mind, alertness and effortlessness are trained. Building human pyramids engenders a feeling of team spirit, a sense of above and below, of supporting and being supported. It boosts strength and the sense of balance, it improves stability and adaptability and fosters a sense of responsibility as well as honing a person's social skills. The individual develops a feel for the other acrobats, who may be far away from them in the pyramid. They become alert to them and the role they are playing. It can take weeks of practice before a large group succeeds in coordinating all the movements necessary to build one pyramid.

In the case of the various balancing acts, students must overcome any fears they might have and take control of the space around them. They must learn to become calm and keep their balance.

They also develop a feel for the particular piece of apparatus they are using, like the tightrope, the unicycle, stilts, the rolling globe, the free standing ladder, the Rhön and Cyr wheels, or the rola bola (or balancing board). Aerial acrobatics uses many elements taken from the above-mentioned activities. There is a greater struggle to overcome not only gravity but also a natural fear of heights, and it requires great physical effort in a confined space such as on the aerial rope, the trapeze, the aerial ring, straps and loops.

Juggling stimulates eye–hand coordination and the ability to recognise and follow sequences of movements. Its important features are rhythm, balance, catch and release, and, especially when working with a partner or in a group, it fosters a keen sense of timing and quick reactions. Alongside balls, rings, clubs, diabolos, devil sticks, plates and cigar boxes, there is also contact juggling, poi* swinging and club swinging.

In the circus, the clowns represent children. They look out at the world with wide-eyed wonder, seeing everything for the first time; they are curious, naïve, spontaneous, always willing to play and to learn something new. Especially during puberty, many young people find it easier to express their feelings through the character of the clown, and the process of creating and developing their very own clown character can leave a lasting impression in an adolescent's biography. As well as having a beneficial effect on emotional flexibility, clowning also helps to develop versatility, creativity and bodily awareness and

language through mime and gesture. Dance in the circus is, on an emotional level, also related to clowning. All kinds of solo and group dancing are forms of expression that can be integrated into a performance.

Performing magic demands an enormous amount of concentration and discipline as well as a knowledge of human psychology and a flair for presentation in order to enchant an audience. The magician uses misdirection to trick the onlooker into watching the wrong hand, and this requires very fine motor skills, intuition and a certain amount of acting ability. The onlookers are not supposed to see how the trick is done, but rather fall under the magician's spell, although the desire to figure it out keeps them watching and thinking. Close-up magic, table tricks that use minimal equipment,

* Poi is both a performing art and the name of the equipment used in a poi performance. Poi involves swinging tethered weights in a variety of rhythmical and geometric patterns. Performers may sing or dance while swinging the poi.

and mental tricks such as mind reading, are good places for students to start. Depending on their passion and skill and available resources, it might even be possible for them to attempt large-scale illusions.

Circus skills for different ages and stages

It is easy to integrate circus activities into the Waldorf curriculum for different age groups, both as an extension to P.E. lessons and in the form of block lessons or projects.

In the case of the younger students, all the circus activities are wrapped up in a world of imaginative pictures and stories. The main thing here is not practice but play. Balls, for example, become frogs hopping over lily pads or squirrels leaping from tree to tree. The acrobatic exercises are known as 'rolling the tree trunk' or 'rolling the snowball'. There is also the 'lion's pyramid' and the 'king's throne'.

In Class 3, it is a good time to start juggling. This can be with one ball or two and is done in a circle to improve children's lateral movements as they pass the balls around. Children at this stage have reached an important point in their development. They begin to see themselves as separate from the outside world, no longer one with it, and this can cause them to experience moments of fear or shock. This phase is known in Waldorf education as 'crossing the Rubicon'.

In Class 4 the children learn to juggle with two balls crossing in front of them. This represents the alternating exchange of information between the cerebral hemispheres.

The students of Class 5 are now old enough to tackle many forms of acrobatic exercises, like the creepy-crawly, the caterpillar, double drummer, the kangaroo, the ant, and forward rolls over a classmate. They can also practise acrobatic leaps.

Class 6 sees the transition from 'playing at circus' to 'practising circus'. The work on the various acrobatic exercises is intensified with handstands, rolls, cartwheels, the first steps towards performing a back flip and forming pyramids. In all of these, the emphasis is on developing and maintaining stability.

In Class 7, following one of Steiner's recommendations, students learn all about inventors and explorers, a topic that relates closely to their inner lives and the outside world. In P.E. lessons, this motif crops up again in a block of lessons dealing with handsprings and somersaults. Practising these, the students experience the rapid change between inside and outside, making themselves small then stretching, tensing then releasing. These are qualities which can be intensified in the circus. The cartwheel is also perfect for this age group, as are the rhythmical swinging movements of juggling with clubs and especially poi.

The students of Class 8 experience first-hand the laws of balance and leverage when they practise partner acrobatics, which can include the handspring (in falling), the support (lying at a slant) leading to the handstand (with partner), the foot-on-hand pyramid, the foot-on-foot pyramid, the shoulder stand, the upper-arm stand, stable lion pyramids and large pyramids.

In Class 9, pushing up and bending at the hip are acrobatic movements that students practise in dynamic partner exercises, including in 'human juggling'. This involves three or more students rolling over and under each other, back and forth along mats, in an interweaving pattern similar to the one created by a juggler juggling with three balls. The backward somersault is also one of the main exercises.

In the Upper School, the students work on combining different elements. They work on juggling acts with partners, practising different formations and incorporating various acrobatic exercises and gym apparatus. They work further on acrobatic exercises such as the somersault and the backflip that give them an enhanced awareness of the space around them, as well as on more demanding exercises such as vaults and building human pyramids. Finally, they get the chance to create artistic choreographies and set them to music, performing them in front of the class or even in front of the whole school. This can be a hugely exciting and rewarding experience.

The circus has something to offer students of every age group. Even those who find it difficult to express themselves in other subjects get a chance to show new skills and accomplishments, and because the circus consists of so many genres and disciplines, everyone can find their place in it.

Sailing: Leaving *Terra Firma*

Malte Pontoppidan

It's the start of a normal school day. Still at home, I make coffee and listen to the news while having breakfast, before driving into school. In the staffroom, I nod to my colleagues and wish them good morning. I sometimes feel, especially in the way I associate with my colleagues, how set in my ways I am. In the familiar surroundings of the staffroom it is safe, nothing changes. I feel sure of myself yet at the same time I feel utterly hemmed in.

Today, however, will be different. As the first lesson approaches, I have a sense of how the day will not only be demanding but also enriching. Just before eight o'clock, I meet my sailing comrade, Hannes, in the school canteen. I treat him to a coffee and we have a quick chat about whose Internet maritime weather report had been right, then we set off to pick up Class 4 along with their teacher. In the meantime, the class has gone through the ritual of chanting the morning verse together and singing or reciting a poem. With our appearance, a mood of eager anticipation grips the children and they surround us in a noisy, excited gaggle. Accompanied by their teacher, we walk to the car park and drive to the harbour.

On the way to the harbour, I stop at a red light and my car soon begins to draw attention. It is rocking from side to side, caused by the compulsive need for movement felt by my passengers, most of whom are affected by ADHD. If I were to tell any of the gawping passers-by that I was, in the next few minutes, about to take this group on board an ancient, open fishing boat without a motor and in gusty winds, they would say I was being grossly negligent.

In my hometown of Flensburg, in northern Germany on the Baltic Sea, we are blessed with the best possible environment for an undertaking of this nature. The large and small traditional sailing vessels of the maritime museum harbour are moored at their berths. As I unlock the gate to our landing stage, there is an immediate change in the children's behaviour: there is no more pushing and shoving, none of the hyperactive behaviour they displayed in the car on the way here; they are calmer. Ever since their first visit in Class 2, the children have loved spending time on the landing stage. They have got to know the ships and the water and the animals and plants that live in and around it; they have marvelled at starfish, mussels and lion's mane jellyfish.

We find the right life jackets and then everyone helps to get the boat ready. Water that has seeped in is bailed out and the sails are prepared, supplies are brought on board and stowed away, and the oars are brought into position. Back in Class 3, during the lesson block dealing with craftspeople and artisans, some of the students got to know the shipbuilder, who is now about to sail with them. During the winter months, the students helped him with maintenance and repair work on the boats.

Of course, even here the children do not always pay attention to what I expect of them. They keep trying to see how far they can get the boat to heel, by moving from one side to the other, rocking the boat more and more, while I am trying to explain the next steps. Nevertheless, their relationship to the hull of the boat, which they have worked on using sandpaper and paintbrushes, seems healthy enough and they do treat the old lady, whose name is *Minna*, with respect. *Minna* is almost three times older than I am and radiates a correspondingly high degree of dependability. The material she is made of has a vital quality, perfect for tactile therapy, but one that constantly reminds us that she needs to be kept in good repair with loving care.

I call my crew together and, with the help of the class teacher, we begin the casting-off manoeuvre, which calls for several well-timed actions. Ropes are untied, oars set into rowlocks. One student takes the wheel while I use the boat hook to push us away from the landing stage. And suddenly, we find ourselves in another world, one with no firm ground underfoot that demands we stay alert. This is a form of wakefulness that makes it quite natural for each and every student to recognise their own rudimental limits, much more so than in the school playground.

Casting off has gone well. Four students are sitting at the oars, doing their best in a headwind to get the boat far enough out of the harbour that we have space around us to set the sails. They have a firm grip on the oars, the same oars they sanded down in Class 3 during the lesson block on artisans and craftspeople. The oars are now smooth in their hands and unlikely to raise blisters. Since that time in Class 3, we have often practised rowing, something that requires good rhythm and balance and the ability to coordinate one's own movements with the rest of the crew. Sailing punishes poor teamwork. We have discovered time and again to our cost that the boat lurches from side to side and struggles to make progress if each rower thinks only of themselves and fails to work together with the rest as a team.

It is no different today, and while the children are busy blaming each other for the chaos that is unfolding, we are drifting ever nearer to the neighbouring landing stage of the customs boat. One of the students, noticing that I am getting restless, takes control of the rowers. They were already working strongly before, but now they put their backs into it under the command of a student who, in school at least, does not often step up to take charge. Soon the boat is back on course and, a few minutes later, the crew hoists the mainsail. Two students are pulling on the ropes with all their might, knowing that to let go would put the whole crew in danger: the gaff with the sail attached would come crashing down like a guillotine. There is no need for me to tell them to concentrate, they are completely focused on what needs doing. The situation itself sees to this.

As a student, and later as a teacher, I have seen many different ways of introducing the subject of local history to the students of Class 4. Teachers like to begin by drawing a floor plan of the classroom, before climbing up onto the roof of the school and thus, step by step, widening the horizon. Street maps of the town and maps of the region follow, taking the students further and further into the outside world. In the light of this, it was not difficult to decide what I should do in this class. Up here on the coast, as well as street maps we also have nautical charts. We looked at some in the lesson and compared them with the maps of the area the children had sketched in their local history books, studying the information they hold and how they are used to find your way at sea.

We have brought these charts with us, and now that we have set the sails and stowed the oars, we have time to study them. The slow, gliding motion of the boat and the fine view over the water enables sailing to play its part in a local history lesson: we recognise the steeples of churches and the silhouettes of high buildings we have visited, and in this way we keep on widening our horizon as we sail along the fjord.

As usual when we go sailing, we have the whole day at our disposal. We always begin with the main lesson and, as a rule, the class teacher comes with us. The curriculum provides a wealth of opportunities for combining different subjects. Two cornerstones are the above-mentioned projects on artisans and craftspeople and local history that students do in Class 3 and 4. Class 4 also learn about Nordic mythology. Instead of using charts, the Vikings followed directions using landmarks. Could we describe our voyages in the same way, using the things we see around us? Furthermore, the intensive work already done braiding ribbons is great preparation for starting to learn about knots. The students learn sailors' knots on board (making drawings of them when bad weather confines them to land) and become so good that some children proudly demonstrate how they can tie them with their hands behind their backs.

In Class 6, the children sail to their favourite beach, where they find a variety of stones to take back to school for their mineralogy project. They also learn how to use a compass, the constant companion in all our planning. During one lesson the previous winter, we hammered a needle of steel and set it on a sheet of paper floating in a tub of water: our first self-made compass. Later, when learning to steer by the compass, we draw on what we have learned in maths lessons. The theme of sailing crops up repeatedly in Class 7, when the students learn about the explorers in the age of discovery.

The interdisciplinary nature of the Waldorf curriculum and the freedom it affords in choosing and adapting lesson content has been essential to the success of our sailing initiative for students with additional support needs. Because the themes of the main lesson do not have to be rigidly interpreted, the teacher can be more responsive to the demands of the moment and what the students need. This is important, especially when out on the water where the elements can continually disrupt our plans and intentions, but also where the experience can be used to look at a theme from a different angle, as was the case in teaching local history using nautical charts as well as street maps.

Another essential element of our work has always been close cooperation with class teachers. Their familiarity with the children is indispensable. They are the ones who can tell us how much we can demand from one student and whether we need to go easy on another one. They are also in a position to advise on which themes from other subjects can be integrated into our project. What is most interesting, however, is the effect on the children when their class teacher becomes one of the students – assuming they are not already an experienced sailor, that is. The teacher invariably sets a good example for their fellow 'classmates' to follow.

In connection with sailing and social learning, one of the most memorable moments I have had was seeing how a class teacher struggled to come to terms with this new world of swaying, rocking, uncertain motion. Happily, she succeeded, along with her students, but what exactly was she battling against? A number of times in the past when I have asked colleagues if they would like to come sailing, they have rebuffed me saying, 'What? On a sailing boat? Wild horses couldn't drag me on one of them.' But as far as I can tell, there is no objective danger at the root of their response, but a fear of the lack of firm ground beneath their feet. And this, for me, is the decisive point. The unfamiliar spatial and social situation on board a sailing boat – which does not allow us to employ our usual redirection and avoidance strategies – forces us to reacquire skills we thought we had already mastered, even one as basic as being able to walk: we have to acquire our 'sea legs'.

It is my conviction that the essence of sailing lies in learning to move confidently in an environment that is unsteady and sometimes precariously lopsided, while also developing a sufficiently strong yet supple sense of ego – a calm, inner poise – to avoid bumping into fellow sailors: something I admit I fail to do myself at times. This approach is neither the quickest nor the most effective way of teaching young people about the sport of sailing, and it is no coincidence that we are working with a sedate historical fishing boat rather than a smart speedboat. This is not the equivalent of acrobatics, for which a racing boat or a kite-surfing board would be more suitable. The key to our work lies in what we accomplish together.

What sort of contribution do I hope to make with this essay? To convince all my readers that sailing is the ultimate in teaching aids? Not at all. What chance then would all those poor souls have, who live and teach on the mainland? No, my aim rather is to encourage others to find new places, new environments, where 'school' can take place. Places of learning, or rather worlds of learning, that are so different from what we are accustomed to that they can help us break out of our usual behaviour pattern. This applies to teachers as well as to students.

I am convinced that we can find such special places of learning everywhere, in particular among traditional trades, crafts and activities like sailing. For our ancestors, these occupations were generally a combination of duty and art, but we tend to avoid putting ourselves in such situations whenever they confront us with our own imperfections. However, if we are courageous enough to take up the challenge, we can learn anew how to walk upright and with firm tread over boards that persist in rocking and swaying.

As a postscript, I would like to express my heartfelt thanks to the Minna Roeder Club who provide the boats for our sailing lessons. The *Minna* has been sailing under the Waldorf flag for twenty-five years and has become a regular part of our programme in recent years. Thanks also to Angelika Caliebe-Hadamovsky and Klaus Hadamovsky for their invaluable help in writing this essay.

Winter Sports: Skiing, Skating and Snowboarding

Barbara Dawid

Winter sports are a good complement to physical education lessons at school, inasmuch as they offer a wealth of enhanced learning opportunities in the areas of movement skills and training the senses. What is more, a few days spent together in the mountains can be a great experience for children and adolescents (as well as for the teachers) and a source of lasting memories.

Each Waldorf school must decide for itself if and when to include these activities and which age group is suitable. There are no general guidelines for this as the conditions and opportunities for undertaking winter sports vary greatly from school to school. But in this essay, we would like to offer a few suggestions.

The main alpine ski on the market is the carving ski, which, with its long, hour-glass shape, makes learning certain skiing techniques, such as sweeping turns, easier. But this ease can deceive the skier into thinking that the movements they are experiencing and the quick progress they are making are wholly the product of their own skill and physical effort. To ski safely on carvers the learner must be aware of the assistance they gain from the skis themselves. Many skiing accidents are caused by a lack of technique and excessive speed.

Below are a few brief suggestions for lessons for the various age groups.

Winter sports for different age groups

Classes 1 and 2

In the early years of Waldorf schooling, children take great pleasure in being active and they are still at the age where they imitate their elders. The teacher therefore aims to present each exercise in such a way that the children want to imitate it, and the best way to do this is to clothe the various tasks in imaginative pictures and stories. This helps the children bridge the gap between the movements they make and their inward experience of them. All the exercises should be varied and eventually lead the children to a degree of skill on skis.[1] For example, the teacher might suggest that the children, moving along on skis, stretch up like giants and then crouch down like dwarves to get through the tunnel.

Classes 3, 4 and 5

Around the age of nine, children put some distance between themselves and the world. The tasks teachers set now can be more purposeful, but they should still be varied and, to some extent, still clothed in images that stimulate the children to improve the way they move. At this age, the students become increasingly aware of their own movement.[2] For example, the teacher might ask the students to swing round the pole on the right, picking up the cloth which is lying there, then continue on one leg.

Class 6

At this age, children enter a new phase of development. Their stature loses its harmonious aspect: arms and legs become disproportionately long, and muscles develop. Students are now able to accept corrections on how they move and put them into practice. Elements of tension and release in muscular dynamics should be introduced into the exercises. This can be strongly felt in cross-country skiing and skating, where there is a direct relationship between movement and muscle growth.[3] More attention can be paid to improving technique, for example, rhythmical skiing alone, in pairs and in a group, and varying the sweeping turns. With Nordic skiing, which includes cross-country skiing, the aims are to improve technique and to manage longer distances.[*]

Class 7

As they continue to grow, pupils experience greater elasticity and resilience in their bodies – two qualities of movement that are associated with the tendons and sinews. For this age group, alongside all the other forms of movement they practise, exercises involving jumping are appropriate. Pupils take pleasure in practising consciously controlled movements, improving their technique and trying out artistic elements.[4]

Developing good technique is the aim in alpine skiing. During skiing, small jumps can be attempted using undulations in the snow as take-off ramps. These involve rapid alternation between tension and release. In the case of cross-country skiing, students should practise deliberately pushing off with both poles and also try to ski longer distances.

---

[*] In Nordic skiing the boot is fixed to the ski at the toe. This allows the heel to rise off the ski and makes sliding across the snow, as in cross-country skiing, much easier. In alpine, or downhill, skiing, the boot is attached to the ski from toe to heel.

Class 8

At this stage, students take up the struggle with the forces of gravity, which requires poise, composure and stamina. The P.E. teacher can set the students tasks with various levels of difficulty, while making it clear that they expect results.[5] In alpine skiing, students might invest time and effort in the slalom, synchronised skiing and striving to achieve an aesthetically pleasing style.

Classes 9, 10, 11 and 12

Having overcome the force of gravity and achieved a certain composure in their emotional life (two of the main challenges of puberty), as well as having attained their own individual experiences of movement and being able to set their own aims, the students can now move with strength, rhythm and purpose.[6]

First lessons in alpine skiing

It is important to convey to students what it feels like to be on skis in a way that is methodical and age-appropriate, and, if possible, without using poles. Typical exercises include 'riding a scooter', which uses just one ski on level ground; skiing in a straight line downhill and learning to go faster or slower as well as learning to brake by shifting one's weight; skiing on one leg; striding uphill, and maintaining balance over bumpy ground. Only when students are comfortable with these tasks can they start to learn basic techniques, such as changing direction. Further steps are then taken to consolidate and expand on these basic skills.

In the skiing curriculum, there are plenty of practical suggestions for a variety of age-appropriate skiing lessons.[7] The more varied they are, the more students get a feel for the underlying flowing motion. They are able to repeat sequences of movement and commit them to memory more easily.

Lessons for advanced learners should be structured so that the various tasks reflect the developmental stages of that particular age group. More challenging artistic elements can be built in, for example, circling (alone and in pairs), synchronised skiing and skiing in formation, transferring weight, changing rhythm, pushing up with both legs or going into a crouch to take pressure off skis, and skiing curves on one leg. The slalom is an additional skill that requires great competence on skis and is a challenge for every student. Most important of all, however, is the sheer joy the students experience while skiing. This is borne of the knowledge and the confidence that the skills they have acquired put them in control of the skis on their feet.

In my experience, the best time to plan a winter-sport class trip is when the students are in Class 6 or 7. At this age, children's muscles, sinews and bones are growing stronger, and everything that was previously done instinctively in play now becomes a conscious exercise. This means that feedback and corrections offered by the trainer can be more consciously applied, thereby improving students' skiing technique.[8]

When skiing, young people feel the grip of powerful physical forces: acceleration, deceleration, braking abruptly, maintaining their balance on uneven ground and when they change direction, and the way their centre of gravity shifts when they lean forwards and backwards. This provides a great opportunity for cultivating qualities such as decisiveness, presence of mind, speed in reacting to new situations, concentration and feel for rhythm, endurance and strength of purpose, as well as good peripheral vision and being able to have a clear overview of their situation.[9] Pupils also enjoy jumping over small ramps and skiing over bumpy ground. This desire for and joy in movement can be channelled into new experiences.

For example, to conclude the class trip, teachers could organise a race in which the various levels of skill are taken into account. The teachers choose teams of two that consist of one student who is confident on their skis and one who is a little less so. Each pair then has the task of skiing over a given course, hand in hand, to demonstrate their skills. It has proven helpful in the past to have several stops spread out over the course, where the students must answer questions.

In a similar exercise, the teachers pick teams consisting of four students of different levels of skill. They are spread out over a longer course this time with the best skier at the start, the second best further along the course and so on. When the first skier passes the second one, the second team member sets off behind them, this happens again with the third and fourth team members. When all four have passed the finishing line, the time is taken. Ideally, there should be a clear view from start to finish so that the starter and the timekeeper can communicate, using agreed signals.

Snowboarding

Having one snowboarding group just for advanced learners has proved worthwhile on school trips. It is easy to organise and the students get the chance to improve their style and gain in confidence. It must be made quite clear to the students that snowboarding is faster, the curves and turns more sweeping, and it can only be done safely if the piste is wide enough and not too busy. This is a valuable lesson in learning to be considerate towards other people on the piste.

The importance of teaching students to be independent and safety-conscious should not be overlooked either and is particularly effective from the age of twelve or thirteen. In addition, depending on the terrain and taking safety aspects into consideration, free riding and jumping might also be practised.

Skating and cross-country skiing

A 'winter week' is a wonderful opportunity to introduce skating or cross-country skiing to students. The rhythmic, sweeping motion, both on the ice and in the hills, is a marvellous experience, and pupils can see how their technique improves over time with the help of their own strength. Despite the exertion, there is a sense of joy. Twelve and thirteen year olds are perfectly suited to these activities. In the course of one week, each student should have at least three sessions of cross-country skiing. If a skating group can be organised, then a session every day is recommended owing to the more demanding technique. This can take place in the morning or in the afternoon, before or after the alpine skiing.

To round off the week, teachers can organise a cross-country relay race. The students are divided into teams of four with a mix of skill levels. Each team completes six laps, which means that accomplished skiers can do two laps, and a lap should be between 800 and 1000 metres, so that the others do not wait too long. The changeover rule from one team member to the next must be explained beforehand.

Hiking in snow

A long snowy hike is an experience that should not be underestimated, especially if it is undertaken at night, setting off after an early supper. The many sensory experiences that students have on an adventure like this can make a deep and lasting impression: the frosty air, the snow underfoot, the night-time noises and the night sky, the extended periods of silence. If you have sledges, then a subsequent downhill run is a marvellous experience. One of the teachers should make sure that the sledges set off at a safe distance from one another, and at least one of the teachers, or accompanying adults, should sledge down to the end of the track first. Everyone is taught braking technique and the correct behaviour when reaching the bottom. If a night hike is not possible, the same venture in daylight hours can still recreate some of the wonderful experiences mentioned above.

Hiking on snowshoes

Hiking on snowshoes requires a special technique that has become well established in recent years. It is easy to learn, and making slow and steady progress through a silent landscape is a source of great pleasure and can be a wonderful experience. However, this form of hiking is only suitable for children of eleven years and older. They must have a certain amount of stamina and be able to fit into the steady, rhythmical stride of the group. They must also be able to develop a feel for the terrain, which contributes to their overall safety awareness.

Skiing trip

It is only possible to carry out a skiing trip with a small group of volunteers and if the necessary equipment is available in the school or can be borrowed. Safety is paramount and during preparation the teacher should brief the students on the various safety precautions, including what to do in the event of an avalanche. The students must be shown how to use an avalanche probe, a snow shovel, and an avalanche rescue beacon. Also during preparation and at the start of the trip, the teacher can point out the nature of the terrain, give a few tips about choosing a route and elaborate on the technique of walking in skis.

Adventure-based Learning: Knowing the Group, Knowing Yourself

Michael Birnthaler

Classical adventure-based learning began around the same time as Waldorf education. As Rudolf Steiner was founding the first Waldorf School in Stuttgart shortly after the First World War, the educator Kurt Hahn was laying the foundation stone for adventure-based learning at the Schule Schloss Salem, the School of Salem Castle. Both initiatives were the result of lessons drawn from the horrors of war. As fate would have it, both Steiner and Hahn, quite independently of one another, handed in peace petitions on the same day in 1917 to the German Reich chancellor, Prince Max von Baden. In both cases, it was to no avail. Hahn, who was in his early thirties at the time, was private secretary to the Reich chancellor, and when the war was over, Prince Max von Baden presented him with a Cistercian monastery, Salem, on Lake Constance. It was here that Hahn established his school for modern adventure-based learning.

The four cornerstones of his school based on therapy by experience were:

- Charity: helping others.
- Projects: manual work of a skilled nature.
- Expeditions: projects conducted outdoors lasting several weeks.
- Sport.

Since Hahn believed in the value of physical education, he introduced a daily sports lesson from the beginning. From early on the sports curriculum included activities such as climbing, sailing, caving, mountaineering, archery, circus skills and fencing. From this epicentre in Salem, similar schools sprung up rapidly, so that by Hahn's death in 1974, a worldwide movement had been established.

Simultaneously, Rudolf Steiner had developed a new type of school, in which physical education also played a significant role. However, Steiner held great store in reforming conventional sports teaching, which he continually castigated as being too mechanical, too physiological and simply vacuous. He even went as far as describing it as practical Darwinism. On the other hand, he was full of praise for sport as an educational means, as long as it consisted of 'meaningful movement'. According to Steiner, a movement is meaningful if it addresses not only the physical body but also the soul. Meaningless movements, on the other hand, such as are often found in conventional sport, exist solely on the physical plane. As Steiner explains:

> Healthy play means being active, so that one feels pleasure in the movement, in healthy thinking and feeling. Sport can be unhealthy if one is simply in motion without thought or emotion, so that one tends to become emotionally lazy.[1]

But what are these meaningful movements that Steiner expressly calls for in sports lessons? They are associated with one of the essential principles of Waldorf education: that lesson content is first taken from archetypal forms and movements and only then led towards abstraction. A well-known example of this principle is the method used in Waldorf schools for teaching children reading and writing, which involves leading them along a road from concrete to abstract forms. The children are first familiarised with the nature of the sounds, which they experience directly as primal movements as they walk and chant these sounds together. Later, the sounds are painted in the form of images and symbols that represent the different letters and help to bring them to life. Finally, they make the cognitive leap from the concrete pictures to the abstract appearance of the letters in our modern alphabet.

Where do we find meaningful movements in the context of P.E. lessons?

In the same way that the abstract letters of the alphabet are preceded by meaningful forms, so too there are corresponding movements in early class exercises that are primal in character. If we go right back to the cultural roots of movement, we come across forms that have religious and devotional significance and that are even embedded in the ancient mysteries. Later on, we find forms of movement arising from the age of hunters and gatherers, then from that of settlers, farmers and artisans. According to Carl Gustav Jung, from the early days of humankind, we discover forms that are deeply embedded in our collective unconscious: ancient rituals and sacred dances, the treading of labyrinths, songs and roundelays, and games that reflect the hunt and the chase and include archery, fencing, sailing, caving and climbing. Even the circus, with all its many performers, suddenly appears as a panopticon of archaic, magic skills: tightrope walking, lion-taming, knife-throwing, walking over coals, fire-eating, sorcery and magic, the flying trapeze, contortionists and feats of strength. These are all vivid images from an ancient time full of mysticism and magic.

It was only in the nineteenth century, the age of industrialisation, that these traditional, meaningful movements became mechanised and artificial. At the same time that industrialisation was taking place, sport, in its modern, artificial, mechanical form, came into being. Its highest aim has always and only been 'faster – higher – further'. Very often, we see the same maxim applied in conventional P.E. lessons, which are basically geared around training students to perform fixed movement sequences that can be measured in order to assess their performance.

A P.E. lesson which encompasses the dimension of experience, which focuses on meaningful movements, and which is sensitive to the above-mentioned archetypal movements, is potentially enriched by four different fields of experience.

The first is satisfying the desire for adventure. In times like these, in which the children of industrial nations live in relative affluence and prosperity, genuine adventures have become rare. But if children and adolescents are not fed with a certain amount of healthy adventure, then they look for substitutes in the fake world of computer games. Uncannily, many action computer games copy the heroic model of outdoor adventure games.

The second experience is confronting one's own potential for violence through activities like fencing, archery and martial arts. These enable young people to find their 'inner warrior'. At the same time, they teach discipline and self-control. They help children channel their more aggressive impulses and teach them to have respect for themselves and each other. In this regard, adventure-based learning goes a long way in preventing violence.

Third is communing with nature. Adventure-based activities take place in the open air; they are, as it were, carved out of the natural world. Whether up in the mountains or deep inside a cave or on the open water in a boat, the natural world is a partner in the various activities. It is no longer simply a backdrop or the extension of a piece of sports equipment.

Finally, there is developing a feel for community. In the case of many sports and games, the main aim is to win. In team games, for example, the members of one team cooperate with each other to beat the opposing team. However, with many adventure-based games and exercises, cooperation is used, not to defeat an opponent, but to cultivate a community spirit. The object of adventure-based learning therefore lies in developing social competence. To this end, a new type of game has been developed: the so-called cooperative adventure games or team games.[2]

Of course, there are challenges in promoting adventure-based learning that should not be underestimated. There is currently a popular trend for extreme experiences like bungee-jumping and skydiving that cater to thrill seekers looking to get their next fix. And while these can be exciting and enjoyable experiences in their own right, they do not reflect the ethos of adventure-based learning. For some years now, work has been carried out in association with the EOS Institute (an experiential, educational organisation in Hungary named after the Greek goddess of the dawn), to finalise a concept for adventure-based learning that sets it apart from this popular trend.[3] Some of the ideas that underpin this concept have already been adapted by some schools and applied in P.E. lessons.[4]

Adventure-based learning has found wide application in many of today's pedagogical areas, from social pedagogy, with its empirically proven effect on preventing violence, and youth welfare, with its potential for preventing addiction, through to working with businesses as a method of team building. However, widespread employment of adventure-based learning in schools is still an aspiration for the future.

Archery: Inner Aim, External Targets

Dieter Bigler

In a world dominated by digital and social media, and with the rise of such affective disorders as attention deficit hyperactivity disorder (ADHD), helping young people to slow down and find their way in the world today has never been more of a challenge for parents and teachers alike. For this reason, being able to offer young people meaningful activities that counteract the attractions of much modern media and help them take responsibility for their actions is of great educational value. Archery is one activity that can be of great assistance in this. When young people practise archery they learn to slow down and breathe deeply, to withdraw their attention from their surroundings and their everyday routine and focus on a single fixed point. They experience a completely new kind of peace and quiet, both physically and emotionally, while at the same time experiencing a state of profound concentration. They learn to let go.

In Waldorf schools, archery often appears on the Middle School curriculum in classes 6 and 7. With expert guidance in woodwork lessons or in a special project, the children can even make their own bows and arrows. At this stage, shooting takes place without the help of technical aids. Archery reappears in the Upper School, ideally in Class 11. As a rule, recurve, or competition, bows are used. This path of learning takes the students step by step from instinctive shooting to using technical aids, for example, shooting with a sight. They learn how to handle the equipment, how to draw the bow, how to stand and how to breathe correctly. This path, from simplicity to increasing complexity, corresponds to the actual state the young people find themselves in and the demands the modern world makes on this age group.

Safety measures

For safety reasons, I recommend shooting in a gym or hall because shooting outdoors on the school grounds, for example, would necessitate comprehensive and costly safety measures. There should be a minimum of two lessons blocks with three to four double lessons.

The recurve bows, arrows (ideally three for each student) and protective equipment such as tabs, bracers and chest guards should be of good quality and professionally maintained. The same applies to the targets. In the gym, a special net strung up behind the targets for catching stray arrows is essential. The targets can be made of various materials and can be made by the students in woodwork lessons.

In the first lesson block, the best shooting distance is around 10 m (33 ft). In the next block, this can be extended to 20 m (65 ft) for the more advanced archers. The other students can still practise with the shorter distance, as the shooting line remains the same regardless of how far away the targets are.

It is important that the teacher introduces this subject thoroughly, not only in terms of providing information on the equipment, but even talking about the history of archery. This is intended to instil in the students the right attitude of respect and restraint for what they are about to do, and to ensure they handle the equipment with care. Any bow with a nocked arrow has the potential to be dangerous, even deadly.

The teacher must be a competent archer. They should have a clear understanding of tournament etiquette and be able to communicate this calm, disciplined behaviour to their students. Strict rules must be observed. If need be, a club archer could be invited to the lessons.

The first lesson

The outline of the lesson given below is based on a ninety-minute teaching block with between twenty and twenty-five students from the Upper School.

Aims

These include:

- setting up the equipment;
- learning about the history of archery and the equipment used;
- ascertaining which eye is dominant;
- learning the three anchor points and the right technique for drawing the bow; and finally
- shooting two or three arrows.

Preparation

A vaulting box without the top section can serve as a rack for bows and arrows, with the upturned top section serving as a holder for the tabs, bracers and chest guards. Place the vaulting box approximately

2–3 m (6–10 ft) behind the shooting line. Place the targets at a distance of 10 m (33 ft) from the line, with four to five students per target. String out the net behind the targets. Give an account of the historical significance of archery as part of the warm-up.

Equipment

Four types of bow can be presented: the longbow, the short bow, the recurve or competition bow, and the compound bow. The bows, arrows and protective gear are studied and explained. Emphasis is laid on the careful handling of the equipment and the strict safety rules that the students must observe throughout the lesson. Give each student a bow of appropriate length, three arrows, a tab, bracer and chest guard. The bows can be marked or numbered so that the students always shoot with the same bow. Carry out a simple test with each student to ascertain which eye is dominant.

Stringing and drawing the bow

The teacher demonstrates how to string a bow and then each student has a go at stringing their own bow. This gives them first-hand experience of the potential power of the bow as it resists their efforts to bend it in order to attach the string.

Next, the teacher demonstrates drawing the bow, showing the three anchor points: the forefinger under one side of the jaw, the forearm roughly horizontal, and the string touching either the tip of the nose, the right nostril or the right cheek (for right-handers). The students practise this technique, finding the anchor points that suit them best. They do this twenty to thirty times by themselves, then a further ten to fifteen times in pairs so that partners can offer corrections.

The first shot

The first shot is special and should be performed with due respect. Indeed, some students are afraid of this moment, having just experienced how strong the bow is when practising the draw.

The students work in pairs. One student prepares to shoot first. Their partner hands them an arrow and observes the student's stance and technique to ensure they are correct. The student draws their bow. Their partner stands behind them, slightly to one side, and looking along the arrow towards the target they give instructions: 'Higher, lower, left a bit, right a bit … now!' The archer simply draws the bow and does what they are told. They do not aim.

The following lessons always begin with a session working in pairs, in which the drawing of the bow is practised repeatedly. The teacher goes around each pair, correcting stance and anchor points if needs be, as well as pointing out any other bad habits that the students might be developing.

Aiming with the help of two orientation points

After the students have had a second lesson shooting in pairs as described above, they then learn how to aim using two fixed points. This will teach them how to aim and shoot on their own.

The shooting line

Each student marks the position of their feet on the shooting line using something they carry with them, such as a key or ballpoint pen. The teacher then gives each student a coloured peg or a painted cork.

The aiming mark

The student now aims at the target as before. Their classmate helps again – 'Up a bit, left a bit…' – but instead of saying 'Now', they say 'Good'. The student, instead of releasing the arrow, makes a mental note of the spot where an imaginary line from their eye, passing over the tip of the arrow, ends on the ground in front of the target (see Diagram 1).

Diagram 1

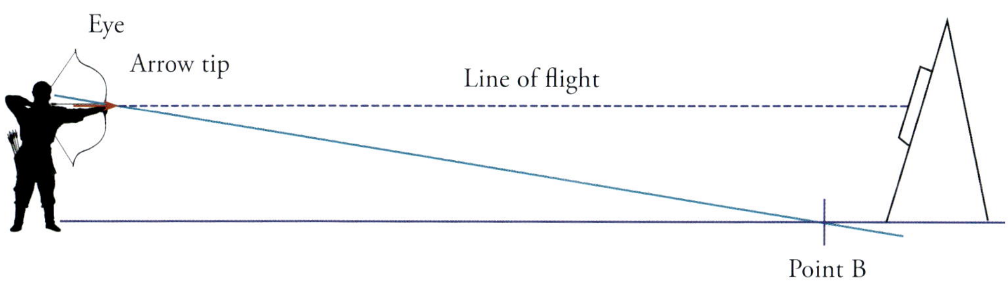

After half of the students have decided where their own individual mark on the ground will be, they lay their bows to one side and walk forward to place their coloured pegs on the spot. Then the other half of the group does the same. Each student now has their own orientation points: one at their feet and one just in front of the target. From the perspective of the archer, standing sideways to the target, both lines C–B and A–B should lie in the same plane (see Diagram 2).

Diagram 2

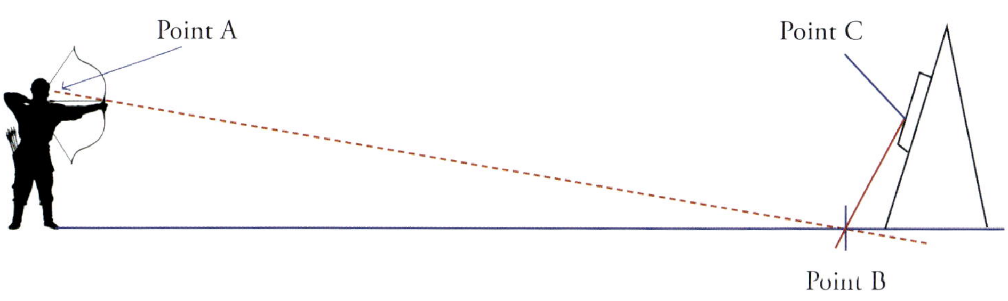

Putting it into practice

Although every student can shoot and (hopefully) hit the target on their own, they continue to work in pairs, with their partner observing and offering corrections if necessary. This is the best way to ensure that as many arrows as possible hit the target and do not fly into the netting.

Now the students can work on improving their aim by adjusting the placement of their coloured peg. If a student's arrows land high on the target then, after everyone has fired their three arrows, the student brings their peg closer to the shooting line. If the arrows land low, they move the peg closer to the target; similarly, if the arrows land more to the left or more to the right. In this way, slowly but surely, the students gain in confidence and accuracy.

It has been my experience that practising this method for at least two lessons is worthwhile. The young archers become surer of themselves and more skilful, which will be to their advantage when it comes to shooting with a proper sight.

Shooting with a sight

At the beginning of the fourth lesson, the students can begin to practise using the sight (until now, if one is attached to the bow, it should simply be turned the wrong way round to render it useless). The students take aim as before, using arrow tip and peg, then they align the sight with the centre of the target. With this simple procedure, most of the students are able to set their own sights and the teacher is free to focus on those who are having difficulty.

In the second lesson block, which ideally takes place three or four months later, the students continue to work on improving their skill in shooting with a sight. This is the time for assessing the finer points of their technique and addressing such questions as, 'Why do my arrows tend to fly to the right?', 'What can I do to prevent my bow arm from jerking upwards at the moment of release?' and 'What is the best breathing technique while shooting?' The teacher, as ever, is on hand to correct any errors and advise on any problems that may have crept in.

Safety

Remember: every bow with a nocked arrow is a weapon! Caution is essential: even a toy bow can be a dangerous weapon.

During shooting, all students must remain behind the shooting line and there should be complete silence. This is necessary in order to create an atmosphere of calm in which every student is able to concentrate on their performance, on their stance, their breathing and their technique. The signals that the teacher gives at the start and the end of each shooting practice must be clear and strictly observed. Only when the signal for retrieving arrows has been given is talking allowed.

If the proper safety measures are adhered to, archery can offer young people many exciting and wonderful experiences.

Climbing: Feeling Your Way and Holding Firm

David Brodbeck

Climbing is one of the basic ways in which very small children explore their surroundings, preceded by crawling and toddling. They grasp at objects to pull themselves up into a standing position and it isn't long before they're climbing higher. They clamber over furniture and other obstacles and struggle up the stairs; later, they climb walls and trees, continually striving for new goals. Each time they get to the top, they feel proud and happy.

It is essential that small children get the chance to indulge in a variety of climbing experiences as often as possible. These are a great way of training elementary forms of movement as well as honing the senses. The four lower senses of touch, life, movement and balance (see p. 15) are of great significance, the senses of touch and balance are especially tested in the act of climbing. Because urban life today does not really lend itself to training the senses, schools must take on the job in order to provide enough opportunities for healthy development. As they feel their way, keeping their balance, overcoming their fears, pausing to assess their situation and look for the next hold, meeting one challenge after another, children move higher towards their goal.

In this sense, climbing can be taken as a metaphor for life as we start out at the bottom and strive upwards towards our goal. It makes us intensively aware of many of life's challenges and can be a help in taking them on and mastering them.

Educational aspects

Other, equally important, aspects also deserve our consideration here. Trust plays a large part in climbing. On the one hand the children and young people must learn to trust themselves and their abilities. What counts in the end is how they perform, how alert and focused they are, and how skilful. But they must also trust the person belaying the rope at the bottom of whatever climbing wall or rock face they are on. They must feel that that person's attention is directed wholly towards them and their welfare, and only when they feel secure in this trust are they free to concentrate on what they need to do. Climbing and a degree of social competence therefore go hand in hand.

Courage is another quality children need to cultivate. The higher they climb, the more they rely on their inner fortitude to reach their goal. There are often difficult stretches to negotiate, but once they reach the top, the children can have the feeling that they can achieve whatever they put their heart into. These are valuable experiences that will prove useful, even crucial, in later life.

Climbing outdoors in nature is a particularly valuable experience. It gets the children outside in the fresh air and allows them to feel part of the natural world – they can feel the rock and enjoy the view. In planning the trip they can research the geographical and geological features, studying the terrain and the weather forecast. They can prepare themselves inwardly for the conditions they will encounter and the challenges they will face.

Climbing according to age and stage

Classes 1, 2 and 3

In the Lower School, children's early experiences of climbing are provided through a variety of obstacle courses made with gym equipment. Through imaginative pictures and stories the courses are transformed into enchanted landscapes that the children clamber over, continually working on and improving their fine motor skills.

Classes 4, 5 and 6

This is the right time to learn the various climbing knots, which are excellent for honing coordination skills and dexterity. It is also important that children get as much free climbing practice – that is, without instruction – as possible. This can take place in the form of games on the lower section of a climbing frame or in the boulder area or the safer parts of a climbing wall. The children can be introduced to belaying methods at this time. Top rope climbing in the hall or at an outdoor climbing wall is a further option.

Classes 7 and 8

Climbing really comes into its own for this age group. Adolescents are trying to find out who they are. They need challenges and want to test their limits, and climbing provides the perfect opportunity to do this. It is a good time to begin work on climbing technique – both bouldering on a climbing wall as well as in rocky areas outdoors. Find tricky sections, with overhangs, and practise them with the students for as long as it takes until they succeed. They want to see how far they can go. If there is an opportunity to climb outdoors, the students could begin climbing longer routes with several lengths of climbing rope. In order to succeed in this, they must learn how to set up the belay station, how to thread and take up rope, and how to fix intermediate belays. Further challenges that can be set might include letting one of the students lead the route and abseiling down the rock face once they've reached the top.

Class 9 onwards

Options for Upper School classes include further work on climbing technique, belaying, top rope climbing, falls and descending routes. Where possible, it is good to find challenging tasks that demand more endurance and stamina. Projects such as the following can offer amazing experiences: longer routes using several lengths of climbing rope; mountain tours, including crossing glaciers and ridge walking; and tours from one ski hut to another can offer amazing experiences.

Spacial Dynamics: Inner and Outer Movement

Jaimen McMillan

Spacial Dynamics is a discipline that explores the manifold properties of human movement and studies the ever-changing relationship of the moving human being to the space around them in any given activity. This encompasses every sort of movement, be it in leisure time, in games and sport, or at work or in therapy. It also considers which conditions affect movement in beneficial and harmful ways.

This essay will address the application of Spacial Dynamics to physical education and movement in Waldorf schools, where it is presently taught in more than thirty countries around the world.

Aspects of Spacial Dynamics

Spacial Dynamics can be characterised in four ways: as a science, a teaching art, an educational speciality and a recognised form of movement therapy.

Spacial Dynamics as a science

Spacial Dynamics develops greater sensitivity for perceiving movement, as well as being a systematic method of organising, assessing and utilising these perceptions.

Spacial Dynamics as a teaching art

Spacial Dynamics can show us how to teach any material, not just physical education, and as such it is used in teacher training programmes and in colleges and universities all around the world. It shows how teachers can use the surrounding space as a means of encountering children in an open and warm-hearted manner, inviting them into the space. It also demonstrates how teachers can regulate their own personal space in order to maintain their health and well-being. The constant invading of personal space, as when a teacher is besieged by children all clamouring for attention, can be a contributor to exhaustion and burnout among teachers.

Spacial Dynamics as an educational speciality

Spacial Dynamics has a growing compendium of age-appropriate exercises, games and interactive activities that support children's physical, emotional and spiritual development, from kindergarten right the way through school. This wide range of exercises help children on their journey of self-development through the different spaces they experience. These are both inner and outer spaces and encompass the discovery of themselves as well as the discovery of the other.

Spacial Dynamics as movement therapy

Spacial Dynamics can also be applied as movement therapy for a number of ailments and complaints. It can help with blockages and delayed motor development as well as integrating reflexes and correcting posture. It improves the sense of balance and increases concentration and perceptive powers.

Training movement perception

Spacial Dynamics offers educators a unique approach to the perception of movement. In this discipline, the definition of movement is not limited to the physical body. Rather, human movement is seen as the interaction of the mover with the surrounding space and the forces at work within it.

The first step towards learning to perceive movement in new ways is for the educator to learn to move in new ways. Differentiated perceptions are thus made possible by spatially differentiated movements. Five of the basic human movements studied and described by Spacial Dynamics are presented below. A person can learn to move in spatial progressions, where the body is designated as 'A' and the surrounding space as 'B'. When properly applied, the differentiated forms constantly provide new ways of interacting with one's surroundings and one's companions.

1. Form

This is the physical body: A

2. Per-form

The individual performs an action that extends their physical body, A, outwards into the surrounding space, B.

A —> B

3. Pre-form

An external, rhythmical impulse – for example, music – takes hold of the individual, prompting them to respond through movement. The individual follows this rhythmical, wave-like impulse, allowing their physical movements to be formed by this wave, which flows on and then fades away.

B —> A —> B

4. Formative forces

In this instance, A, the physical body, is drawn out by B, which here represents an *ideal space rather than a physical one*. This experience is like being influenced by something that is not yet manifest, something that acts like an impulse of the future, a force of becoming.

B < A

5. In-form

This is formed by the interaction with another individual, C. The first individual, A, performs an action or sequence of movements within the surrounding space, B. The second individual, C, receives what flows from that space and then responds as they feel moved to do so. This creates reciprocation and communication within the space.

A <==> B <==> C

Spacial Dynamics uses this model of spatial differentiation in educational settings to progress from observing movement to analysing, evaluating and, ultimately, enhancing movement.

Spacial skilfulness and the art of teaching

Meeting children where they are

Children at every age have different physical, emotional and developmental needs. In addition, they also have a need to be met and addressed in a way that takes account of and respects their own personal space. There are teachers who are very successful with children of a particular age, but who are often less successful when interacting with children of other ages. It is a rare teacher who can be effective with students of all ages, but those who are all share one particular ability: they are able to meet children as they are, where they are.

Teachers can develop a greater sensitivity for these educational encounters by studying the art of spatial communication. Nonverbal communication plays an important part in all human interaction. What we want to communicate, the power of our spoken words, can be amplified and supported when accompanied by the silent language of our gestures and posture and the way we move and inhabit a space. This in turn affects the mood and the quality of that space, and it is this flexibility of the spatial context, not simply what is contained within it, that allows the teacher to encounter and address each child and each age group in the appropriate way.

This ability to modulate the quality of a space to suit a variety of encounters also helps teachers become more effective in communicating with their students. The children are at ease in their space as the teacher is in theirs, and the effective teacher will be able to 'hold' the space and command the attention of the children. They will be able to hear and understand the teacher better. However, this does not mean that the children are addressed as in the movement described above: A —> B, teacher —> children, where the children are passive receptacles of what the teacher is expressing. Rather, the teacher will be heard and understood better because the children themselves have become the source of the teacher's attention and dedication, which in turn determines the content, intonation and volume of their voice.

Training movement through the use of space

One idea that offers a whole new approach to teaching acrobatics, circus arts and sport is that a movement in space can be anticipated by the teacher before a child carries out that movement. The teacher prepares the path and location in advance, making it easier for the children to slip into it. As a result the teacher intervenes less and observation becomes less intrusive.

Mastery

Spacial Dynamics was developed out of the study of skill and mastery. Classical physical education, as the term suggests, has always laid emphasis on the physical aspects of training. Those who are unsuccessful at certain exercises are told to develop more stamina and try harder. However, the secret of mastery lies not in trying harder, but in developing a sense of ease, in perceiving the flow of the movement itself and flowing with it, rather than trying clumsily to force it.

Spacial Dynamics reveals the movement 'behind' any game, exercise, sport or other activity. This movement is visualised as dynamic patterns in space that the body can learn to follow. Our muscles, in addition to their reflexive, automatic and protective functions, are trained to perceive and ultimately follow a certain movement.

In this way Spacial Dynamics helps us to cultivate a greater awareness of how we move, and this can also have therapeutic benefits. By becoming more sensitive to movement and by identifying and connecting with the essence of every movement, we are led to a more authentic, intuitive experience of ourselves, one that is born out of the will in the act of doing. The most important human achievement is the ability to change, but often we resist change. We may be hurt by something or, even worse, traumatised. By directing our awareness to the archetypes and the ideals of the space around us, and learning to follow them with our bodies, we are presented with a basis upon which change becomes possible. For we now begin with what is changeable, what is not yet manifest, we begin to engage with a whole world of unlimited possibilities.

The foremost method of teaching Spacial Dynamics is demonstration. This presents the teacher with a huge challenge. Their posture, bearing and movements must represent the ideals behind what they are teaching. A large part of Spacial Dynamics training consists of recreating the archetypes in one's own space, and then training one's own body to move in accordance with these ideals. Through this rigorous training, the teacher's movements will give children and adolescents glimpses of the archetype. This movement training represents, at the same time, a process of self-development for the teacher.

Learning to experience oneself in this way, as initiator and director of one's movements in the surrounding space, is a wonderful way to develop a will that is not solely based on the physical body. Having moments of mastery is a prerequisite for becoming a movement educator.

Incarnation and excarnation

The process of incarnation, of taking hold of and inhabiting one's body, is not the only goal of development. Excarnation, laying aside and going out of one's body, must also be learned. Spacial Dynamics aims to help children feel at home in their physical bodies as well as in the space around them. An education in meaningful movement should go beyond forming and training the physical body, the domain of traditional physical education, and shape awareness of personal, interpersonal and wider social spaces. This will open pathways for children in later life that will help them make meaningful connections with people and the world around them.

Working with space in Waldorf schools

Space is not void. Space is alive. Growing up is much more than a vertical experience. Healthy development consists of the vital interplay of internal and external growth. One important aim of the Spacial Dynamics curriculum is to cultivate students' awareness of their own movement, which itself develops out of a counter-movement. The students' spatial journey from birth onwards progresses from being held and moved by their parents or caregiver as an infant, to the childhood days of exploring and conquering the neighbourhood, then to the roaming and roving of the adolescent, culminating in the experience of independence and freedom, to free play, music, rhythm and dancing, and imaginative pictures. As regards early childhood, all the activities of Spacial Dynamics are based on emulation. This is what ultimately contributes to a spatial reversal, to the morphogenesis of the space we occupy. Long before the development of quantum physics, Rudolf Steiner postulated that matter was congealed movement. If this is the case, then it is imperative that movement education in Waldorf schools enhances children's experience of the forces of space.

Eurythmy, the Bothmer exercises and Spacial Dynamics are taught in Waldorf schools around the world. Eurythmy makes the forces behind speech and music visible through specific movements. The Bothmer exercises are an approach to physical education developed Fritz Graf von Bothmer for the Waldorf schools (see pp. 196f). Both are largely characterised by their use of geometrical forces. Spacial Dynamics, developed by Jaimen McMillan and inspired by the work of Rudolf Steiner, supports both of these disciplines in the Waldorf curriculum by contributing exercises that work with the formative forces of curves, spirals, lemniscates and vortices. The exercises are characterised by dynamic, fluid rhythms and the flowing qualities of water. In this sense, Spacial Dynamics has developed the PACT model for schools (Pentathlon, Arts, Cooperation, and Truce). Developed by Thom Schaefer and Jaimen McMillan, this model has adapted the five classical Greek disciplines to the needs of pre-adolescent children. Combining the arts, athletics and a non-competitive scoring model, this is now found in hundreds of Waldorf schools worldwide.

As well as being used in schools, Spacial Dynamics is also employed in curative education worldwide as a form of movement therapy. The integration of reflexes, postural problems, scoliosis, ADHD, balance disorders and learning difficulties are just a few of the developmental challenges that can be supported through the use of Spacial Dynamics as movement therapy. Licensed Spacial Dynamics teachers and therapists are qualified to carry out this work in Waldorf schools.

Space is the human fabric that each person wears according to the situation they find themselves in. Through a corresponding sequence of games, space can become a social fabric, with which we can weave a tapestry of cooperation, respect and healthy challenges.

For further information on Spacial Dynamics please see www.spacialdynamics.com.

Football: The Individual and the Team

Christian Boettger

No other team game has caused more controversy in Waldorf schools than football. In this essay, I would like to make the case for a creative and innovative debate on the topic. My thoughts have been inspired by the book, *Rettet das Spiel. Weil Leben mehr als Funktionieren ist* (*Save the Game: Life is More Than Just Existing*) by Gerald Hüther and Christoph Quarch. To begin with, the authors describe how important it is that human beings cultivate a form of learning and living that is, in the best sense of the word, playful:

> Playing together renders development and innovation possible. Playgrounds are landing grounds, allowing something new to come into the world.[1]

This type of human being, known as *homo ludens*, which, loosely translated, means 'playful human', has an adversary in *homo economicus*, the 'economic human'. The authors show how financial incentives place games within an economic monoculture that sees them in purely business terms.[2] To counter this, they develop a phenomenology of play that postulates three inherent qualities: connectedness (I and you), freedom and presentation. When these three qualities coincide, space is created for potential development.[3] The authors also state that there are:

> Five basic categories of game, which encompass all the games in the world: games of skill, competitive games, cult games (those that do not have mass appeal or have reached a mass audience but still have a dedicated following), play-acting and games of chance.[4]

Games that manage to combine as many of these categories as possible are particularly attractive, not only to players but also to spectators. Interestingly, the authors come to the following conclusion: all five types of game, as well as the three inherent qualities of play, are reflected in the game of football, right up to international level.[5]

Although there are many team sports, it is football that has provoked the most vehement discussion in Waldorf schools.[6] There are many weighty arguments against football.[7] It is undeniable that the game focusses largely on the movement and skills of the legs and feet, with the head being used as a kind of third limb so to speak whenever a player heads the ball. There are also a number of arguments against football that deal with the commercialisation of the sport, the behaviour of crowds at games and the almost tribal mentality that can prevail. Any Waldorf school that wants to introduce football into P.E. lessons should consider these issues with parents and Upper School students before arriving at a decision.[8] However, one conclusion that can be drawn from the discussions mentioned above, and one that I would like to put on record, is that banning football in Waldorf schools cannot be justified by claiming that Rudolf Steiner disapproved of the game.

If we take a look at how active children and young people are today, we must accept that the conditions in which they are growing up are completely different from those of the early twentieth century, when the first Waldorf school was being established and its curriculum drawn up. P.E. lessons alone will not provide children and young people with enough exercise to ensure their healthy physical development. Dexterity, stamina, coordination and all-round awareness are some of the qualities that P.E. lessons can cultivate, but constant, independent practice is necessary to develop true mastery. Therefore, those games and sports that children can easily play in their free time and that encourage them to meet up and be active outside of school are worth considering for inclusion in school during P.E. lessons. This can help push back against the increasing amount of time that children spend using digital media these days. It should also be noted that a general lack of movement and too much sitting have a particularly adverse effect on legs, feet and back.

No other game, including rounders, dodgeball, hockey, handball, basketball and volleyball, is as undemanding and as easy to organise as a game of football. It makes no difference how many players turn up, how big the playing field is or even what sort of ball is used: two players, a ball and jumpers for goalposts are all that are needed to get a kickabout started. In my experience, this is what makes the game so popular, both in the playground and after school, and in order to get children up and moving, we should set the bar as low as possible. It is also important that children learn to deal with the social aspects of games themselves, such as enforcing rules and deciding on variations to the game, as well as resolving discussions on alleged infringements. Along with the exercise the children get, this aspect of social encounter is of great importance. In the playground, however, one rule is obligatory, namely that ball games only take place in the designated area, to keep accidents and injuries to a minimum.

In P.E. lessons, some students never tire of asking to play football, but it can be difficult to cater for the greatly varying levels of skill shown by children and adolescents. What is more, there is never enough time to achieve a satisfactory level with the majority of the students, unless additional sports groups are on offer after lessons or the students choose to practise in their free time.

Nevertheless, in any given ball game, it is worthwhile trying out all sorts of variations and, where necessary, adapting the rules. In this respect, the game of football is perhaps the most versatile. For example, many sorts of ball can be used: playing with a softball can help those students with less experience of the game develop confidence and be less afraid of the ball; a tennis ball, being much smaller, can help students develop quicker reactions and finer coordination skills.

Other variations of the game include sliding football, in which the players move around the floor of the gym on their bottoms. Then there is crab football, in which players support themselves on their hands and move with their feet in the manner of crabs. Similarly, there is three-legged football, in which two players on the same side have two legs tied together like in a three-legged race, meaning they must move together and coordinate the way they control the ball. It can be an interesting, not to say delicate, task deciding who partners whom.

Football can also be played while applying the rules of other team games. What a difference it makes when, for example, ice hockey rules apply and the game is played with a small ball and small goals. Then there is football tennis, perhaps not quite so suitable for P.E. lessons, because only a small number of children can play at any one time. This is also the case with footvolley, where football is played according to the rules of beach volleyball.

Siefried Eith, a member of the GEW Sport Commission (the German trade union for education and science), recommends the following variation:

> In each corner of the gym, not too near the walls, two cones are placed to form a small goal. A goal only counts if a fellow teammate stops the shot behind the goal. My teammates must put themselves in the right position. It is no good simply thumping the ball towards one of the goals. Which goals do I defend? Where might I score one? Nothing is fixed, it all depends on how the game develops.[9]

In conclusion, I would like to reiterate my plea that if children are keen to play and exert themselves then we must encourage them, and if they wish to play football, we should react calmly and imaginatively, not dogmatically. Children should be able to play to their heart's content and learn as many skills as possible. What is more, when young players learn to agree on and stick to the rules in team games then they are on the road to social competence. The question of how best to integrate this game into P.E. lessons should be considered regularly in the corresponding P.E. teachers' conferences.

Appendix: Guidelines for P.E. Lessons in Waldorf Schools

The guidelines presented below were laid down in the autumn of 2016 by colleagues participating in a training course for physical education teachers in Waldorf schools. They arose from a need to exchange ideas about basic principles of P.E. teaching and to lay down meaningful guidelines to underpin pedagogical work in schools. We also hope that they contribute to quality control in lessons and cooperation in teacher training.

Where at all possible, we believe that P.E. lessons in Waldorf schools should pursue the following aims:

- To be co-educational and take into account the different cultural background of students.
- To include the Bothmer exercises as a central element of the P.E. curriculum.
- To be taught, where possible, by one male and one female teacher, whereby they are both involved with the whole class.
- To be double lessons.
- To take into account the developmental stage of children, and take care to avoid activities that, from an anthroposophical point of view, the children are not yet ready for. Similarly, learning targets should be adapted to the developmental needs of the children.
- To be carried out holistically, addressing body, soul and spirit. This approach is reinforced by a rhythmical repetition of activities, in the form of block lessons over a period of time as well as within single lessons.
- To contribute towards social learning and community spirit. Extracurricular activities such as circus projects are an extension of these aims.
- To be open to students with additional support needs and to guarantee specialist assistance where required.
- To aim to make movement a pleasurable experience and lay the foundation for a life of activity.
- To take place in the appropriate surroundings, with appropriate equipment, in order to provide a wide range of activities.
- To profit from a lively exchange with other members of staff in order to find common themes in other subjects that might be taken up in P.E. lessons.
- To require teachers to invest time in further training, with an emphasis on the anthroposophical background to Waldorf education.
- To require teachers to keep up to date with current developments in their subject.

Acknowledgements

We would like to thank the contributors to this book who have made their specialist knowledge and years of experience available to readers; the photographers, especially Elisabeth Steffe, who is responsible for most of the photographs; and Christian Boettger of the Pedagogical Research Section of the Federation of Waldorf Schools. Thanks to our colleagues, Alexander Koekebakker and Leif Büchner.

Special thanks also to the many students, parents and colleagues of the Waldorf School in Freiburg-Wiehre, who gave this project enthusiastic support and donated their time to help us.

We would specially like to thank Geoff Hunter for translating this book into English

Gerlinde Idler and Lutz Gerding

Editors and Contributors

The editors

Gerlinde Idler

Born near Vienna in 1968, Gerlinde Idler has been a teacher of physical education in Waldorf schools for over twenty years. She is a lecturer in Waldorf education at the Kassel Teacher Training College in Germany, where she helps people from other professions train to become physical education teachers, and a guest lecturer at Waldorf teacher-training courses around the world. She holds a Masters degree in sociology, educational and political science as well as in Bothmer Movement and Spacial Dynamics.

Lutz Gerding

Born in 1963, Lutz Gerding began his teaching career at the Waldorf school in Bremen. After further training in adult education he became a tutor at Kassel Teacher Training College in Germany, helping people from other professions train to become physical education teachers. He is currently a lecturer and coordinator for teacher training in China.

The contributors

Dieter Bigler

After completing his Waldorf teacher training at the teacher training college in Dornach, Dieter went on to work as a class teacher in institutions for children with additional learning needs throughout southern Germany. Further training at the College of Physical Education led to him teaching movement, games and sport. Dieter has trained in Spacial Dynamics (Levels 1–3), and in game pedagogy at the Academy for Movement, Games and Coaching. Since 2005, he has been the head of Movement and Body Therapy in the psychiatric clinic in St Urban, Lucerne. He is a founder member and board member of the Verband Spacial Dynamics Europa, and a founder member and board member of the IAABT (International Association for Anthroposophic Body Therapy of the Medical Section of the Goetheanum).

Jürg Bigler

Born in Zürich, Switzerland, in 1958, Jürg did his teacher training in Zofingen, Switzerland, and then a pedagogical course in physical education in Heidenheim, Germany. He also undertook a year's scientific study course at the Goetheanum. He is a class teacher, with a focus on English and sport, at the Bergschule Avrona as well as at the Rudolf Steiner school in Bern Ittigen, Switzerland. Since 2005, he has been the course instructor for the International Conference of Sports Teachers (athletics).

Michael Birnthaler

Michael studied Sport, Art and Educational Science before training as a Waldorf teacher and going on to teach physical education at various Waldorf schools in Germany. He carried out his research project on adventure-based teaching and Waldorf pedagogy, and was awarded his doctorate on the subject of adventure sports. Michael is the founder and head of the organization EOS-Erlebnispädagogik (www.eos-ep.de). He has contributed to various publications and is a guest lecturer at several universities.

Christian Boettger

Christian studied aerospace engineering to become a chartered engineer before doing his Waldorf teacher training in Stuttgart. For nineteen years he taught maths and physics, with sport as a secondary subject, for the Upper School in Waldorf schools in Karlsruhe and Schopfheim. Since 2006, Christian has been the managing director of the Federation of German Waldorf Schools and the Pedagogical Research Section. He has worked on many research projects and publications dealing with Waldorf education. Since 2011, he has worked in extra-occupational teacher training.

David Brodbeck

David attended the Waldorf school in Basel, Switzerland. After working as a carpenter, David did his teacher training at the college in Heidenheim, where he focused on teaching sport, and then, later, at the college in Stuttgart, where he trained as a class teacher. From 1988 to 1999, he taught P.E. and was a class teacher at the Waldorf school in Ittigen, Switzerland. After further training in curative pedagogy, David worked as a special education teacher at the Bergschule Avrona in Steffisbur. Alongside this, he also set up various circus projects, and led climbing and skiing trips.

Adrian Constantinescu

Born in Bucharest, Romania, in 1971, Adrian has many years' experience working in curative education teaching P.E., as well as working with individual pupils with additional learning needs. Since 2008, he has taught P.E. at the Waldorf school in Kassel. He also teaches Bothmer Movement to children and adults. Adrian is a lecturer and trainer for the International Bothmer Gymnastics Training College.

Claudio Czak-Lindemann

Born in Salzburg, Austria, in 1974, Claudio attended college for physical education and the Bothmer School for Gymnastics and Movement Therapy. From 1994 to 2014, Claudio taught P.E. at the Waldorf school in Markgräferland and is presently working at the Rudolf Steiner school in Basel. He is a board member of the committee running the Waldorf sports teachers' conference, a guest lecturer for acrobatics at the University of Stuttgart and, until 2016, at the Academy for Anthroposophical Pedagogy in Basel, lecturing in gymnastics and Bothmer Movement. He is a founding member and supervisor of a training initiative begun in Kassel, Germany, in the summer of 2012, for people looking to switch from other professions into teaching physical education.

Barbara Dawid

Born in 1950, Barbara trained as a P.E. teacher, with secondary subjects in woodwork and technical drawing, at the state training college in Munich, Germany. She went on to teach the subject for classes 1 to 12 at the Waldorf school Chiemgau in Upper Bavaria, Germany. She lectures at the teaching colleges in Munich and Bochum-Langendreer.

Dr Elisabeth Frank

Born in Vienna, in 1951, Dr Frank is a general practitioner and paediatrician, qualified in anthropososophical medicine and psychotherapy. She has worked as a school doctor in Austria, Switzerland and Ghana, and was the school doctor at the Rudolf Steiner school in Vienna-Mauer for twenty-four years. She has taught in hospitals, schools, kindergartens and training colleges. Dr Frank currently works as a paediatrician.

Astrid Jochens

Astrid studied sociology and psychology in Munich, Germany, before attending the teacher training college for Waldorf teachers in Stuttgart, where she trained as a class teacher with a focus on sport. Astrid trained in curative education in Bonn, and later did a course in dance pedagogy. Since then, Astrid has been a class teacher at the Waldorf school in Reutlingen. Astrid runs various dancing groups for children and adults.

Alexander Koekebakker

Alexander was born in Toronto, Canada, in 1965. After attending the Waldorf school in Toronto, Alexander studied German language and literature at the University of Toronto and the University of Freiburg, in Germany. He later trained in Bothmer Movement. Since 1995, he has been the teacher for P.E. and English at the Waldorf school in Freiburg-Wiehre. He is also a founder member of the school circus. Since 2009, he has been the chairman of the committee running the Waldorf sports teachers' conference. Alexander is guest lecturer for gymnastics and acrobatics at Stuttgart University and, until 2016, at the Academy for Anthroposophical Education in Basel, Switzerland. He is a founding member and supervisor of a training initiative begun in Kassel, Germany, in the summer of 2012, for people looking to switch from other professions into teaching physical education.

Jaimen McMillan

Born in 1950, Jaimen has dedicated his life to the study of human movement. He is the founder of Spacial Dynamics and, since 1985, has been in charge of the Spacial Dynamics Institute. For over twenty years he ran the Graf Bothmer Gymnastics School Stuttgart e.V. together with Alheidis von Bothmer. As an author, lecturer and trainer, he has made significant contributions to the fields of movement education, movement therapy and leadership development for over forty years. Jaimen McMillan runs training programmes for P.E. teachers, counsellors and doctors.

Malte Pontoppidan

Born in Flensburg, Germany, in 1976, Malte graduated from the Waldorf school in Flensburg in 1995 and spent the following year doing voluntary social work in anthroposophical institutions in Israel (Beer Sheva) and Hamburg. From 1998 to 2001, he did an apprenticeship and worked as a boat- and shipbuilder in Plön and Kappeln, in the Schleswig-Holstein region of Germany. After a two years at sea as a nautical officer's assistant from 2002–03, Malte trained to become a woodwork and class teacher at the training college in Kiel. He spent three years as a class teacher at the Waldorf school in Braunschweig. Since 2009, he has been the woodwork and sailing teacher at the Waldorf school in Flensburg.

Alfred Schachl

Alfred was born in Morbach, Germany, in 1961. After graduating from school, Alfred did a basic training course in acrobatics in Cologne. This was followed by a course in rural home economics and training in Bothmer Movement in Stuttgart. After two years of freelance work, he started teaching P.E., circus skills, and technology at the Rudolf Steiner school in Lüneburg. Alfred is the founder of the Tabasco circus, which still performs regularly, and is the co-author of a book on circus games.

Benz Schaffner

Born in Peru, in 1959, Benz attended the Waldorf school in Basel, Switzerland, and then teacher training college where he trained as a P.E. teacher. Since 1982, he has taught P.E. at the Rudolf Steiner school in Basel, where he later became a class teacher. He is a founder member of the P.E. teachers' workshop in Heidenheim, and an instructor for youth and sport at the sport college of Switzerland. Benz is also a founder member of the European committee of sports teachers at Steiner schools. Until 2016, he was the supervisor of gymnastics and sport at the Academy for Anthroposophical Pedagogy. As well as lecturing, Benz continues to work with teachers on the subject of movement and P.E.

Silvia Tampe

Silvia was born in Heidenheim, Germany, in 1959. After graduating from school, Silvia did a one-year study course at the College for Eurythmy and Speech Formation in K] ngen, followed by a three-year course at the Graf-Bothmer School of Gymnastics in Stuttgart. She finally completed her studies at the pedagogical college for physical education at the Waldorf school in Heidenheim. Since 1987, Silvia has been a P.E. teacher for classes 1 to 12 at the Waldorf school in Heidenheim. She also lectures at conferences.

Bernard Thiry

Bernard was born in Namur, Belgium, in 1967. After studying eurythmy in London and Birmingham, Bernard trained in Bothmer Movement and Spacial Dynamics. He has worked as a dancer in a variety of genres and made numerous international appearances. Bernard is the founder of a dance school in France.

Christiane Weide

Born in Kassel, Germany, in 1962, Christiane studied sport and gymnastics in Stuttgart, before attending the sports teachers' college in Heidenheim, Germany. Since 1985, she has taught P.E. for classes 1 to 12 at the Emil Molt School in Berlin. Christiane is a member of the committee providing further training for sports teachers, and runs a course with emphasis on gymnastic games for small children and apparatus gymnastics. For many years, she was lecturer for methodology and didactics in apparatus gymnastics at the Waldorf teacher training college in Berlin.

Eric van Wijnen

Born in Eindhoven, the Netherlands, in 1958, Eric studied at the Christian Academy for Physical Education in Arnheim. An introductory course for Upper School teachers led to his first encounter with Bothmer Movement, which he went on to study in Stuttgart. Eric taught at the Parcival College and the Boerderijschool in Groningen. Since 2012, Eric has taught P.E. at the Waldorf school in Märkisches Viertel, Berlin. Alongside his work with Bothmer Movement International, Eric is also a guest lecturer for various educational institutions. He is a founding member and supervisor of a training initiative begun in Kassel, Germany, in the summer of 2012, for people looking to switch from other professions into teaching P.E.

Picture Credits

Elisabeth Steffe: almost all photographs

Charlotte Fischer: photos of child movement development, football and inclusion

Ashraf El-Gammal: photos for the article on Bothmer Gymnastics

Ulrike Prasch: skiing photos

Johannes Nitsche: fencing photos

Astrid Jochens: folk-dance photos

Malte Pontoppidan: sailing photos

Alexander Koekebakker: photos of pupils at athletics and on the gymnastics equipment

David Brodbeck: photos of outdoor climbing

Michael Birnthaler: photos of adventure-based learning

Severin Bigler: close-up photos of athletics

Marc Wilhelm: photos of Upper School students at athletics games and on gymnastics equipment

Stefano Pilloni: sailing photos

Clarissa A. Hempel: photos of Spacial Dynamics

Jaimen McMillan: photos of Spacial Dynamics

Sample lesson concepts

The sample lessons in Part Two were devised by G. Idler, C. Weide, S. Trampe, A. Koekebakker, J. Bigler, C. Czak-Lindeman, and E. van Wijnen.

Endnotes

Part One: Introduction

Fundamental Aspects of Physical Education in Waldorf Schools

1. Richter, Tobias (ed), *Pädagogischer Auftrag und Unterrichtsziele. Vom Lehrplan der Waldorfschule [The Educational Tasks and Content of the Steiner-Waldorf Curriculum], Verlag Freies Geistesleben, Stuttgart 2003.* See also: *Avison, Kevin and Rawson, Martyn, The Tasks and Content of the Steiner-Waldorf Curriculum,* Floris Books, UK 2019.
2. ibid. p. 25.
3. ibid. p. 26f.
4. Steiner, Rudolf, *Study of Man: General Education Course* (CW293), Rudolf Steiner Press, UK 2011.
5. Steiner, Rudolf, *The Education of the Child,* Anthroposophic Press, USA 1996.
6. Treichler, Rudolf, *Die Entwicklung der Seele im Lebenslauf: Stufen, Störungen und Erkrankugen des Seelenlebens [The Development of the Soul in the Course of Life: Stages, Disorders and Diseases in the Soul Life],* Freies Geistesleben, Stuttgart 2012, p. 21.
7. See Soesmann, Albert, Die zwölf Sinne. *Tore der Seele [The Twelve Senses: The Gates of the Soul],* Freies Geistesleben, Stuttgart 2011.
8. See Lipps, Peter, *Temperamente und Pädagogik. Eine Darstellung für den Unterricht an der Waldorfschule [Temperaments and Pedagogy: A Guide for Teaching at the Waldorf School],* Freies Geistesleben, Germany 1998.
9. Kischnick, Rudolf, *Leibesübung und Bewusstseinsschulung [Training in Awareness and Physical Exericse],* Zbinden Verlag, Switzerland 1989, p. 29.
10. Steiner, Rudolf, *Study of Man,* p. 125f.

Movement in Childhood

1. Steiner, Rudolf, *Chance, Providence and Necessity* (CW163), Anthroposophic Press, USA 1988, p. 68.
2. Steiner, Rudolf, *Anthroposophy (A Fragment)* (CW45), SteinerBooks, USA 1996, p. 96.

All Education is Self-Education

1. Steiner, Rudolf, *The Child's Changing as the Basis of Pedagogical Practice* (CW306), Anthroposophic Press, USA 1996. Lecture of April 20, 1923.
2. Der Spiegel, 39/2017, p. 17.

Part Two: Physical Education Lessons from Class 1 to Class 12

Class 1: From Imitating to Following – Teaching Through Images and Stories

1. Nietzold, Jochem, *Geistige Struckturen sinnvollen Turnens [Mental Structures of Sensible Gymnastics],* J Ch Mellinger Verlag, Germany 1994, p. 43.
2. Meyer-Fischer, Sophia, *Reigen und Spiele 1./2. Schuljahr [Roundelays and Games for Class 1 and 2 (notes from the Conference of Sports Teachers, 1999)],* Germany 1999.
3. Steiner, Rudolf, *Soul Economy and Waldorf Education* (CW303), Anthroposophic Press, USA 1986.
4. Kischick, Rudolf and Haren, Wil van, *Dreh dich nicht um - 300 Bewegungsspiele für Kinder und Jegendlich [Don't Turn Around – 300 Games and Exercises for Kids and Everyone],* Germany 2008, p.32.
5. Kischnick, Rudolf, *Leibesübung und Bewussteinsschulung [Training in Physical Exercise and Awareness],* Zbinden Verlag, Switzerland 1989, p. 51.

Class 2: Games and Discoveries – Fables, Legends and Tales of the Natural World

1. Meyer-Fischer, Sophia, *Reigen und Spiele 1./2. Schuljahr [Roundelays and Games for Class 1 and 2],* p. 7.

Class 3: Being Active in the World – Crossing the Rubicon

1. Brounts, Tonnie and Daniel, Helga, *Bewegt ins Leben: Eurythmie In Den Klassen 1 Bis 4 [Moved into Life: Eurythmy in Classes 1 to 4],* Pädagogische Forschungsstelle, Germany 2008, p. 28.
2. ibid. p. 28f.

Class 4: Face to Face – Meeting Each Other

1. Brounts, Tonnie and Daniel, Helga, *Bewegt ins Leben: Eurythmie In Den Klassen 1 Bis 4 [Moved into Life: Eurythmy in Classes 1 to 4],* p. 36.

Class 6: Accuracy and Geometry – the Emergence of Rules and Laws

1. Kischnick, Rudolf, *Leibesübung und Bewussteinsschulung [Training in Physical Exercise and Awareness],* p. 73.
2. ibid. p. 54.
3. ibid. p. 84.

Class 7: Inner and Outer Limits – Inventors and Explorers

1. Kischnick, Rudolf, *Leibesübung und Bewussteinsschulung [Training in Physical Exercise and Awareness]*, p. 40.
2. ibid. p. 40.

Class 9: Tension and Release – the Turbulent Years

1. Avison, Kevin and Rawson, Martyn, *The Task and Contents of the Steiner-Waldorf Curriculum,* Floris Books, UK 2019, p. 201f.

Class 10: From the Centre to the Periphery – the Discus

1.Gießler, Harald, Turnen im Rahmen der Waldorfpädagogik [Gymnastics as Part of Waldorf Education], dissertation, AFRA Verlag 1997.

Class 11: Taking Aim – the Javelin

1. Bothmer, Alheidis von, *Die Bothmer-Gymnastik: Pädagogische und Therapeutische Anwendungsmöglichkeiten [Bothmer Gymnastics: Pedagogical and Therapeutic Aspects], Schattauer Verlag,* Germany 2004, p. 116.

Part Three: Exploring a Range of Games and Activities

Bothmer Exercises: A New Form of Physical Education

1. Steiner, Rudolf, *Study of Man,* p. 179.
2. Hörnlein, Katrin, interview in *Die Zeit [The Time],* 34/2015.
3. Steiner, Rudolf, *Study of Man,* p. 151.
4. A more complete description of the exercise can be found in *Bothmer, Alheidis von, Die Bothmer-Gymnastik [Bothmer Gymnastics],* p. 68.

The Bothmer Exercises in Practice: A Personal Experience

1. See Bothmer, Alheidis von, *Die Bothmer-Gymnastik [Bothmer Gymnastics]* for a more detailed description of the twenty-eight exercises.
2. ibid. p. 59.
3. ibid. p. 56.

P.E. Lessons in Classes 1 and 2: Age-appropriate Movement and the Significance of Images

1. Thanks are due to Sophia Meyer-Fischer, a former Waldorf P.E. teacher, for having noted down this verse.
2. Thanks to Johannes Hörner for this verse.

P.E. Lessons in Classes 3 and 4: 'What are we playing today?'

1. Steiner, Rudolf, *The Kingdom of Childhood* (CW311), Anthroposophic Press, USA 1995. Lecture of August 18, 1924.

An Anthroposophical Approach to Play: Cultivating Confidence and Empowerment

1. Lievegoed, Bernard, *Phases of Childhood: Growing in Body, Soul and Spirit,* Floris Books, UK 2005.
2. ibid.
3. Isenberg, Joan Packer, and Quisenberry, Nancy, *'A Position Paper of the Association for Childhood Education International – Play: Essential for all Children',* in Childhood Education, 79:1, 2002, p 33.
4. Lievegoed, Bernard, *Phases of Childhood.*
5. Schiller, Friedrich, *On the Aesthetic Education of Man, Penguin Classics,* UK 2016.

Apparatus and Floor Gymnastics: Between Tension and Dynamics

1. Steiner, Rudolf, *Menschengeschichte im Lichte der Geistesforschung [Human History in the Light of Spiritual Research] (GA 61),* Rudolf Steiner Verlag, Switzerland 1983, p. 430.

Athletics: A Wealth of Challenges

1. Steiner, Rudolf, *Speech and Drama* (CW282), Anthroposophic Press, USA 1986. See lectures of September 5 and 12, 1924.
2. See Unminger, Walter, Helden, Götter, Übermenschen. *Eine Kulturgeschichte menschlicher Höchstleistungen [Heroes, Gods, Supermen. A Cultural History of Human Excellence],* Ex Libris, Switzerland 1962, p. 24.

Swimming: The Pool as a Classroom

1. On the subject of the temperaments, see Lipps, Peter, *Temperamente und Pädagogik. Eine Darstellung für den Unterricht an der Waldorfschule [Temperaments and Pedagogy: A Guide for Teaching at the Waldorf School].*
2. Kischnick, Rudolf, *Leibesübung und Bewussteinsschulung [Training in Physical Exercise and Awareness],* p. 143f.
3. Gunther Frank, *Koordinative Fähigkeiten im Schwimmen: Der Schlüssel zur perfekten Technik [Coordination Skills in Swimming: The Key to the Perfect Technique],* Hofmann GmbH, Germany 2008, p. 159.
4. Excellent methodical tips for practising swimming technique can be found in, *Bayrische Landesstelle für Schulsport (publ.),* Schwimmen unterrichten, Auer Verlag, Augsburg 2013.
5. Stockmeyer, E. A. Karl, *Rudolf Steiner's Curriculum for Steiner-Waldorf Schools: An Attempt to Summarise his Indications.*

Folk Dancing: Expressing Soul and Character

1. Stingel, Manfred, *Geschichte des Tanzes, Broschüre der Volkstanzgruppe Frommern [History of Dance: A Brochure of the Frommern Folk Dance Group]* p. 1.
2. Neff, Kurt, Vom Tanz. *Ein Lesebuch [Dance: A Reader],* p. 24.
3. Teichmann, Frank, *Der Mensch und sein Tempel: Griechenland [Greece: Man and His Temple],* p. 121.
4. Klein, Gabriele, Frauen Körper Tanz. *Eine Zivilisationsgeschichte des Tanzes [Female Dance: A History],* p. 35.
5. Steiner, Rudolf, *From Mammoths to Mediums* (CW350), p. 9.
6. ibid. p. 11.
7. Kügelgen, Helmut von, *'Von der Würde des Kindes' ['On the Dignity of the Child'],* published in *Erziehungskunst [Waldorf Education],* p.365.
8. Neff, Kurt, Vom Tanz. *Ein Lesebuch [Dance: A Reader],* p. 38.
9. ibid. p. 38.

Rhythmic Gymnastics and the Bothmer Exercises

1. Hardtmuth, Thomas, *Das Verborgene Ich: Aspekte zum Verständnis der Krebskrankheit [The Hidden Me: Understanding Cancer],* Amthor Verlag, Heidenheim 2003.
2. ibid.
3. Wallmann, Alina, *'Rhythmische Sportgymnastik' ['Rhythmic Gymnastics'],* diploma thesis at the Free University Stuttgart, 2012.
4. Illustration taken from *Bothmer, Alheidis von, Die Bothmer-Gymnastik [Bothmer Gymnastics],* p. 98.
5. ibid.
6. Aristotle, De Anima 432a1.
7. Bothmer, Alheidis von, *Die Bothmer-Gymnastik [Bothmer Gymnastics].*
8. ibid.

Winter Sports: Skiing, Skating and Snowboarding

1. Richter, Tobias (ed.), *Pädagogischer Auftrag und Unterrichtsziele. Vom Lehrplan der Waldorfschule, Verlag Freies Geistesleben [The Educational Tasks and Content of the Steiner-Waldorf Curriculum],* Stuttgart 2003, p. 381.
2. ibid. p. 381.
3. ibid. p. 381.
4. ibid. p. 385.
5. ibid. p. 385.
6. ibid. p. 387ff.
7. *Skilehrplan Band 1: Ski alpin; Band 2: Skilanglauf; Band 3: Kinderskilauf [Ski curriculum – Volume 1: Alpine skiing; Volume 2: Cross-Country Skiing; Volume 3: Children's skiing],* BLV Verlagsgesellschaft, Munich 1999.
8. cf. Nietzold, Jochem, *Geistige Strukturen sinnvollen Turnens [Mental Structures of Sensible Gymnastics],* p. 54.
9. ibid. p. 152.

Adventure-based Learning: Knowing the Group, Knowing Yourself

1. Steiner, Rudolf, *Konferenzen mit den Lehrern der Freien Waldorfschule 1919 bis 1924 [Conferences with the Teachers of the Free Waldorf School, 1919 to 1924]* (GA300), p. 300.
2. See Birnthaler, Michael, *Teamspiele. Die 100 besten Gruppenspiele [Team Games: The 100 Best Group Games],* Verlag Freies Geistesleben, Stuttgart 2014.
3. Further information available at www.eos-ep.de.
4. see Birnthaler, Michael, *Praxisbuch Erlebnispädagogik [Experiential Education: A Practice Book],* Verlag Freies Geistesleben, Stuttgart 2010.

Football: The Individual and the Team

1. Hüther, Gerald and Quarch, Christoph, *Rettet das Spiel [Save the Game],* p. 17.
2. ibid. p. 116.
3. ibid. p. 125.

4. ibid. p. 125f.
5. ibid. p. 151.
6. On this theme, I recommend Karl-Reinhard Kummer's essay 'Anthropological Aspects of Football', which appeared in the 1997 edition of the journal *Erziehungskunst [The Art of Education]* and which throws light on the anthroposophical side.
7. In 2006, just before the World Cup took place in Germany, two articles appeared in the journal *Erziehungskunst [The Art of Education],* written by Werner Neudorfer and Michael Birnthaler. The articles dealt with how the discussion on football had developed in Waldorf schools and summed up the most important arguments against playing the game (see www.erziehungskunst.de/suche/archiv-suche/?search=Fußball). A similarly intensive discussion took place in the run-up to the 2014 World Cup (see www.erziehungskunst.de/suche/?sorting=2&search=Fußball).
8. Cf. Frielingsdorf, Volker, *Waldorfpädagogik in der Erziehungswissenschaft [Waldorf Education in Science Education],* Beltz Juventa, Weinheim 2012, p. 142f. Also, Gießler, Harald, *Turnen im Rahmen der Waldorfpädagogik [Gymnastics as Part of Waldorf Education],* dissertation, AFRA Verlag 1997, Chapter 2.2.6: *Das Problem des Fußballs [The Problem of Football],* p. 101ff.
9. See www.gew-sportkommission.de/spielidee/fussballvari.html

Further Reading

Avison, Kevin and Rawson, Martyn, *The Tasks and Content of the Steiner-Waldorf Curriculum,* Floris Books, UK 2019.

Bothmer, Alheidis von, *Die Bothmer-Gymnastik: Pädagogische und Therapeutische Anwendungsmöglichkeiten [Bothmer Gymnastics: Pedagogical and Therapeutic Aspects],* Schattauer Verlag, Germany 2004.

Brooking-Payne, Kim, *Games Children Play,* Hawthorn Press, Stroud 1996.

Brounts, Tonnie and Daniel, Helga, Bewegt ins Leben. *Eurythmie in den Klassen 1 to 4 [Moved into Life. Eurythmy in Classes 1 to 4],* Germany 2008.

Bucher, Walter, *1001 Spiel- und Übungsformen im Schwimmen [1001 Swimming Games and Exercises],* Hofmann Verlag, Germany 2010.

Gunther, Frank, *Koordinative Fähigkeiten im Schwimmen: Der Schlüssel zur perfekten Technik [Coordination Skills in Swimming: The Key to the Perfect Technique],* Hofmann GmbH, Germany 2008.

Hüther, Gerald and Quarch, Christoph, *Rettet das Spiel. Weil Leben mehr als Funktionieren ist,* Hansa Verlag, Germany 2016.

Kischnick, Rudolf, *Leibesübung und Bewussteinsschulung [Training in Physical Exercise and Awareness], Zbinden Verlag,* Switzerland 1989.

—, *Was alle Kinder spielen: 250 Bewegungsspiele für Schulkinder [What all Children Play: 250 exercise games for school children],* Freies Geistesleben, Germany 1995.

Kischnick, Rudolf and Haren, Wil van, *Dreh dich nicht um - 300 Bewegungsspiele für Kinder und Jegendlich [Don't Turn Around – 300 Games and Exercises for Kids and Everyone],* Germany 2008.

Klein, Gabriele, *Frauen Körper Tanz. Eine Zivilisationsgeschichte des Tanzes [Female Dance: A History],* Heyne Verlag, Germany 1994.

König, Karl, *The First Three Years of the Child,* Floris Books, UK 2004.

Kügelgen, Helmut von, 'Von der Würde des Kindes' ['On the Dignity of the Child'], published in *Erziehungskunst [Waldorf Education],* Germany 1984.

Künstler, Alois, *Das Brünnlein singt und saget [The Fountain Sings and Speaks],* Freies Geistesleben, Germany 2012.

Lievegoed, Bernard, *Phases of Childhood: Growing in Body, Soul and Spirit,* Floris Books, UK 2005.

Lipps, Peter, *Temperamente und Pädagogik. Eine Darstellung für den Unterricht an der Waldorfschule [Temperaments and Pedagogy: A Guide for Teaching at the Waldorf School],* Verlag Freies Geistesleben, Germany 1998.

Meyer-Fischer, Sophia, *Reigen und Spiele 1./2. Schuljahr [Roundelays and Games for Class 1 and 2 (notes from the Conference of Sports Teachers, 1999)],* Germany 1999.

Neff, Kurt, Vom Tanz. *Ein Lesebuch [Dance: A Reader],* Insel Verlag, Germany 1993.

Nietzold, Jochem, *Geistige Strukturen sinnvollen Turnens [Mental Structures of Sensible Gymnastics],* J Ch Mellinger Verlag, Germany 1994.

Pikler, Emmi, *Lasst mir Zeit. Die selbstständige Bewegungsentwicklung des Kindes bis zum freien Gehen [Give Me Time: Independent Movement Development of the Child Up to Free Walking],* Richard Pflaum Verlag, Germany 2018.

Soesmann, Albert, *Die zwölf Sinne. Tore der Seele*

[The Twelve Senses: The Gates of the Soul], Freies Geistesleben, Stuttgart 2011.

Steiner, Rudolf, *Anthroposophy (A Fragment)* (CW45), SteinerBooks, USA 1996.

—, *Becoming the Archangel Michael's Companion: Rudolf Steiner's Challenge to the Younger Generation* (CW217), SteinerBooks, USA 2007.

—, *Chance, Providence and Necessity* (CW163), Anthroposophic Press, USA 1988.

—, *The Child's Changing Consciousness as the Basis of Pedagogical Practice* (CW306), Anthroposophic Press, USA 1996.

—, *Education for Special Needs – The Curative Education Course* (CW317), Rudolf Steiner Press, UK 2015.

—, *Inner Reading and Inner Hearing* (CW156), SteinerBooks, USA 2008.

—, *The Kingdom of Childhood* (CW311), Anthroposophic Press, USA 1995.

—, *Konferenzen mit den Lehrern der Freien Waldorfschule 1919 bis 1924 [Conferences with the Teachers of the Free Waldorf School, 1919 to 1924]* (GA300), Rudolf Steiner Verlag, Switzerland 1992.

—, *From Mammoths to Mediums: Answers to Questions* (CW350), Rudolf Steiner Press, UK 2009.

—, *Menschengeschichte im Lichte der Geistesforschung [Human History in the Light of Spiritual Research]* (GA 61), Rudolf Steiner Verlag, Switzerland, 1983.

—, *Riddles of the Soul* (CW21), Mercury Press, USA 1996.

—, *Soul Economy and Waldorf Education* (CW303), Anthroposophic Press, USA 1986.

—, *The Study of Man – General Education Course* (CW293), Rudolf Steiner Press, UK 2011.

Steiner, Rudolf and Wegmann, Ita, *Fundamentals of Therapy – An Extension of the Art of Healing through Spiritual-Scientific Knowledge* (CW27), Mercury Press, USA 2010.

Steinke, Michael, *Bewegungssinn und Gleichgewichtssinn, Anthropologische Grundlagen [The Sense of Movement and Balance: The Anthropological Basics]*, manuscript of the Arbeitsgemeinschaft Heilpädagogischer Schulen auf anthroposophischer Grundlage [The Working Group of Special Education Schools Founded on an Anthroposophical Basis], 1993.

Stockmeyer, Karl E. A., *Rudolf Steiner's Curriculum for Steiner-Waldorf Schools: An Attempt to Summarise His Indications*, Floris Books, UK 2015.

Teichmann, Frank, *Der Mensch und sein Tempel: Griechenland [Greece: Man and His Temple]*, Verlag Urachhaus, Germany 1985.

Wenz, Josef, *Die goldene Brücke [The Golden Bridge]*, Bärenreiter, Germany 1963.

Index

You may also be interested in...

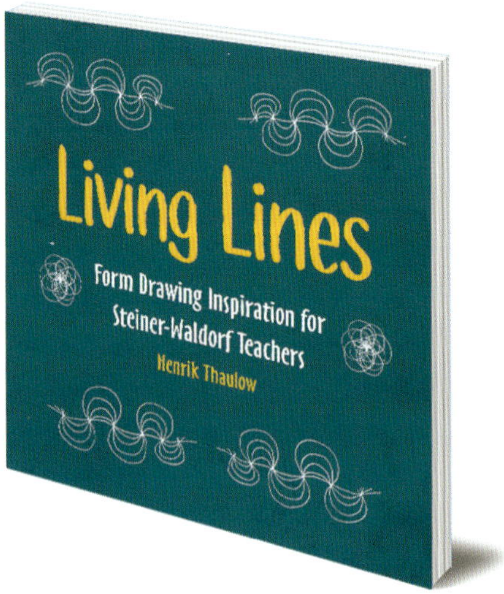

Living Lines

Form Drawing Inspiration for Steiner-Waldorf Teachers

Henrik Thaulow

'This book provides a valuable resource, full of ready-to-go ideas... Whether a newcomer to this activity, or a seasoned practitioner, there is much to discover and use.'

– Martin Hardiman, Former Steiner-Waldorf Class Teacher and Form Drawing Teacher

This unique book first explains form drawing and its role in Steiner-Waldorf schools, while also tackling practicalities such as advice on suitable paper and pencils. It goes on to offer a wide selection of exercises for classes 2 to 5, with step-by-step instructions on how they can be taught, arranged both by class and by theme, drawing on examples of pupils' work and images of forms from nature and cultural heritage. Teachers can use these lessons as an inspiring starting point.

This fascinating and beautiful book will allow Waldorf educators, at school and home, to confidently teach form drawing to their pupils.

florisbooks.co.uk

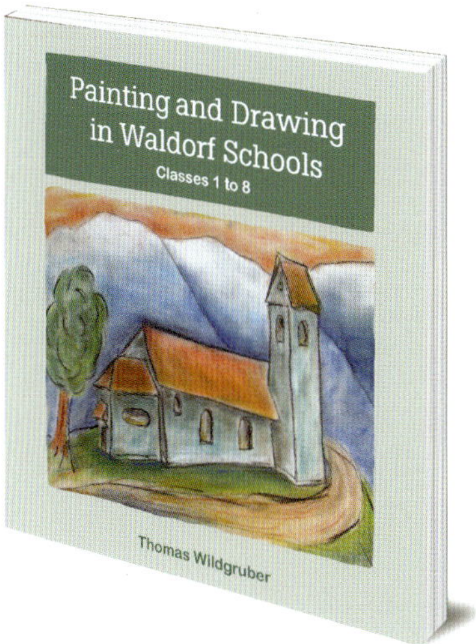

Painting and Drawing in Waldorf Schools

Classes 1 to 8

Thomas Wildgruber

'A superbly structured manual on drawing and painting in the class teacher years. In over twenty years as a class teacher in Britain and Germany, this is one of the most inspirational and useful books I have come across.'

– Sven Saar, Freie Waldorfschule Wahlwies, Germany

This comprehensive teachers' manual provides a complete artistic curriculum for classes 1 to 8 in Steiner-Waldorf schools (age six to fourteen).

At each stage, the book demonstrates the skills that teachers can help children to develop. There are 280 practical exercises for teachers to use, and over 800 drawings and paintings as inspiring examples of artistic possibilities. The curriculum moves from free drawing, to guided colour exercises, to precise perspective drawing.

florisbooks.co.uk

More books for Steiner-Waldorf educators

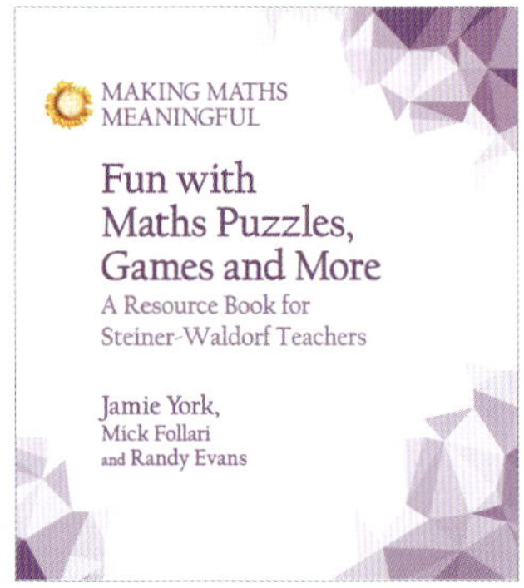

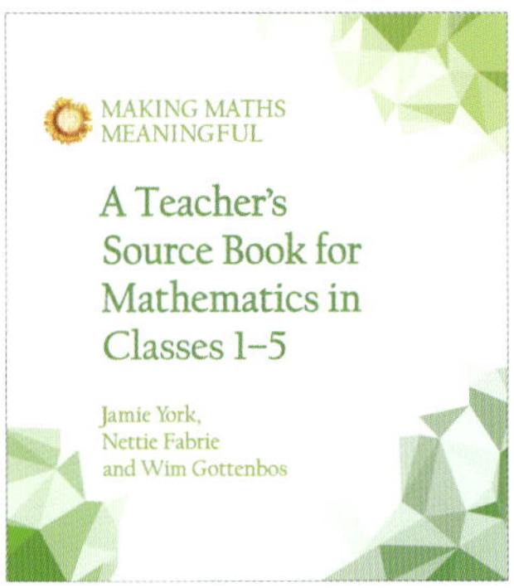

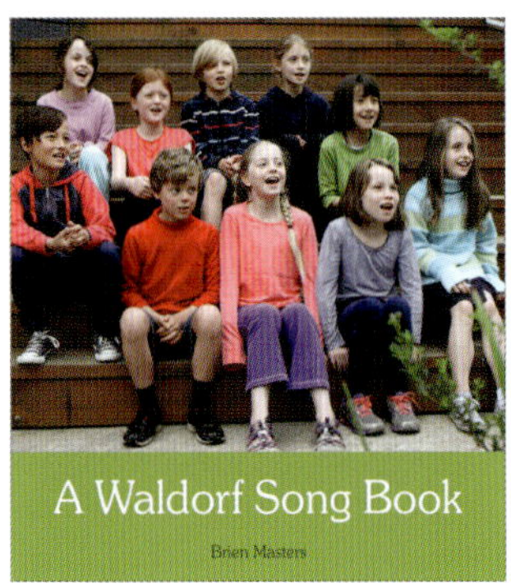

florisbooks.co.uk

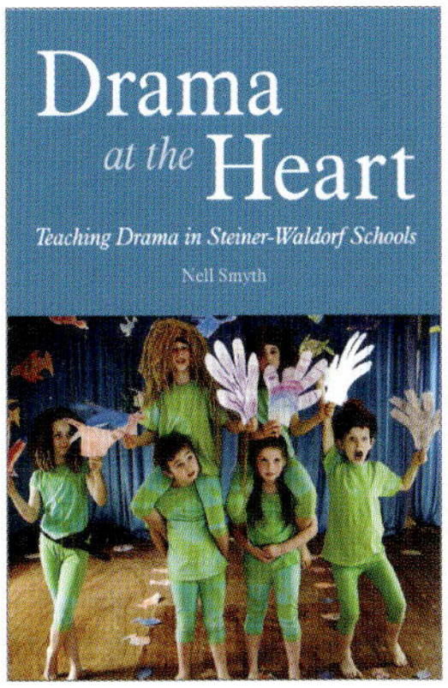
Drama
at the Heart
Teaching Drama in Steiner-Waldorf Schools
Nell Smyth

Gardening
Classes in
Waldorf Schools
Birte Kaufmann

A Journey
Through Time
in Verse
and Rhyme
Poems
collected by
Heather Thomas

A JARGON-FREE GUIDE FOR PARENTS
Understanding
Waldorf
Education
Teaching from the Inside Out
Jack Petrash

THE LEGEND
of
Parzival
The Epic Story of his
Quest for the Grail
RETOLD BY ROBIN COOK

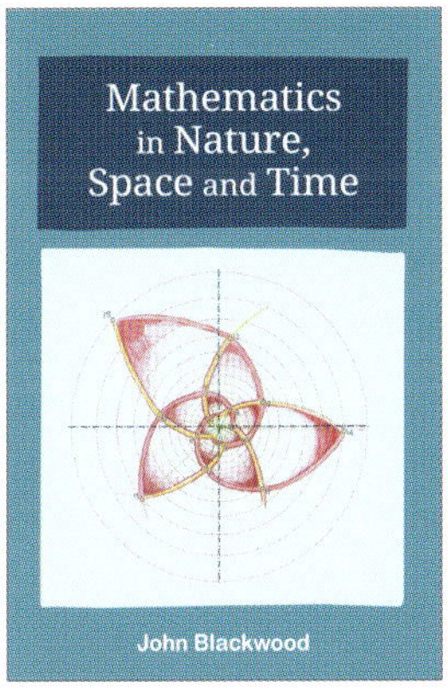
Mathematics
in Nature,
Space and Time
John Blackwood

Botany
Charles Kovacs

TOWARDS
CREATIVE
TEACHING
Notes to an
Evolving Curriculum for
Steiner Waldorf Class Teachers
EDITED BY MARTYN RAWSON
AND KEVIN AVISON

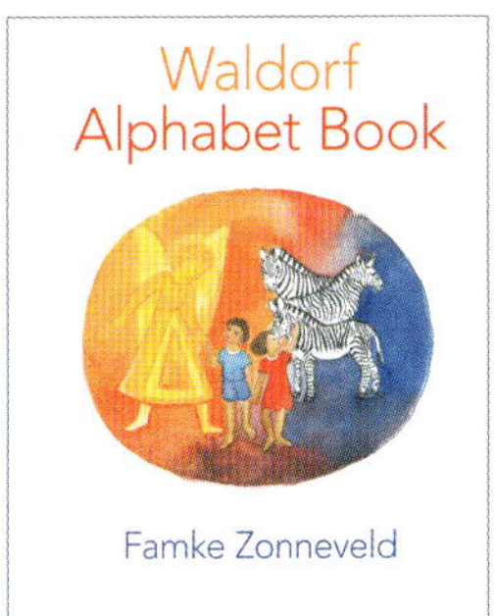
Waldorf
Alphabet Book
Famke Zonneveld

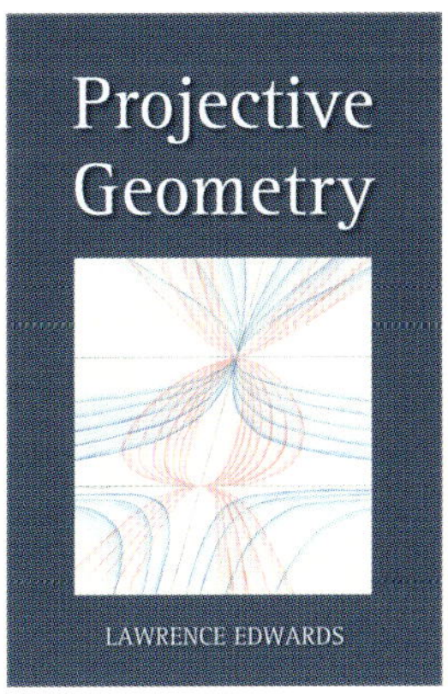
Projective
Geometry
LAWRENCE EDWARDS

Stories of the Saints
A Collection for Children
Siegwart Knijpenga

THE
WISDOM
OF
Waldorf
100 Reflections
on Waldorf Education to
Enrich and Inspire